This book belongs to:

Kathleen Farstad

The End of
American
Childhood

The End of American Childhood

A HISTORY OF PARENTING FROM LIFE ON THE FRONTIER TO THE MANAGED CHILD

Paula S. Fass

PRINCETON UNIVERSITY PRESS

Princeton & Oxford

Requests for permission to reproduce material from this work
should be sent to Permissions, Princeton University Press

Published by Princeton University Press
41 William Street, Princeton, New Jersey 08540

In the United Kingdom: Princeton University Press
6 Oxford Street, Woodstock, Oxfordshire OX20 1TR

press.princeton.edu

Jacket illustration by Asia Pietrzyk / Marlena Agency

Library of Congress Cataloging-in-Publication Data

Fass, Paula S., author.
The end of American childhood : a history of parenting from life on the frontier to
the managed child / Paula S. Fass.
pages cm
Includes bibliographical references and index.
ISBN 978-0-691-16257-7 (hardback) — ISBN 0-691-16257-3 (hardcover) 1. Families—
United States—History. 2. Parenting—United States—History. 3. Children—United
States—History. I. Title.
HQ535.F37 2016
306.850973—dc23
2015031606

British Library Cataloging-in-Publication Data is available

This book has been composed in Sabon Next LT Pro, Montserrat, and Matchbook

Printed on acid-free paper. ∞

Printed in the United States of America

1 3 5 7 9 10 8 6 4 2

With love for Jack, Bibi, Charlie, Beth, Chelly, and Judah
Three generations learning from each other

CONTENTS

ACKNOWLEDGMENTS

This book has occupied me for years, and it has accumulated many debts. Some of these cannot be fully acknowledged, but happily its publication allows me to note the kindness and assistance of institutions and individuals who have helped me to think through the issues I write about and gave me the time and space to conduct the research on which it is based. The Center for Advanced Study in the Behavioral Sciences (CASBS) at Stanford welcomed me to its haven for a second time in 2006–2007 at a crucial stage in the evolution of my research and provided resources for excellent fellowship and conversation. My stay at the center was funded by the John Simon Guggenheim Foundation, whose assistance I am delighted to acknowledge.

The center's intense intellectual life was further enriched by the presence of my close colleagues Bengt Sandin, Maria Sundqvist, and Steven Mintz. Claude Steele, the center's then director, made it possible for me to hold several mini-conferences on childhood that expanded the numbers as well as the range of our small group to include Stephen Lassonde, Michael Grossberg, Kriste Lindenmeyer, and Mary Ann Mason. Together we became a set of adventurers who stretched the boundaries of how childhood could be understood and imagined. Dolores Hayden and the late Peter Marris also provided excellent companionship on the hill and helped me to think and write more clearly.

Some of my ideas were developed in a variety of presentations to groups of students and colleagues over the past seven years. I am especially pleased to acknowledge Tema Barn (the Department of Childhood Studies) at Linköping University, Sweden, where I was the Kerstin Hesselgren Professor and spent a splendid semester in 2008, with special thanks to Bengt Sandin; the Center for Advanced Studies at the

Ludwig-Maxmillian Universität, Munich, Germany, which kindly invited me to inaugurate their Program in Children's Studies in April 2013; the Child Speaker Series at Palo Alto University (2012), with thanks to Robert Russell; the University of Victoria, Canada, where I was Distinguished Guest Woman Scholar in 2012, with thanks to Rachel Hope Cleve; the History Department at Tel Aviv University, Israel (2011) with thanks to Eyal Naveh; the Eugene Lang College of the New School, New York, where I spoke in 2011; the Child Studies Department at Rutgers University, Camden (2010); the American Academy of Arts and Sciences and Felton Earls, Cambridge, Massachusetts, for hosting an important conference on Children's Rights in 2009; the Strong Museum of Play in Rochester, New York (2009); the History Seminar at the University of Lund, Sweden (2008); the Seminar on Polity, Society and the World in 2008 at Bilkent University, Ankara, Turkey, with special thanks to Dennis Bryson; Kastamonu University, Turkey (2008), where my friend and colleague Nihal Ahioglu Lundberg provided a very warm welcome. I most fully anticipated the themes and arguments of this book at presentations at the American Philosophical Society in Philadelphia (2013) and the Annual Lecture at the German Historical Institute in Washington, DC (2013). The Society for the History of Children and Youth has been a sustaining presence in my life since its founding, and its conferences have provided me with the occasions to present ideas and work in progress, the company of kindred scholars, and opportunities for learning.

Through all this time, my efforts have been supported and encouraged by colleagues and staff at the History Department of the University of California at Berkeley, where funds from the Margaret Byrne Professor Chair have underwritten my research. I will always be grateful for this assistance, so basic to the book's evolution. For secretarial assistance, I want to thank Alex Coughlin. So, too, my colleagues in the Child and Youth Policy Center at Berkeley have generously financed several conferences that I sponsored on the Berkeley campus over the years. Most recently, Jill Duerr Berrick, its director, provided funds to pay for the illustrations in this book. This center and the Berkeley Family Forum have been an important part of my intellectual formation, and its influences will be evident in the book. I want to acknowledge especially my friends Mary Ann Mason,

Steve Sugarman, and Neil Gilbert. Berkeley has excellent graduate students, several of whom have been actively involved in this book. I note, with special thanks, the contributions of Amanda Littauer, Caroline Hinkle McCamant, Julie Stein, Candace Chen, Gabriel Milner, Don Romesburg, and Jennifer Robin Terry. To my delight, Lisa Shapiro and Meghana Ravikumar volunteered to "intern" with me during the summers when I was starting and completing this book.

As I was finishing the book, I imposed on several people to read it. These included Stephen Lassonde, Mary Ann Mason, Julia Grant, Howard Chudacoff, and John Demos. John probably does not know how important his encouragement and the example of his skill as a historian have been to me. The production of this book was handled with exemplary care and attention at Princeton University Press, where my editor Brigitta van Rheinberg was alert to its potential and has been generous with her praise and suggestions. It is the kind of support that authors crave. The book was expertly edited by Karen Fortgang and Molan Goldstein, and its path to the public carefully supervised by Julia Haav, James Schneider, and Quinn Fusting. Jill Marsal is an exceptional agent, responsive and alert, an editor as well as an advisor. My thanks go out to this whole team.

My children, Bluma Lesch and Charles Lesch, have been a constant inspiration. Charlie, himself an excellent writer, read the draft I sent to colleagues and provided important comments and suggestions. Above all, Jack has been my companion through the research, the thinking, the writing, and the years of learning about children and parenting. My life and work have been enriched in so many ways by his presence, his help, and his love; it is difficult to recount completely the contribution he has made.

The End of
American
Childhood

Young in America[1]

For a very long time, being a child in the United States included certain privileges and risks. So did being a parent. Americans were prosperous and their opportunities seemed without limit. Their children could move in directions not even imagined by the previous generation. With seemingly endless landed resources, a dynamic economy, free schooling, and laws that did not restrict them to following in their parents' path, succeeding generations could define their own futures. This appeared to liberate generations from each other to create a dazzling sense of change. Taking this all for granted, Americans then offered these possibilities to immigrants who, we proclaimed, came for their children's sake as much as their own. The sense of an unfolding future spilling into the welcoming land was what the American landscape painter Thomas Cole conveyed in the inviting second installment of his cycle of the Four Ages of Man (1840), the one he called *Youth*. America was about youth and youthfulness, new futures, and open doors.

These images also conveyed risk, both for children and for their parents. Parents had less influence, and children were on their own. Parents would have less power to control; and children, fewer shoulders to lean on. The future itself was far less knowable, and there were always those unable to adapt fast enough. Parents were not sufficiently respected, and their wisdom easily discarded as old-fashioned and out of date. Much was expected of children who had to fulfill not only their own desires but immigrant expectations. This mythological past has, of course, never been the reality for all parents and children. Generations of well-to-do and well-placed families passed their privileges forward, and poverty was often inherited. Slipping into lesser

The Voyage of Life: Youth (1842). Painting by Thomas Cole. Courtesy of the National Gallery of Art, Washington, DC.

positions always posed a threat as a possibility of intergenerational failure. Some children were deeply restrained by personality or upbringing or circumstances, while others were more freely risk takers. And even the myths could not blot out the reality of slavery and race in our historical memory. These have stained the experience of generations, past and present. Still our self-image had enough substance to remain vital to American institutional and political life. We acted in ways that made the images become part of the real life of the nation.

Today, Americans are asking if any of this system of beliefs and values still holds true. Are there any advantages to being raised in the United States? Do parents have too much control over their children? Are immigrants even offered the illusion of a better future for their children? Are we still raising a nation of risk takers or has globalization made us like everyone else? Is the promise of American childhood over? In exploring how we came to define the American generational promise, what it meant, how it functioned in the past, and if it has changed over time, this book tries to provide a way to answer these questions. It lays out the historical terrain within which these questions and their answers first emerged and the points in our history when childhood, parenting, and generational relations changed in deep and important ways.

Historians have not often asked these questions about parents and children and how their experiences relate to our national identity. Creators of grand opera and great theater recognize the dramatic importance embedded in the relationship. They are aware that the intensity of the bonds between parents and children and their intimate variety not only serve as the basis for deep emotions, but also connect the audience to fundamental questions about society and history. And they have long tied the large concerns of the state to the small arenas of fathers and their sons or daughters, of mothers and their children. We learn this from Shakespeare and Verdi, Euripides and Arthur Miller. On a much smaller scale, this lesson is also part of what the public responds to in sensational news. A mother or father who mistreats and kills a child, either through negligence or intent, is telling us something about the society of which they are part.[2] These stories make headlines or run as a ticker under the television news. The audience is shocked and overcome by pity and grief. The existence of such unfortunate and unforgivable members of our society leads us to reflect on the nature of evil, the realm of psychopathology, the terrible unpredictability of life's circumstances, the inadequate protections of the state.

Historians are only now catching up to what theater, opera, and daily news have known for some time, as we begin to understand just how important the relations between generations are to who we are as nations and as societies. Our individual histories take place in the small theaters of our personal lives, but these are deeply entwined in a larger world of politics and culture. In the realm of popular culture, as in that of high culture, the audience knows the difference between the grandly dramatic and the ordinary. We never assume that stories in which mothers kill their children are what childhood or parenting is about. They are aberrational, recalling the extremes of behavior or misfortune, and they call us back to what we should and do expect when we think about childhood or parenting. We know that such terrible stories define the limits on behavior, not its content.

Historians of childhood and of the relationship between parents and children also understand the difference between the ordinary and the exceptional. But their task is more challenging, since they need to demonstrate that ordinary behaviors are the most historically vital and consequential, and further complicated by the elusive search for historical tracks. While generational relations may be connected to powerful changes in politics and society, it is the repeated, the expected, the ordinary that tells us what childhood and parenting was like. In this book, I have sought out these traces of past relationships and experiences in the descriptions of sociologists and the prescriptions of ministers, psychologists, and childrearing advisors; in parenting journals, popular magazines, and personal memoirs; as well as in the circulars of the government. Together such sources provide us with a record of the lives of Americans as parents and children.

Over the course of the more than two hundred years of the nation's history, parenting and childhood—what parents owe their children and what children can expect—have not only changed in many of their details. In an always diverse and uncommonly heterogeneous population, they have varied significantly by group and locale at any specific time. I therefore include stories about many different kinds of parenting relations and children's experiences. Nevertheless, I will argue that American parent-child relations also demonstrate a cultural particularity that developed from the specifics of the American context and of American history.

In the United States, much earlier and more emphatically than elsewhere in the West, authoritarian controls over children gave way to a more relaxed relationship between the generations. This pattern and its consequences drew the attention of European and American observers quite early in the nation's history, and Europeans often described American children as rude, unmannerly, and bold. Americans were eager also to see themselves as different—fresher, newer, younger. From the time of the Revolution, some Americans believed that childrearing had to adapt to the changed possibilities of their New World environment. Americans were more open to endowing their children with greater independence and flexibility in choice because they believed that the future held better possibilities and opportunities for their children.

This view, together with the availability of land (on a breathtaking scale) and an absence of laws that specifically determined inheritance (as was common in Europe), did, I believe, recast the relationship between American parents and their children from the start of the nation's life, as it lowered the degree of publicly approved control that parents exercised over their children's future. This did not mean that American parents were indulgent toward their children or that children had a longer or more leisured or more playful childhood. The contrary was often the case. American children went to work early because land and labor ratios made their work desirable and necessary. That work was not, however, just a form of subordination as it tended to be elsewhere in the Western world. Instead, it often provided the young with a sense of the importance of their contribution and of their ability to create their own place in the world. It made innovation seem possible and creativity valuable. In a society expanding through immigration and where slavery was a fact of life for many, this could never simply be a description of all parents and all children. But from early in our national life, it did become an identifiable American pattern.

Instead of imagining that this pattern applied to all parents and children in the United States, it is useful to think of the early American experience as defining a formula or recipe that shifted the standard of what might be expected in the relationship between parents and children. It established a baseline that would often be invoked as desirable and legitimate, even as the initial circumstances that created it changed and then finally disappeared. As we shall see, it was this formula—one that emphasized children's independence and limited parental control—that dominated the American vision of childrearing even as parents struggled against its boundaries, and as new Americans with very different pasts brought alternative visions. It is also a pattern that has deeply influenced American childrearing advice. Parents today still struggle with this legacy, but it remains a fundamental part of our conversation.

In attempting to set out in broad strokes this most intimate relationship, I have made certain kinds of choices. I try to tell stories that help us to understand intergenerational relations at particular moments in time and to examine the changes that made those times

especially significant. The chapters are organized in broadly chronological fashion, each focusing on selected themes and problems that
best capture the issues facing parents, children, and the public during
that period. But because historical changes and people's lives do not
obey arbitrary chronological limits, the chapters also overlap as they
proceed. I am fully aware that the United States has always contained
a great diversity of peoples and experiences, but I have emphasized
only parts of this diversity at specific historical moments because it
allows me to focus on particular aspects of the evolving story, not
because they tell us everything that was happening at that point. In
many cases, a later discussion will bring these other experiences to
the fore. Readers may recognize some of the people whose lives I
describe—Ulysses S. Grant or Margaret Mead, for example—but be
much less familiar with others. All lives are historical, but some tell us
more of what we need to know and I have made my choices accord-
ingly. This book is full of people's lives and describes many experiences, but it cannot and does not try to be comprehensive. Similarly,
many historical events have meaning for individuals and families, but
some are more urgent and broadly consequential. I have drawn often
on the self-descriptions of individuals, some of whom are remem-
bering their childhoods, knowing full well that most of us are not
completely reliable in how we tell our stories or in what we remember, but with the hope that this is less of a problem when we read
broadly among many such self-descriptions.

The American Revolution first endowed children with an important role in the unfolding of the nation's future. The circumstances
of land ownership and the early maturity that accompanied rapid economic expansion gave substance to that inheritance. American society
circumscribed patriarchal authority, and women had greater authority
over their children's lives than elsewhere in the Western world. Together
these factors, as I suggest in the first chapter, set a basis in the early
republic for children's access to more independence in their choices
and in their destinies. At a time when the boundaries of childhood
were fluid, early maturity gave even young people roles to play and a
range of prerogatives.

Americans admired and rewarded the initiative of the young. But
greater autonomy could also be a threat to order, and the problem

of children who were inadequately cared for, abandoned, and adrift became a major focus of public attention by the second half of the nineteenth century. In chapter 2, I suggest that the turmoil of the Civil War, which had devastating effects on family life and brought the problems of freed slaves and their children to public attention, altered the conversation about parents and children in important ways. These changes were compounded by industrialization, particularly as it accelerated at the end of the nineteenth century. As many of the young engaged in unhealthy indoor work, rather than self-directed outdoor activities, while others were lost in urban disarray, Americans reconsidered the nature of family authority, elevating a new vision that focused on the protections children needed, and began to use public institutions when parents seemed inadequate to the task. Middle-class Victorians reimagined family roles and began to hedge childhood with new restrictions by the late nineteenth century. How to salvage independence and self-direction became a problem for educators and others as new scientific values became prominent.

By the end of the nineteenth century, saving children who needed care and providing advice to mothers about effective nurture became the central commitments of public life. These continued forcefully into the early twentieth century. Drawing on the prestige of science and the lever of statistics, even the federal government became a critical actor in this realm, with the establishment of the first and only federal agency devoted to children's welfare. As chapter 3 shows, this was underwritten by a new professionalism in the twentieth century that enlisted pediatricians, psychologists, childrearing advisors, and experts in juvenile delinquency. Together they reframed the parent-child relationship as mothers, in particular, were urged to look outside the home for counsel. By the 1930s, this "expert" knowledge about children produced a national vision of a normal childhood.

Especially important for immigrants, these extra-home agencies grew in variety and number in the first two decades of the twentieth century. The presence of so many newcomers and their great diversity changed American institutional life, the public schools most prominently. In raising the stakes and the age of school leaving, immigration made the high school a uniquely American institution and turned adolescence into a prominent cultural experience. The large number of immigrants created the conditions for these institutions to grow in ways that, as I show in chapter 4, transformed the relationship between immigrants and their children and had significant consequences for generational continuity. In fact, by changing what it meant to grow up in America, the high school and adolescence recreated childhood for everyone in the United States. A sign of America's new wealth and growing self-confidence on the world stage, the high school meant that the United States continued to be a very different place for children and adolescents than was the case elsewhere in the Western world. In extending childhood while separating children from their parents, it endowed the young with a different kind of independence.

In the context of the elevated role of schooling, it was unsurprising that education became the social pivot around which Americans chose to address race and racial inequality in the 1950s and 1960s. In chapter 5, I discuss how black children and youth became objects of national policy. The postwar period also saw a special delight in childhood, as the enormous increase in the child population defined the era and Dr. Benjamin Spock presided over a renewal of family life deeply centered on childrearing. In the context of the emphasis on both equality and the importance of children, the period became the site of a startling intergenerational revolt that took place not only at lunch counters in the segregated South but in high schools, in colleges, and on the streets throughout the country. Affirming their independence even as schooling began to shrink its reality, the youth of the time were, in fact, deeply dependent on the institutions that had been created for them. But the young also helped to refashion practices and alter institutions that affected children for the rest of the twentieth century. These changed intergenerational relations in the twenty-first century.

In chapter 6, I turn to where this tangled set of events has left us, as parents and children face each other across the divide of shrinking independence for the young and growing fears by their parents, and in the context of a new immigration and a globalized world. As American confidence has eroded and our institutions appear to have lost their coherence, the young have become the repositories of our many anxieties. The chapter asks whether and how the American difference still matters in a world grown smaller and American prosperity less distinctive, while our children's prospects seem no longer as bright as they once were. Today, our conversations remind us of both the tradition we still value and the vast changes that have taken place in the past half-century.

In writing, I have focused on the significant moments of change while also keeping in view certain common beliefs and expectations that created a tradition against which and around which discussion about parenting, childhood, and generational relations took place and continues to revolve today. *That tradition emphasizes the desirability and possibility of making children independent of their parents and giving them the tools to become so.* In the United States, themes of independence, autonomy, self-definition, and individual success have been viewed as essential to cultural identity, and, as a result, they have been deeply embedded in our views about children, childhood, learning, and family obligations. Even as Americans today try to make their children safer and more secure, they hope to maintain a certain edge that would allow their children to succeed by being independent and innovative. Economists, too, are beginning to look to this quality as essential to successful "flourishing."[3] Americans have from their earliest times looked to a future different from the past and to their children to define and fulfill it. As a result, I argue, even today there is something very American about how we discuss and worry about parenting and childhood.

While the United States' population today is drawn from everywhere on earth, these American cadences remain very much alive and part of our national conversation. Whether these are still useful or possible or desirable is something the reader will have to decide. The book introduces the reader to the historical basis for these beliefs as they grew from our earliest sense of nationhood, and to the changes that have challenged and tempered them as they became a tradition over the course of more than two centuries. These include several domestic and foreign wars, fundamental transformations in the economy, the massive elaboration of schooling, changing religious and scientific beliefs about the nature of the child, and recurrent migrations of people who came from societies with very different visions of these matters. It also includes important moments when we have tried to address if and how race has been an exception to these patterns.

Having inherited the consequences of these many changes means that childhood and parenting today are quite different than they were in the early nineteenth century when this story begins. Households are much smaller, with far fewer children born, and all are expected to survive into adulthood. Our lives are much more urban, lived more indoors, more hedged around with legal provisions (which are sometimes protections), and children are expected to remain children and to be taken care of by their parents for much longer periods of time. Parents are usually more self-conscious regarding good parenting, although they are not necessarily better parents as a result. Today's parents, especially in a middle class that expanded dramatically in the middle of the twentieth century, discuss and read about parenting regularly, from scientific and medical experts, from psychologists and educators, even from cookbook writers who advise them about what is safe for children to eat. Much of this knowledge has extended the life, well-being, and education of children but also circumscribed their freedom and narrowed their path to self-defined maturity. That paradox—a better, longer childhood that at the same time seems to make raising and being a child more problematic—lies at the heart of the story I tell in this book. Even as we protect them, we still want our children to have access to those characteristics that we believe made them successful in the past when they were far less protected, and we pay lip service to their autonomy and right to self-definition. Whether the many changes in our history can be reconciled with these values is something the reader will be asked to think about as we follow the lives of the many different parents and children detailed in this book. I hope the reader will also realize that there are many ways of being a good parent and that our judgments should be much more cautious.

When I describe the treatment of children and the relationship between the generations in the United States as different than in Europe through most of the nineteenth and twentieth centuries, I am aware that this comparison is fluid, the differences are variable, and the sharpness of contrasts has receded over time. In 1800 when this book begins, the United States was small and very self-consciously a new kind of society. Its population, slave and free, was four million, almost all of it rural. By 2015, the American population had passed well beyond 300 million, and the world from which that population is drawn has changed massively. Today, the United States resembles Europe more than it did in the past, so much so that historians have come to speak about the West as a single entity in ways that would have been unfamiliar even half a century ago. In that light, Americans today not only are Western in their generational patterns but have been extremely influential in their creation. While differences remain between Americans and Europeans in their views and practices regarding parenting, childhood, schooling, and what generations owe each other, those differences are much narrower than they were in the past. The changes in economy and industry, governance and social welfare, work and schooling, mortality and disease, scientific outlook and religious sentiments over the past two centuries that helped to create the Western world as we know it deeply affected the intimate sphere of the family, generational relationships, and how we understand and expect to treat children. Even in the shrinking global world of the twenty-first century, however, generational relations, family patterns, and parenting still distinguish the United States from most parts of Asia, South America, and Africa—the places from which most newcomers now come as immigrants. As we absorb the newcomers today, our sense of what is American will almost certainly continue to change. If asked, however, Americans will likely offer the view that they remain different even from those in Europe today, and certainly from the rest of the world. That difference is the result of our historical attachment to certain practices and values regarding what the generations owe each other. The following book explores the origins and development of those views, in the hope that our current conversations about parenting may become much better informed and meaningful. I also hope that the centrality of family, parenting, and childhood to society, economics, and politics will become evident as a fundamental feature of national life.

One of the aims of this book is to show Americans what has changed in their past and how the relationship between parents and children filters into other historical changes. Today, as parents and their children face very new circumstances domestically and internationally, they want to know how to respond, what to reinvent and adjust, and what they can still call upon as part of their tradition in order to move confidently into the future. I hope that this book can serve as something of a guide in that process. History is never a road map to the future, but even a modern GPS system requires knowledge of older landmarks and a familiarity with the basic terrain. As a scholar who has explored commonalities in Western childhood and who is keenly interested in these matters globally, and as a parent with a deep personal stake, it is my contention that knowing what has been different about our past will allow us to better organize the quest for guided change in a more emphatically global world. As will soon become clear, I am firmly convinced that there remains something useful and necessary in understanding *American* childhood, *American* parenting, and *American* generational relations.

We will begin, therefore, not exactly at the beginning—that is to say in 1776—but at the beginning of the nineteenth century, when a new president from a new political party, who articulated the very basis of American independence, Thomas Jefferson, became head of the nation he had helped to create. All that newness also brought deep reflection on how children should be raised and why they had the right to expect that their lives would be better than those of their forebears. Through two centuries of national life, civil and foreign wars, new sciences of man's evolution and a child's development, innovative schooling institutions and visions of the life cycle, and migrations from many continents, we will wind up asking ourselves in this book what we are continuously asking ourselves in books, in newspapers, on television, on the internet, and in person—what is happening to American childhood and parenting, and what do the generations need in order that we may move together into the future?

CHAPTER 1

Childhood and Parenting in the New Republic

Sowing the Seeds of Independence, 1800–1860

When Americans declared their independence from Britain and royal authority, they left behind not only a political system but also a way of understanding the world. Rather than a single ruler, they adopted the idea of the republic and of the shared authority for governance among its citizenry. Rather than submit to a dominant father figure, they looked to secure their future through divided authority. Americans continued to be connected to the European world in many essential ways, but they also altered these in important aspects. They maintained the English language and many English institutions, like the common law. They inherited a long tradition of Western philosophy and the basics of the Protestant faith. They ate foods familiar to their ancestors. Each of these practices was naturalized and subtly altered in the American environment: American intonations and rhythms changed the language; American sectarianism freed the nation from state-sponsored religion; some philosophical perspectives became part of the American grain at the expense of others; they added an array of New World foods to their diets.

In 1800, as Thomas Jefferson, whose famous Declaration had launched the Revolution, was elected president of the republic, the United States was on its way to becoming a distinct nation, with a culture that was both Western and unique to the American continent. In its various consequences, the American Revolution was thus far more than an expression of political difference with Great Britain. It expressed the changed circumstances of the environment that Americans inhabited and also created an impulse toward change as Americans began to see themselves as inheritors of a revolutionary tradition and reflected on its consequences for social life.[1] The intimate sphere of family life was probably the most fundamental location of this change, as Americans reimagined how parents and children should relate and what the generations owed each other.

In the first half of the nineteenth century, Americans elaborated this difference in generational practices and attitudes. Deeply embedded in the politics of revolution and the economics of a new environment, the differences also reflected changes in gender roles and the allocation of power in the family as well as revised views of the reach of the law. They were connected to alterations in Protestant beliefs about the child as a trembling being who needed to be made ready for life as well as for death. Some things had not changed very much. The devastating mortality rate of infants and young children still bound Americans into the circle of sorrow that all Western parents, even those who saw themselves as harbingers of a new future, had to confront.

As they created their special variant of childhood and parenting, Americans were creating a social revolution fully in line with the political changes that began with the famous revolt of 1776.[2] Both rejected entrenched hierarchy, and embraced independence and more personal autonomy. Both revolutions were uneasy and often hazardous undertakings. Together they made the United States into a very strange place in the world.

I

That strangeness is captured in many of the opinions voiced by articulate Americans in the first sixty years of the republic. "Our children," Nathaniel Willis declared in 1827 as he launched his new publication, *The Youth's Companion*, "are born to higher destinies than their fathers."[3] This vision has become a cliché to us today. But it was alien to most Europeans and would have been unfamiliar to American colonists. For centuries in the Western world, elders reigned and were assumed to possess knowledge and wisdom as well as power. Their welfare and needs were primary and their dictates unquestioned. This perspective is still common in many parts of the world today. Lady Elphinstone of Scotland captured its essential meaning when she declared, "My children from the youngest to the eldest love me and fear me as sinners dread death. My look is law."[4] Views like these dominated Old World values regarding the appropriate reverence and obedience of children toward their parents.

American revolutionaries had rejected this tyrannical posture in the political arena. In the circumstances of the world they were creating, Americans also rejected such views as a guide to household affairs. Although Europeans, too, were changing their perspective on childhood as they absorbed the lessons of the Enlightenment, and as they responded to the political revolutions erupting throughout the continent, the social conditions of European life made it more difficult for them to change as rapidly or as fully as Americans in regard to how the generations treated each other.[5]

Why and how had things become so different in the nascent United States? Historians of the American Revolution have long understood that the changes articulated in that event were deeper than politics, that they had roots in cultural and social life, and affected the domestic realm and private relations. American children, famed historian Bernard Bailyn speculated over fifty years ago, needed a different, more open-ended kind of schooling. Since they needed to adapt to the new circumstances of a changing landscape, following in their fathers' footsteps was not good enough. That knowledge was often inadequate to the circumstances. Individual resourcefulness and the willingness to adjust to the unexpected and to create the still unimagined became basic values as Americans defined a new type of individual adequate to the possibilities of the new world they were creating. Children, who were less constrained by ingrained habits, had an advantage over their elders in the American environment. At a time when European Enlightenment thinkers were seeking to throw off the shackles of custom and tradition, Americans reorganized their lives in ways that unselfconsciously adapted those perspectives, removing layers of tradition and encrusted custom.

Even before the Revolution, Enlightenment European thinkers, such as John Locke and Jean-Jacques Rousseau, were read with marked appreciation by Americans who believed that these philosophers' views about children, and about childhood as a formative phase of life, were especially relevant to their environment. John Locke is best known today for political writings that helped to establish the basis for America's commitments to liberty, for opposing tyrannical rule, and for ideas that Jefferson and others used in formulating their views about freedom of religion and conscience. But Locke was also looked to as a pioneer in ideas about how children could be raised to become responsible citizens and trusted to exercise their independent judgment. He believed that children were malleable and childhood was a time when habits were laid down that would shape later life. He urged parents to appeal to children's reason, not to their fear of punishment. Fewer restraints and adult impositions during childhood and a willingness to accept a child's natural inclinations as a basis for learning underwrote Rousseau's more radical beliefs in the innate wisdom and natural sensibilities of children. Rousseau looked to rid society of traditional ideas and social patterns by giving children more leeway to grow and time to exhibit that wisdom. In tracts written from the late seventeenth through the mid-eighteenth century, these two philosophers helped to shape modern ideas about children that were important throughout the West. For Americans eager to be informed, Locke and Rousseau captured the special importance of childhood to the ideals of a reformed society.

By the beginning of the nineteenth century, questions regarding parents and children and what they owed each other were very much part of the American conversation. After the Revolution, Americans eagerly addressed parent-child relations, sometimes with considerable urgency, because they saw the Revolution and republican government as setting special requirements for childrearing. Fathers' injunctions, like kings' dictates, were problematic in the new society they sought to create. The American revolutionaries spoke regularly of the rule of law and argued that they were trying to maintain liberties threatened by British imperial action. But even as they spoke about conserving older liberties, they turned toward more radical social notions. In attacking the legitimacy of the king—the most revered of earthly authorities—they undercut the unquestioned authority of fathers.[6] That authority remained elsewhere the guiding basis for domestic and social relationships. In France, whose own revolution similarly raised fundamental questions about the rule of kings and fathers, republican beliefs initially dismantled patriarchy after the Revolution of 1789, but it was reassembled within a decade as the French republic tumbled and fell. In the United States, preexisting conditions and the continuity of republican and democratic ideas created a context in which social and family changes were sustained and elaborated.[7]

Not only were old-fashioned fathers deeply suspect in the United States, but Americans were asking what kinds of children were needed to maintain the revolution that Americans continued to embrace. This made matters regarding childrearing part of the national agenda from the very beginning of the republic. Most American historians have not fully appreciated how radically the American environment and the revolution that it spawned were revising the most fundamental of human bonds.

European visitors to the United States in the half-century after the Revolution saw it clearly. As they witnessed the behaviors and demeanors of the old and the young, they witnessed a series of historically important changes. The great observer and French political theorist, Alexis de Tocqueville, devoted a chapter of *Democracy in America* to the unusual nature of American family relations. Among chapters registering his observations about (and sometimes disdain for) Americans' peculiar cultivation of the arts, their transformations of the English language, and their neglect of traditional philosophy, Tocqueville was much more admiring when describing "The Influence of Democracy on the Family." That influence, he argued, was in line with other leveling effects of the greater equality experienced in the United States. "It has been universally remarked that in our time [1830s] the several members of the family stand upon an entirely new footing toward each other; that the distance which formerly separated a father from his sons has been lessened; and that paternal authority, if not destroyed, is at least impaired."[8]

Societies throughout Europe and the Americas were also starting to feel the crosswinds of change, as the Western world came under the influence of democratizing conditions,[9] but Tocqueville found it to be "even more striking" in the United States. Speaking of young people beyond the earliest years, he observed: "The same habits, the same principles, which impel the one to assert his independence predispose the other to consider the use of that independence as *an incontestable right.*" In Tocqueville's view, independence in children was more than a practice; it had become a conscious part of a child's self-understanding. This all took place peacefully, since there was no struggle between the generations. Fathers feel "none of that bitter and angry regret which is apt to survive a bygone power." Instead the expectations had become an instinctive part of the culture as "the father foresees the limits of his authority long beforehand, and when the time arrives, he surrenders it without a struggle."[10]

Tocqueville went on to contrast the quality of feelings in more traditional societies with those in the United States. In the one, the father "is listened to with deference, he is addressed with respect, and the love that is felt for him is always tempered by fear." But in democratic America, as fathers yielded authority, "the relations of father and son become more intimate and more affectionate; rule and authority are less talked of, confidence and tenderness are often increased, and it would seem that the natural bond is drawn closer in proportion as the social bond is loosened."[11] Tocqueville was probably too quick to identify these two—the social, with its weakened emphasis on hierarchy, and the emotional, whose qualities Tocqueville argued resulted in an increase of "tenderness" on both sides. We would do well, for the moment at least, to separate these two aspects of the changed relationship between parents and children. Many memoirs from the period document the former; few tell us much about the latter. Tocqueville's observations about greater warmth and affection may have been (and not for the first time) an instance of wishful thinking by a social observer eager to believe that natural "feelings" and natural "bonds" would grow when social ties were loosened.

Somewhat later than Tocqueville, another observer of American domestic relations, Polish count Adam de Gurowski, concluded that in the United States, children matured early and were early "emancipated . . . from parental authority and domestic discipline." In this way, Gurowski accounted for the observations common at the time that "[c]hildren accustomed to the utmost familiarity and absence of constraint with their parents, behave in the same manner with other older persons, and this sometimes deprives the social intercourse of Americans of the tint of politeness, which is more habitual in Europe."[12] Many Europeans commented on the rude manners of American children, but few appreciated, as Tocqueville and Gurowski did, that this resulted not from parental laziness or indifference to child governance but from a different kind of disciplinary regime.

One who did and who made the contrast with European children explicit was the author of a volume called *America as I Found It*. "English children in the presence of strangers are reserved and shy. They feel that the nursery and school room are their proper sphere of action. . . . Most unlike to these is the sentiment of the American, both parent and child. The little citizen seems to feel at a surprisingly early age, that he has a part on the stage of the world, and is willing enough to act a little before his time."[13] The notion that children believed they had a part to play on the stage of the world was an unusually effective way of seeing that American children had large expectations and they were early trained toward the appropriate habits of mind and demeanor.

Probably nowhere else in the Western world could one visit the homes of respectable families and find children who so easily took part in the family circle and were so comfortably regarded as equals, not as subordinates or dependents. In fact, throughout the West during the nineteenth century, middle-class opinion was endowing children with special appeal and setting childhood apart, and family practices were distinguishing children's activities from those of their parents. While Americans, too, saw something precious and important about childhood as a stage of life, their cruder conditions and more demanding economy made it far less likely that children would inhabit an exclusive world in nurseries and at play away from the travails of the world.

II

Ulysses S. Grant, who would become a great Civil War general and then the eighteenth president of the United States, grew up in the kind of household that Tocqueville or Gurowski may have observed as they traveled through rural Ohio (a state that produced more than its share of generals and presidents). Grant's father was a prosperous leather tanner, and in "comfortable circumstances," according to Grant, but young Ulysses was expected to do his share of work on the land that his father owned. His father, Jessie, did not force him to labor in his own trade, which his son "detested," but Ulysses began to work in the woods from the time he was seven or eight years of age "hauling all the wood used in the house and shops."

BIRTHPLACE OF U. S. GRANT, POINT PLEASANT, CLERMONT
COUNTY, OHIO.

"Birthplace of U. S. Grant, Point Pleasant, Clermont County, Ohio." Illustration from
the Rev. P. C. Headley, *The Life and Campaigns of Lieut.-Gen. U. S. Grant: From His
Boyhood to the Surrender of Lee* (New York: Derby & Miller, 1866).

"When about eleven years old I was strong enough to hold a plow,"
Grant recalled. "From that age until seventeen I did *all* the work done
with horses, such as breaking up the land, furrowing, plowing corn
and potatoes, bringing in the crops when harvested, hauling all the
wood, besides tending two or three horses, a cow or two, and sawing
wood for stoves, etc., while still attending school."[14] As he did almost
all the tasks of farming, young Ulysses was playing a significant part
in the affairs of the Grant household, and he knew that this part was
important and valuable. He was assuming a role on the world's stage.

Grant's early life reflected the kind of special American circumstances that Gurowski had in mind when he said that in the United
States, "the space, the modes to win a position by labor were unlimited,

and thus children began early to work and earn for themselves. Thus ...
they became self-relying and independent, and this independence continues to prevail in filial relations." What in our eyes might seem to
be young Grant's hard childhood, burdened by early responsibilities
and physical labor, was a response to the American labor shortages of
the day that made the work of children valuable and a household necessity. It also made this work, as Gurowski understood, unusually
liberating.[15]

Grant also understood this. He explained that since he did everything expected of him, he was never scolded or punished but was
given the right to both "rational enjoyments" and a large degree of independence. This independence allowed him to roam freely and travel
widely, often for many miles beyond the family home and frequently
overnight, even as a ten-year-old boy. He was allowed to trade horses
(not always successfully) on his own account.[16] John Locke would
have approved of both the absence of physical punishment and the "rational enjoyments" as well as the increasing measure of self-direction
allowed to Ulysses as he proved his abilities.

Grant was early trained both to responsibility and to freedom. By
his early adolescence, he knew that he could engage in the world's
tasks and was rewarded for it. His father did not scold him, but Grant
says nothing about his father's affections, or whether he was kind. He
does not discuss his father's feelings. We would surely not describe
the elder Grant as a solicitous parent, since he expected much of his
son (it was he who requested that his son be nominated for West
Point). In return, he gave him very little—except the opportunity
to develop a large measure of self-possession and independence.
Grant knew he did well, and his growing sense of competence (despite various mistakes made on the way), made him strong. Grant
had been making an important contribution to his household since
he was seven, and more over time as his capacities were proven and
expanded.

Ulysses Grant's experience of a midwestern childhood was not
unique. Other boys also worked hard at many tasks, enjoyed leisure,
and were early invested with the ability to operate independently and
to succeed as adults.[17] In 1800, when Daniel Drake was fifteen, this
"country boy from Kentucky" was brought to Cincinnati, where his

father abruptly left him to be apprenticed to a physician. "Father remained a day, when to my dismay, he took leave of me." One can
well understand this "dismay." It is harder to imagine that this rapid
separation radiated a sense of warm affection from his father. But
Daniel persevered, and he became a capable and honored physician.
The Drakes were originally from Plainfield, New Jersey, but the elder
Drake sought a better life and a richer future for his family. So after
suffering significant losses during the American Revolution, he
moved them West. "Not contented with their position," his father and
uncle moved in 1788 to a place that seemed to offer more potential
than comfort, to the then still new state of Kentucky, only recently
admitted to the Union. They lived there in a traditional log cabin,
described in Daniel's memoirs as being "the size and form of Dove's
[his aunt's] dining room—one story high—without a window." By
the time Daniel was nine, his father had acquired land covered in
forest, which young Drake and his father cleared together. The father
and son not only worked together, but each was soon wounded at the
tasks (wounds inflicted by jackknife and axe). Daniel was given adult
tools, a mark of his father's trust that he was able to handle adult work.
Daniel's satisfaction with this assumption was clear. "Then forth
for 6 years I passed a happy life of diversified labor. . . . From the age
of 8 to 15 I had much care of our stock; for boys can do that kind of
work."[18]

The common work of American pioneer children has become an
essential story of frontier life. Less well known or acknowledged is
that gender boundaries were often disregarded in the course of this
experience. Daniel worked not only at tasks with his father but also
at those normally seen as women's work. To help his mother, he dyed
cloth, carried water from the spring, helped to nurse the younger
children, and cooked. His work was indeed diverse as he did what
was needed with little complaint—or so he remembered years later
when writing his memoir. Then at fifteen, he was separated from all
of it—from his physical labor and from his pious parents (his mother's favorite word was "wicked"). She was hardly indulgent of him,
either in the work he was required to do or in the virtues he was expected to display while doing them.

Many boys did female work. Henry Clarke Wright, who became an outspoken educator and a radical abolitionist, spent his childhood helping his stepmother by babysitting, and much more. "He cleaned, he cooked, he washed." In upstate New York, where his family lived in the early nineteenth century, he also did more masculine work "riding the horses, yoking and driving the oxen, bringing in the cows, harnessing and all the rest of the hard labor of the frontier farmer." After his farming experience, Wright was left to become an apprentice in April 1814. Lonely, "home-sick" and with a "feeling of wretchedness," Wright learned to grow up fast. He also learned his own mind and how later to defend his extremely independent and unpopular views.[19]

The American boys of the early republic grew early into independence. They were neither indulged nor coddled. They were given some say in the objects of their labor and, when possible, free time to play. But the children were also seen as "little citizens"—persons with capacity as well as potential. Some visitors were shocked by the results, but others were impressed. One Englishwoman observed, "You will see a little being that has not seen the sun make one circle of seasons, lay hold on a toy, not to cram it in his mouth and look stupidly at it, but to turn it curiously over, open it if he can, and peep in with a look as wise as that of a raven peeping into a marrow bone. One mark of early observation and comprehension never failed to excite my wonder. Little creatures feed themselves very early, and are trusted with cups of glass and china, which they grasp firmly, and carry about the rooms carefully, and deposit unbroken."[20] There is, perhaps, a degree of exaggeration in such observations, finding the precocious engineer within the child not yet a year old. But in light of current findings by cognitive psychologists about the "scientist in the crib,"[21] perhaps it is less a matter of exaggeration than a willingness to see even young children as more fully capable of independent thought and action than most Americans are accustomed to today.

Americans at this time assumed that children needed less supervision and direction. This was true for girls as well as boys. By the time she was six years of age, Caroline Stickney (later Creevey), who grew up to be a nature writer, was expected to go to the doctor alone after she had fallen and severely injured her arm. It turned out to be broken. "Mother was too busy to accompany me and there was nobody else. Besides children were taught to stand upon their own feet in these days." Caroline's regular tasks included bringing the cow to pasture in the morning and retrieving her at night, and, like Ulysses Grant, she was able from an early age to roam freely in the woodland that this future botanical enthusiast loved to explore and whose trees she climbed regardless of risk. At ten, she was allowed to ride the family horse; when she asked her father for directions to find a certain path, he made clear to her that she could find her own way.[22]

Anna Howard Shaw had a more extreme experience, as her father sent his young family from Lawrence, Massachusetts, to which the family had migrated from England after Thomas Shaw's bankruptcy, to the north woods of Michigan. There the children and their mother were left alone to establish her father's claim to the 360 acres he had acquired, while he remained East to settle his affairs. Shaw's mother, overwhelmed by grief and disbelief at the raw and trying circumstances, collapsed emotionally and was "practically an invalid." This left the enterprise entirely to the five children. Barely twenty years old, Shaw's oldest brother, James, was in charge. Anna was recruited to lay floorboards on the earth and frame windows and doors. When even James left because he needed an operation that took him back to Massachusetts, the young children were left to fend for themselves, through a variety of "nerve-wracking" conditions and winters that "offered few diversions and many hardships." Anna eventually took advantage of opportunities for schooling that led to her unflinching grasp at independence as a professional woman. In later life, Shaw was a crusader for women's suffrage, and managed to become both a medical doctor and a minister. This kind of brutal induction into resourcefulness and independence, while not representative, was also not uncommon.

Girls and boys matured early, and Tocqueville, for one, believed that American children did not have or need an adolescence. The very young child, given the right to handle glassware or crockery, is a child invested with the capacity to act responsibly. Dr. Spock would note more than a century later that such confidence acknowledged that a child is eager to do "grown up things," like feeding herself in the same way as the adults around her. And early work laid the basis for later habits. Anna Shaw noted that work had "always been my favorite form of recreation."[23]

The English commentator who saw precocious infant explorers poking around their toys was observing a different model of child development, one that was becoming as alien to middle- and upper-class Europeans of the nineteenth century as it is to us today. While European children of the middle classes were being treated as precious objects of solicitude, needing careful protection, American children who later became presidents, doctors, writers, and reformers were exposed to adult work and responsibility. And they were far less supervised. It was not only that class was more fluid in the United States in this period but that the specific expectations about children remained more fluid than in Europe. Later in the nineteenth century, middle-class Americans, too, would begin to separate children from adult activities and treat them, as we usually do today, as fragile beings who needed special toys and risk-proof furnishings. But during this initial period when American society was being formed and the culture was laying down historical tracks, children were much more integrated into adult activities and given both more responsibility and more freedom.

Most Americans in the first half of the nineteenth century viewed their children's early maturity as natural, an expression of both the helping qualities they required in the young and beliefs about children's abilities to be useful from an early age. It was a widespread phenomenon in many parts of the new country and remained an active part of the culture up to the end of the century, while elsewhere in the Western world, children were sentimentalized. It was true for girls as well as for boys, observed in the eastern United States as well as the West, common among rural folk especially but in cities as well. Rachel Buttz's father, Tunis Quick, was raised in the Shenandoah Valley in the early nineteenth century. His father was a well-meaning "generous, kindhearted man," but his decision to back a neighbor's loan impoverished the family, and soon after his mother's death young Tunis was "hired to a neighbor who required him to do almost as much work as a full-grown man." Just past ten years of age, Tunis quickly became responsible in other ways as well. Tunis objected to the slavery that was a feature of the area in which they lived, so at fifteen he urged his father to move the family to the North. They stopped first in Ohio "where [he] was variously employed in farming, hauling goods and keeping a ferry on the Scioto River." Having worked hard and impressed his employer, young Tunis obtained the means to buy a home in Indiana where the family finally settled.[24] Tunis Quick learned early to assist his family as they struggled, and his sense of responsibility also gave him the ability to think independently and to have his views heard and respected. By what we would consider his mid-adolescence, he had not only directed his family's migration north, but he was buying property for them. Tunis's desire to leave a section dominated by slavery is also noteworthy, since it was the South, where slave ownership defined the society, that was the major exception to the developing democracy within families.

To some extent, the independence given to children grew from the ideals and values expressed in the Revolution since Americans believed that future generations had to acquire the characteristics that would maintain the principles enunciated in that event. But more than ideology was involved. No simple commitment to an idea can completely explain the behaviors so widely observed and the general willingness to heed children's independent judgment. Ideology will not necessarily loosen a father's grip over his sons when he had always expected to be obeyed and to have his commands met, even when he is committed to republican ideals. In the Southern United States, of course, this loosening of paternal power never happened, since slavery reinforced its grip. And even in other parts of the United States, some observed the loosening of parental reins with concern and attempted to inhibit the young through new institutions of supervision, such as schools, as they recognized how much mischief could be loosed in a world guided by revolutionary principles. Not all Americans took kindly to the idea of children acting on their own. But a widespread independence among the young continued nevertheless. American life in the first half of the nineteenth century was defined by conditions that made such views about children necessary while the restless temperament of Americans made them ready for change and improvement. Together, these conditions provided children with the leeway to become more independent as they became more useful. Utility as well as ideology needs to be taken into account if we are to understand the families that produced a Grant, Drake, Quick, Shaw, or Wright.

The changing circumstances of the early republic resulted from both material conditions and political institutions. Together, these were widely understood as fundamental to the difference between Americans and Europeans. A shrewd, early observer of the difference, the Reverend Enos Hitchcock, sought to sustain the new revolutionary ideology through appropriate childrearing and education. "The systems of education written in Europe, are too local to be transferred to America; they are generally designed for a style of life, different from that, which is *necessary* for the inhabitants of the United States to adopt: *they do not reach our circumstances, and are not suited to the genius of our government.*"[25] To understand the American regime of domestic relations, we need to grasp just how unsettled, raw, and unpredictable the American land and the developing economy were during the important first half of the nineteenth century, since the experiences of American children and their parents were an expression of that reality. This dynamic new economy revised expectations about youth and what it could achieve. So did the laws governing inheritance and generational relations. The changes in American domestic life also transformed power relations between men and women, husbands and wives, and this, too, affected generational relationships in important ways.

III

Certain characteristics of the new nation had important consequences for how children and parents treated each other, as well as for politics and economics. The American Constitution had made no provisions for political parties of the kind that brought Jefferson to office peacefully in 1801. But it did foresee the immense expansion of the economy and the possibilities for territorial growth that defined the United States during its first century of existence. A limited population, largely hovering along the Atlantic coast, exploded in size and in ambition after the Constitution took effect in 1789. New territories, resulting from treaties, purchase, and conquest, brought the United States to the limits of its contiguous continental expanse by the beginning of the Civil War in 1861 (Alaska would be added during the war). Rural expansion and a vigorous and voraciously expanding farming population that spread onto the rapidly acquired new territory meant that there was always more work to do than workers available to do it. This gave young people opportunities to test their independence. But working on the land was not the only option. Young people began also to look to new industrial production as manufacturing and the factory system expanded choices for young laborers in towns and cities on the East Coast. Even young women were rapidly absorbed into these new occupations. Despite the existence of poverty and inequality, the United States opened doors for young workers from among its own people and from abroad, tantalizing and welcoming immigrants from countries such as Germany, Norway, Switzerland, Ireland, and the rest of the British Isles.

Catherine Beecher, an educator, pioneer in ideas about household efficiency, daughter of an influential preacher, and sister of the famous novelist, described the buzzing and humming consequences. "Everything is moving and changing. Persons in poverty, are rising to opulence, and persons of wealth are sinking to poverty. The children of common laborers, by their talents and enterprise, are becoming nobles in intellect, or wealth, or station; while the children of the wealthy, enervated by indulgence, are sinking to humbler stations."[26] It is worth noting that even in this early period, some Americans were concerned about "indulgence" and its baneful effect on children and their future success. Beecher was concerned especially with the "domestic economy," and she quickly focused on children as the necessary beneficiaries (or victims) of this loosened social system. The uncertainties of station were directly influenced by the tumult of the economy. Children could not expect to follow in their fathers' paths, nor could fathers' influence be too heavy-handed, if they were not to squash their children's potentials—or lose their willingness to reside at home.

Beecher also recognized the consequences of the labor shortage that defined the times. Her own concern centered on domestic service. "There is such a disproportion between those who wish to hire, and those who are willing to go to domestic service, that . . . were it not for the supply of poverty-stricken foreigners, there would not be one domestic for each family."[27] The absence of adequate domestics and their sloppy service would be a constant plaint of middle-class housewives of the time, whose many duties and many children made some kind of assistance a necessity. The absence of help from a permanently designated servant class would have significance for the kinds of work that the children in the house, even middle-class children, could be expected to perform. This shortage helps to explain why young Henry Clarke Wright, with no sisters available, could be found alongside his stepmother at various domestic tasks. American labor shortages made gender as well as age assignments more fluid in the household.

Labor shortages both for in-home tasks and for those on the land and in the factory made youthful work profitable and desirable. It also meant that young people would move often from one kind of work to another. Young female school teachers became mill workers when factories opened up in places like Lowell, Lawrence, and Chicopee, Massachusetts. Men became clerks, taught school for a while, and then studied law or medicine. The fluidity of occupations and the scarcity of labor destroyed older apprenticeships, since few people wanted to invest years in such training when work was unstable and new options beckoned. It was a young person's world—full of opportunities and risks. This economic pattern helped to make young people more independent of their parents. It also gave them a sturdy sense of their ability to take chances and to exercise their judgment.

Another source for the changes in domestic relations was the nature of American law. Starting early in his career, Thomas Jefferson had actively opposed the kinds of inheritance laws that stymied personal independence and success, laws that maintained family order, hierarchy, and prestige at the cost of the future of children. He was vehement in rejecting primogeniture and entail, two aspects of British property law that put land in permanent and deeply undemocratic patterns of family descent. By the time Jefferson wrote against them in the 1780s, they were fast declining in practice, but he understood how important even lingering remnants of this older land-based family system could be, and he was vociferous in denouncing them where they still applied. As one historian of the law has noted, "It is significant that at least one influential Revolutionary American perceived that the logic of republican revolution pointed toward radical reevaluation of the law of inheritance."[28] By 1800, not only sons but also daughters inherited equally. In the new United States, the traditional obstacles created by laws that governed inheritance and the relationship between parents and children were removed. These impediments had maintained both patriarchy and hierarchical distinctions within the family.

Jefferson's thoughts on this matter appeared in a letter to James Madison in 1789 (at the point that the new constitution was going into effect): "'that the earth belongs in usufruct to the living': that the dead have neither powers nor rights over it."[29] For those unfamiliar with the quaint term "usufruct," it means the fruits of property gained through labor. Jefferson embraced the right of future generations to acquire and work the land equally and to own it in full. The land, for Jefferson, was the basis for all economic prosperity as well as independence; it should not be withdrawn from usage by laws that upheld the rights of past or present generations. Not held hostage to family tradition, or to the laws that supported it, children could venture forth to enjoy the fruits of the new society.

To grasp what the new legal regime meant for children in the new nation, it is hardly necessary to cross the Atlantic. Even in North America, some of these older patterns persisted—but not in territory contained in the new republic. In Alta California, still under Mexican jurisdiction and Mexican law, land was not divided equally among all children, as the law allowed in the United States. Mexican law still kept land in entail, holding it within the family estate, even after the father's death. This upheld a vision of the family as an institution with substance and traditions of its own, whose honor and prestige took precedence over the individual needs or desires of its members. Indeed, the power of patriarchy was unchallenged as fathers in Alta California determined whom their children should marry in order to increase family power and prestige, and constrained the choices their sons made about their future occupations.[30] In fact, wherever the law codes enacted in the Napoleonic period were adopted, they defined the responsibilities of parents and the obligations of children through inheritance, and these laws affected much of Europe and South America.[31]

Americans did not attempt to restrain children or impose an older view of the family through inheritance laws. Even children born out of wedlock found conditions much more flexible in the United States as brutal laws (once applied in the American colonies and still potent in other places such as Latin America) were relaxed so that children born outside of marriage could inherit and be recognized by their fathers. As one Texas court noted in 1850, "the rights of the children do not depend on the legality or illegality of the marriage of the parents. If there be a crime . . . they are considered unconscious of the guilt, and not the proper subject for the infliction of its retributive consequences." And Timothy Walker, one of the most significant legal scholars of the first half of the nineteenth century, thought the old common law practices (no longer applied in the United States) in this regard were devoid of "justice and humanity" because "the sins of the parents" were imposed on the "unoffending offspring."[32]

Law in the United States also had few provisions regarding the specific obligations of children to their parents. Parents were free to use inheritance for their purposes, and children could reject the offer. Walker, who found few laws that obligated children at the time he produced his legal compilation in 1837, was impressed by how much had changed since the colonial period. "From unlimited authority over the person, property, and even life of the child, the parent is now curtailed to a very guarded and qualified authority during the years of minority. And even this authority finds but little aid in the law in case of resistance." Where previously a child "might be whipped if he presumed to strike a parent," there was no longer any "legal provision for compelling even an affluent child, after majority, to support an indigent parent. . . . [F]ilial, like parental, duty is left as they should be by the legislature to depend upon natural affection."[33]

In the United States, inheritance of land that defined obligations within families and relations between generations were no longer regulated as in the Old World in ways that upheld patriarchal authority and subordinated the children's future to the will of the family. Outside of the South—where in the nineteenth century the desire to maintain the patriarchal order that underwrote slavery affected laws regarding families and children—American laws did not enforce traditional hierarchical obligations. Their emphasis on individual choice gave children a new status.[34] The relations between parent and child could more flexibly adapt to the circumstances and respond to the "natural" feelings of family members. This is how Tocqueville understood affection. But to fully understand the meaning of affection in the early nineteenth century requires that we look beyond the new economic and legal refashioning taking place to consider the critical role of mothers in these more "naturally" regulated families, where the quality of affection rather than laws were expected to define intergenerational relationships.

IV

"When as a little child I first looked into my mother's eyes, I found them full of gentleness and love, and their color was heaven's own blue. . . . She had a sweet disposition, a sunny smile and a pleasing manner." This is how Rachel Buttz remembered her mother. Sweet and mild, mothers at midcentury were pictured as the source of gentle childrearing and of wonderful memories.[35] In so portraying the mothers of the republic, nineteenth-century Americans endowed motherhood with a new value and growing power.

Mother's roles had traditionally been important but limited, constrained by patriarchal power in both law and custom. Women were subordinated to their husbands and dependent on them for their position and authority. Fathers ruled the family and oversaw the welfare of their children. Since women were regulated by the law of coverture—a married woman's political and legal existence was "covered" or incorporated into that of her husband—they had no independent authority in law over their children, and their own inherited property was to be administered by their husbands. This subordination was one of the key anchors of patriarchy, and it left women very little room to maneuver if and when they were forced to seek legal recourse.

Sabrina Ann Loomis Hills, who remembered her childhood as one of constant movement from place to place as her family spread throughout New England in the nineteenth century, provides us with a biblical image when she remembers previous generations: "A visit to my great uncles, Ely and De Forest Hyde, impressed my mind with the idea of the patriarchs of old as they stood at the back of their chairs while saying grace."[36] This was a fitting description since everything historians have learned about colonial America suggests that patriarchs ruled on this side of the Atlantic much as they did on the other. In New England, their rule was underwritten by biblical precedent and religious injunction; in the South by a slavery regime that emphasized the power of masters.[37]

Even well into the nineteenth century, in the public realm, legal patriarchy was still the rule of the day. It was only gradually and unevenly, state by state, that women were able to gain some of the means to correct this inequality in the ownership of property and the legal authority over their children. In 1848, when they gathered to demand their rights at Seneca Falls, New York, no state yet provided women with protections from male control and none gave mothers control over their own children.

In practice, however, American women were gaining a measure of private authority nevertheless, as Americans after the Revolution emphasized the contractual nature of the marriage relationship, and "the consensual nature of marriage."[38] The Revolution had substantially questioned authoritarian relationships of all kinds, and while women were by no means incorporated into the full array of citizenship rights, they did benefit from this general change, and one historian has even argued that it empowered women to begin making choices in regard to childbearing.[39] The tension between public life, where women remained handicapped, and private life, where they increasingly were given recognition and respect, defined the nineteenth century.

Changes in domestic relations were also responding to an economy that took men out of the home for work in factories and offices, a change that accompanied the Industrial Revolution. In colonial America, work was usually performed in complex households defined by the father's occupation and supervised by him. But as paid employment moved out of the home, women were left in charge of daily family life and children came under their control. This encouraged what historians have called the "cult of domesticity" in which the spheres of male and female influence were radically divided, and woman's home duties were elevated and came to define her sphere. This "enthronement of the mother" in the home, in Anne Kuhn's words, emphasized the power of "maternal example" and shifted "the authority-centered regime of the patriarchal family government to the more female culture of the nineteenth century."[40]

Operating in a vibrant and unpredictable economy, men pursued success and wealth more than ever or struggled to make a living in an increasingly competitive market economy. They found little time for their children. The Reverend John S. C. Abbott, a famous advisor on family life and childrearing and a critic of this lapsed authority, described the situation in 1842 as one of "paternal neglect." "The father . . . eager in the pursuit of business, toils early and late, and finds no time to fulfill . . . duties to his children."[41] This resulted in a vacuum of authority filled by mothers who, despite legal restrictions, remained at home and ready to take charge.

The sharp economic division that made this possible was never complete, even as women gained more control over the household. Catherine Beecher hoped women would not only take it over entirely but also transform it, rationalizing housework and making it more efficient, just as their husbands were systematizing the work process in factories. Beecher looked to women to become domestic engineers. But that never happened. Many forms of productive work continued to take place at home, including work for which women found remuneration. In rural areas especially, considerable overlap between the men's work sphere and women's home sphere continued for a long time, and much of America remained heavily rural throughout the nineteenth century.

The change was cultural as much as it was economic, as gender images distilled what were believed to be men's and women's essential qualities and characteristics. By the mid-nineteenth century, men and women, once viewed as distinct and separate versions of humanity, became almost like different species or races, with characteristics sharply divided: piety, chastity, and nurturance were seen as traits of women's personality, while entrepreneurial energy, sexual drive, and assorted nasty habits (swearing, drinking, smoking) were overwhelmingly associated with men.[42] This radical division of "natural"

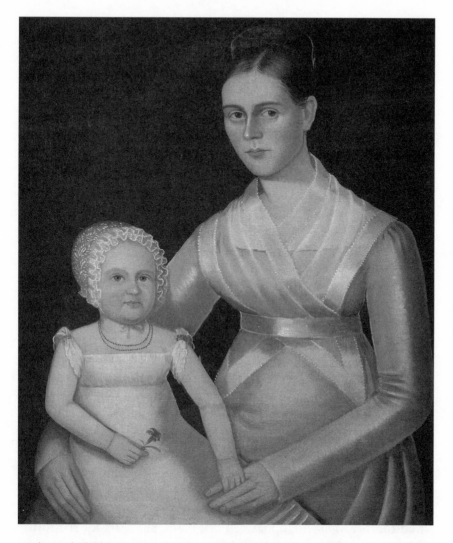

Mother and Child (c. 1820–1830). Painting by Ammi Phillips. Fenimore Art Museum, Cooperstown, NY. Gift of Stephen C. Clark, N0267. 1961. Photograph by Richard Walker. Courtesy of the New York State Historical Association, Cooperstown, NY.

attributes helped to keep women and men apart in their social worlds, encouraging a variety of same-sex associations.[43] As this happened, the management of children gravitated into women's domain, not only because children were usually raised within the household from which men were increasingly absent but because women alone were believed to possess the right attributes to raise them. Children's proper nurture, as it was now defined, needed the very special traits that women possessed.

Horace Bushnell, a prominent midcentury minister, presented women's special qualities of nurture in the most lofty terms. Mother's love, he asserted was "semi-divine," the result of no "mere animal instinct," and "measurable in no scale of mere earthly and temporal love." With such special religious qualities, mothers provided the young with the moral guidance to ballast character in a world of temptations, uncertainty, and rapid change. Women were both naturally maternal and divinely inspired as they looked through "the body into the inborn personality of the child—the man or woman to be."[44]

In invoking the special qualities of women, ministers like Bushnell were also radically transforming earlier Protestant beliefs about children's nature and the importance of childhood experience. Once viewed as born in sin and naturally inclined to evildoing, children were now portrayed as beings ready for grace. "This motherhood may more certainly plant the angel in the man, uniting him to all heavenly goodness by predisposition from itself, before he is united as he will be by choices of his own."[45] Because of their exquisite qualities of nurturance, only mothers had the means to make children, now viewed as impressionable from earliest infancy, into beings who were moral, religious, and good. Drawing on their natural predispositions, women would prepare children for their heavenly futures and their roles in a radically transformed nation.

Sarah Pugh's diary registered these new views at the time of her mother's death. As Pugh mourns the loss of "the one who, above all, loved me, *my Mother* [emphasis in original]," she fears for the future without her. "What to me will be my future life without this central point of love and devotion?" But she draws strength from her knowledge that her mother's profound love would guide her life and actions as a "good and faithful servant!"[46] Pugh's mother's love provided for inner strength and the ability to continue on the right path even without her.

The emphasis on the centrality of a mother's love was spread broadly in the first half of the nineteenth century in sermons and women's magazines. Lydia Maria Child, probably the most influential magazine publisher of her day, devoted an entire chapter to the subject in her *Mother's Book*, published in 1831. Child believed that maternal affection was so strong that it was able to subordinate selfish drives to the needs and wants of the child. But a mother's love was no simple matter of uninhibited feelings. It required self-knowledge, disciplined devotion, and an ability to "govern her own feelings." She needed to be consistent as well as fond, serene as well as gentle, as "the mother holds . . . the hearts of her children in her hand."[47] Proponents of affectionate mothering, like Child, were clearly aware of the dangers as well as benefits of affection-based childrearing as women previously accustomed to administering harsh forms of discipline began to adopt a softer style. Subsequent American advisors on childrearing would spend more than a century trying to tame this "natural" maternal affection that emerged prominently in the middle of the nineteenth century as the key ingredient for child nurture.

The elevation of female nurture in childrearing in the first half of the nineteenth century accompanied a new religious orientation. The Protestant Christianity that ministers, such as Bushnell, promoted was a more benevolent religion than that practiced in colonial America. A patriarchal God, once portrayed as harsh and punitive, was replaced by a gentler divinity whose distinctively female qualities are nicely captured in the following poem (one of many of its kind):

> Jesus can make a dying bed
>   Feel soft as downy pillows are,
> While on his breast I lean my head,
>   And breathe my soul out sweetly there.[48]

If we leave aside, for the moment, the poignant reminder in this ode to mortality of just how vulnerable a child's life was understood to be at this time, we are left with a very strong association between Christianity and female virtues. Fathers' authority, bolstered by a fierce paternal God, was elbowed aside as women's qualities and women's role as childrearers became the basis for real households as well as the religious ideals and sentimental imagery that sustained them.

This connection between a nurturing mother and a benevolent God became part of childrearing strategy. Caroline Stickney's (later Creevey) mother consciously made the association. When she found

Caroline, sobbing because she had blasphemed, her mother "caught me to her breast and comforted me as only a loving mother can." She then advised Caroline to confess to God, since He was very like a mother, offering forgiveness and love—someone in whom a child could confide. "After that," she recalled, "I tried to feel that this dreadful Being was more like mother than I had supposed, and that, perhaps, He cared for me."[49] Caroline Stickney captures the very transformation taking place at the time in how God was imagined.

Did this association between a yielding divinity and the nurturing, almost angelic mother give women power? It certainly did, though it was not easily measured in law or politics. As the American family was reframed by the revolutionary heritage, the law, and a changing economy, American women were given a perch from which to alter the future. The importance of this imagery of "natural" motherhood was so great that it could even overcome lingering legal patriarchy. By the mid-nineteenth century, judges in child-custody cases regularly gave mothers custody of young children, despite the fact that fathers continued to have a legal right to those children. In *Mercein v. People* (1842), a case that defined the change, the judges of New York's highest court noted that "the law of nature has given to her an attachment for her infant offspring which no other relative will be likely to possess in an equal degree, and where no sufficient reasons exist for depriving her of the care and nurture of her child, it would not be a proper exercise of discretion in any court to violate the law of nature in this respect."[50] This case became the basis of the "best interests of the child" doctrine that still governs matters relating to children. Although the case's circuitous route through the courts left the law of child custody in "a deeply confused state" at midcentury, according to one legal historian, the confusion itself suggests the degree to which even legal reasoning was influenced by the belief that mothers were the best guardians of their children during their "tender years."[51]

Schools, too, responded to this vision of women's natural ability to raise children. As publicly funded schools spread in the middle decades of the nineteenth century, school boards turned to women as teachers of the young, thereby feminizing the teaching profession in the United States far earlier and more fully than anywhere else in the Western world. While labor shortages made female work with children attractive as the ideal of democratic schooling spread, women's natural characteristics also made it desirable. Other countries, in keeping with burgeoning nationalisms, also established public school systems and requirements for literacy, but nowhere else did the care of children in school become so thoroughly a female fact. As a result, American women enjoyed more advanced schooling themselves, going first to academies and then eventually to the women's colleges and state universities that grew up by the second half of the nineteenth century.

Not all mothers were consistent in adopting new childrearing guidelines laid out by women's magazines, advisors, and preachers. Cornelia Gray Lunt (whose adventurous and ambitious family helped to found the city of Evanston, Illinois) remembered her mother as loving. "Oh Mother!—Mother! Did I ever give thanks enough for you and your love?" "How good God is to me to give me such Parents." But it was a love punctuated by anger. In recalling her midcentury Chicago girlhood, she describes episodes when she was harshly reprimanded and disciplined.

Cornelia's mother could be loving and gentle, but also erratic, exacting obedience to her word and punishing freely by withdrawing love or objects of play. And she administered spankings that shook her daughter to the core. Sometimes, Cornelia hardly knew what she had done; sometimes she was innocent of the accusations. During her first severe punishment, she was shocked and shrieked because her "mother's gentle hand had become a sledge hammer to me." At one point, after being asked to take care of her three-year-old brother, Cornelia was punished for taking him into the yard and getting his and her shoes dirty, a transgression her mother claimed was compounded by lying: "her eyes were fixed on me from which all softness had fled. My Mother was suddenly a mystery." Cornelia remembered that she had been "rudely taught by something within to adjust myself to harsh contrasts of life."[52]

Hardly a beacon of warmth and reason, mothers like this could be inconstant in their affections and demanding in their expectations as they exercised new authority over their children. S. G. Goodrich, a children's book and magazine editor, nevertheless concluded that even poor or ignorant mothers were a positive influence. "The majority of mothers do in fact temper their conduct to their children, so as, on the whole, to exercise, in a large degree, a saving, redeeming, regenerating influence on them."[53] Despite the hedging language, the mother's new role was viewed as beneficial. Having replaced a patriarchal father and an angry God, Americans in the early republic turned to mothers and their redeeming love as the guide to childrearing.

V

A century later, the American mother had become a very different parent, more indulgent and prone to remain a presence in her child's life well into adolescence as more elaborate demands for schooling and a variety of other changes altered the patterns of growing up. By then, some observers were beginning to suspect that maternal affection was less a promise than a threat, one that undermined their children's independence and attached sons, especially, too closely to the refuge of their mother's love. One of the most prominent analysts of American family life and childhood of the mid-twentieth century, psychoanalyst Erik Erikson, argued that mothers had once demonstrated a different, less embracing kind of love. In a famous essay, "Reflections on an American Identity," he argued that American mothers of the nineteenth century loved and nurtured their young but then briskly rejected them and sent them out to venture by themselves. These mothers were "not overprotective" and demonstrated "a certain lack of maternalism"[54] as they prepared children to conquer a continent. This maternal restraint accounted for Americans' independent spirit and sustained their adventurous nature.

Erikson was writing about the mothers we have been observing gaining power over their households and their children. Although his views on the relationship between mothering and the American national character is almost certainly too simple, it is worth thinking about how the mothers who were portrayed as warm and kind in the nineteenth century could be viewed as harsh and "rejecting" a century later. Making this contrast in perspective encourages us to confront some of the differences in environment and beliefs that distinguish contemporary parenting from America's earliest approved-of parent-child relations.

In the nineteenth century, ministers and publicists for women's influence were concerned to quell the formerly harsh treatment of children who were believed to harbor evil inclinations, and the patriarchal power that supported it. (Remember that Daniel Drake's mother's favorite term was "wicked.") They urged women to express their love more emphatically and embrace their roles as mothers of the republic and channels of a gracious God. They described motherly devotion as a force for good and enshrined it as a divine inclination.

But the meaning of affectionate mothering was never simple or uniform, even before extensive immigration from a much larger European and then global realm brought ever more variety into the picture. The instructions for mothers to raise their children with love were meaningful in a particular kind of religiously guided universe. Many nineteenth-century women, themselves raised strictly to be obedient and God-fearing, sought to form their daughters and sons along similar lines. They quickly punished evil inclinations or plain mischief rather than inspiring good through their own steady affections. Others, like Caroline Stickney's mother, made a serious attempt to use their influence toward new goals. Some, like Cornelia Gray Lunt's mother, responded with less consistency.

Men in patriarchal societies had once instructed their sons in the work they were expected to perform and the roles they would have to assume. They chided and they punished. And they taught obedience. But paternalism was rejected in ideology and also by the circumstances of America's environment. Americans changed their ideals of parenting and the texture of generational relationships. Children were given more freedom for independent action, and they learned to exercise their own minds. They matured early. American women gained a more powerful role in their children's lives. Once women took over the task of raising their children beyond infancy, the task became both more consequential and more complex, but it was not mothering alone that would determine their children's futures.

Parenting was framed not only by political ideals, economics, religion, and changing domestic regimes but by the brutal facts of mortality. The high rate of child mortality that defined childrearing for all parents before the twentieth century creates a wide gulf between us and these parents of the early republic, a gulf in understanding and possibly even in sympathy. The emotional life of everyone in the family, but especially that of women, could be deeply tested by the death of children. While all parents before the twentieth century came to expect child loss, it became a special dilemma for mothers enjoined to show love to their children and to raise them in a new nurturing spirit. What kind of mother did it take to watch a beloved child die at an early age, as so many did in the nineteenth century?

Child-labor reformer Florence Kelley's mother lost five daughters at midcentury, all of them "in infancy and early childhood"—one at age two, one at eleven months, another two at seven and four months, and one at six years. Kelley describes her mother as demonstrating "utter unselfishness," but after the last death, her life was marked by "a settled, gentle melancholy which she could only partly disguise for the sake of my two brothers and myself, her only surviving daughter."[55] Kelley's mother was exercising self-restraint, as good mothers were advised to do, both as she watched her children die and as she thought about her living children, but she could not hide her melancholy from her perceptive and admiring daughter.

The death of a child affected everyone. Four children eventually died in the New England household of Caroline Stickney (Creevey). Her father was devastated by the death, in infancy, of the first-born son. He had "passed from the parental nest," in Caroline's words, "when he was six months old." His death was "a terrible blow to my parents"; her mother feared for her father's sanity because of "his wild grief." As a child, Caroline, too, learned to mourn the early death of a sibling. Her "first really great affliction" came when she was nine years old and her sister, Lizzie, "a winsome, happy little cherub," died of cholera infantum at eighteen months. "I had loved her so," Caroline recalled. She remembered the grief that overcame the entire household. "In the sitting room my father sat, holding the baby on a pillow in his lap. Tears were falling down his face. Mother was silently crying." Early the next morning, Caroline found the house "dreadfully still" and, creeping down the stairs, she found her baby sister in her crib "marble-like." The nine-year-old screamed and fell unconscious.[56] Even younger children could be deeply affected. For

Sabrina Ann Loomis Hills, "the burial of my infant brother particularly impressed my mind, though I was not three years old."[57]

Once it becomes the defining quality of family relations, affection can take many paths as it ensnares the human heart. Repeated deaths of children could test its limits in those who survived, and the desire to put children on the right path in anticipation of an early death could affect how it was expressed and managed. Women might prepare their children with the soft and downy pillows of the poem that heralded a milder Christian faith or with the harsh warnings about lying and disobedience of Cornelia Lunt's mother. Some expressed their depths of feelings "in agonies of grief";[58] some were restrained and stoic; others became melancholic over time. And separations and partings, either by death or by children exercising their early independence and moving away, were a constant feature of the lives of these families. Daniel Drake's mother had to exercise self-restraint when he left home to be apprenticed at fifteen. It was unlikely that she would see him for years, as he moved to a faraway city where transportation was crude, and she (or he) might die before he returned.

Instead of calling this mother either strict or fond, it is best to observe her growing power in the household as women redefined their place in the world of childhood. Where patriarchy had ruled, in Europe and colonial America, family life was defined by subordination and obedience. After the American Revolution it was mothers to whom tribute was paid. Mothers enlarged their roles at home and in childrearing while overseeing the newly laid basis of an unfolding tradition of children's competent independence. Americans would contend with these two traditions for a long time as they hoped to maintain the characteristics of self-direction, competitiveness, and resourcefulness even as childrearing standards changed. How much love was the right amount?

Fathers had not disappeared. Far from it. They also sorrowed at the loss of their children, and their legal authority remained intact. By the end of the century, the image of the father would be re-created around a more loving figure. But the revered American patriarch was, by the middle of the nineteenth century, a historical relic. Instead of relying on patriarchal demands and filial obedience, Americans had created a new kind of family relationship against which many were now ready to measure all comers. It would exercise a powerful influence for a long time to come, since it enshrined independence as the essence of what Americans expected of their children. In this family pattern, children were given freedom and responsibility at a young age in the expectation that they would use it to become independent citizens and innovative workers ready to take on new tasks.[59] That ideal would remain a vital aspect of American identity. Mothers had the central role in this regime as the primary parent who was valued and rewarded with praise for that work; remembered as gentle, her "affection" was the natural glue of generational relations. Fathers were important participants in this new family, but increasingly as only one voice among many. This was the fruit of the social revolution that Americans had initiated as they became the citizens of a young republic. As Americans would discover after midcentury, children could also become a source of great social concern when their independence and their relationships with parents were not always what Americans had imagined them to be.

CHAPTER 2

Children Adrift

Responding to Crisis, 1850–1890

The death of infants and young children was widely expected as a hazard of everyday life in nineteenth-century America, as it was elsewhere in the Western world. In 1861, another hazard arrived to afflict adolescents and young adults in the United States as the scourge of war brought death in the hundreds of thousands to soldiers, and the deprivations and diseases accompanying war afflicted both soldiers and the civilian population. The Civil War was both metaphorically and actually the great destroyer of the American republican illusion of innocent perfection, a conflict that wreaked more havoc than any other single event in American history. As Americans divided into North and South, battlefield casualties were doubled by innovative tactics of destruction and the circumstance of American fighting American on American soil. The latest estimate of war deaths is 750,000, as battlefield mortality and the diseases that afflicted those imprisoned and hospitalized took an almost unthinkable toll. No war was bloodier, more painful, or more of an assault on civilized habits. As Drew Faust has observed, the war altered basic American "conceptions of how life should end."[1]

Very young men were sometimes among the battle dead and wounded. But the casualties of war included children, widows, and other family members left without support.[2] The resources of many families previously adequate to the task of bringing up their children became overburdened as husbands, fathers, or sons disappeared, often forever. And the war precipitated a series of new concerns that modified, though they did not overturn, the American commitment to children as capable and valuable in their independence.

These concerns initially focused on the children of freedmen in the South, former slaves who had not previously been a serious part

of conversations about American generational relationships. Reformers eager to do good moved south after the war to help children of
former slaves find their kin and to learn to read and write. They soon
shifted their attention to children in cities, in factory work, and among
the lower orders more generally, many of them orphans or the children of immigrants perceived to be inadequately parented. The decades after the war witnessed a tumult of changes that deepened ap-
prehensions about America's children and their future. Triggered by
the chaos of war, these anxieties soon merged into the realities of a
world that had moved very quickly beyond the familiar life of the
early republic.

These anxieties would make Americans aware of childhood in a
new way and lean much more on sentimentalized images of childhood already widely available in the Western world. A new attachment to visions of the betrayed innocent child infused concerns about
children who were abandoned or abused, all of them seemingly lost
in a new society. These changes also brought new players into the public arena, citizens whose orientation to the next generation was informed by questions regarding safety and social resources: Who should
supervise children whose parents could not or would not do so?
When were children, even the most resourceful children, no longer
safe in a world full of unexpected hazards? In this context, Americans
developed a new network of caretaker institutions to supplement or
substitute for the family. These institutions and officials then openly
articulated views that had previously been taken for granted—how
parents could best care for their children.

I

When Lieutenant John Townsend Ketcham wrote his mother about
his brother Edward Hallock Ketcham's death at the Battle of Gettys-
burg, he noted, "Mother, yet a little time thee and I have to walk this
earth, when we compare it to the great eternity beyond, where father
and Edward are gone before us." He could not then have known how
little time remained to him. John Ketcham was taken prisoner and
sent to Libby Prison where he died on October 8, 1865 (after the war
ended), joining his father and brother in death but leaving his mother

alone.[3] John and Edward Ketcham were among the hundreds of thousands of combatants whose death or severe incapacity changed the nature of generational expectations, as mothers or children were left to fend for themselves in a war that showed no pity.

Ulysses Grant, the hardworking Ohio boy, became a great general during the war as his successful military strategies demonstrated his immense gifts as a tactician and a leader. On April 9, 1865, Grant accepted the surrender of General Robert E. Lee at Appomattox Courthouse, bringing the bloodiest and cruelest war in American history to a conclusion. By leading the Army of the West, Grant had played a large part in securing the victory. While the war's causes lay in the past, its aftermath would help to define the future of families and children throughout the second half of the nineteenth century.

"The cause of the great War of the Rebellion against the United States," Grant observed in his memoirs, "will have to be attributed to slavery."[4] Slavery was an exploitative labor system that directly contravened American beliefs in giving freedom to children and greater household authority to mothers. The right of laborers to make their own choices was an important ingredient in the events that eventually impelled Northerners to fight their Southern compatriots. Before the war, Southerners gloried in the belief that their form of slavery exemplified the best kind of patriarchy, with strong fathers protecting their wives and all their "children," black and white. Most Southerners had not owned slaves but the region's leadership, culture, and politics were defined by those who did. The subordination of children, women, and slaves to this patriarchal ideology had separated the region from the Northeast and Midwest in its family ideology as it did in its labor system. So did the laws governing family life.[5] Southern women exercised far less control over their children, and slave households stood apart entirely from the patterns we have observed developing in the United States in the early republic. For the vast majority of Southern blacks who were slaves, neither children nor adults were free to express their desires or define their destiny. While Southern white fathers had the right to supervise and the authority to protect their children, enslaved black parents were entirely deprived of this ability; their wills were subordinated to the desires of their masters, whose control over the children of slaves was absolute as the owners

Five generations on Smith's plantation, Beaufort, South Carolina (1862). Photograph by Timothy H. O'Sullivan. Civil War Glass Negatives and Related Prints Collection, Prints & Photographs Division, Library of Congress, Image # LC-DIG-ppmsc-00057.

of their bodies and future labor. Almost all slave children recognized this crucial fact of life at some point in childhood, and when they did it was both painful and clear.

 Even though Jacob Stroyer was given some small say in the work he was to perform—like Ulysses Grant, he enjoyed working with horses—when he was thrown from a horse he was quickly beaten by the master's groom. Jacob complained to his father, expecting some redress for his ill treatment, but was told, "Go back to your work and be a good boy, for I cannot do anything for you." His mother, too, proved powerless. "Then the idea first came to me that I, with my dear father and mother and the rest of my fellow Negroes, were doomed to cruel treatment through life, and defenseless." Other slave children, too, realized not only their own defenselessness but that of their parents, because "they themselves had to submit to the same treatment."[6] Slavery contradicted the beliefs of Americans in myriad ways, but never more than in the fact that the work children did was built into the enslaved condition, never an exercise in self-direction, and never, as it had been for young Ulysses Grant, a part of learning to become a competent and independent adult.

In wrestling over slavery before the war, Americans often invoked the image of the child. Southerners emphasized the benevolence of slavery, under which kind masters cared for the needs and took responsibility for the welfare of their black and white children. Northern opponents of slavery used sentimental visions of childhood in publications of all kinds to attack slavery and the wounds it inflicted on families and children. Northerners rejected the supposed benevolence of patriarchy as hypocritical, abusive, and cruel. And most Northern opponents of slavery differentiated their own reverence for family from what they saw as the intrinsic abuses of familial relationships for whites as well as blacks in a society based on slavery.

The most prominent text to use this imagery, the novel that Abraham Lincoln claimed had helped to start the war, was *Uncle Tom's Cabin* (1853). By connecting the wounding of childhood and the destruction of innocence to the institution of slavery—to its exploitation, systematic degradation, and insensitivity to family ties— Harriet Beecher Stowe underscored the domestic treachery of a political problem. The book's beautiful heroine, Little Eva, more an angel than a child, dies because her innocence, goodness, and charitableness cannot withstand the South's harsh realities. The death of children was a common experience in the middle of the nineteenth century, but the death of Little Eva used knowledge of that pervasive reality to political purposes. It also provided a monument to the sentimental impulses that became part of nineteenth-century views of childhood throughout the Western world.

Enslaved Africans worked hard to find some place for family life from the beginning of their experience in North America, and they negotiated "for a modicum of domestic security."[7] In the Chesapeake region, for example, Ira Berlin has shown that they created certain conventions regarding their rights, which included naming their children, and visitation between husband and wife if they lived on different plantations. But their masters ultimately had the upper hand, and the families that slaves created were fragile. Most slave children were part of families, broadly defined to include kin of several generations as well as fictive kin, but none had been immune from the fear of separation that *Uncle Tom's Cabin* used to such great effect in its portrayal of a slave mother fleeing with her child from the threat of separation. And few slave children came to adulthood without experiencing some deep loss—of a father, mother, or sibling. American slaveholders and slave traders had treated children as useful and important parts of a profitable enterprise. As a result, very young children were rarely parted from their mothers, but older children could be sold or transported to other plantations; some were used to pay debts. By the time they were sixteen, one-third of all slave children had been removed from their parents by sale or transfer, and this was likely an underestimation because it is based on the experiences of former slaves interviewed in the 1930s who were still young at the end of the war.[8]

Work, not nurture, was the destiny of slave children whose fragmented families, deprived diets, and foreshortened periods of development were part of their rigidly defined status and their destiny. Even very young children were given tasks to perform for the master and his household, not just to accustom them to work but to enforce their subordination. A two-year-old might be asked to rock a baby or open doors, five-year-olds could do farm tasks and could be punished for disobedience or inattention. One slave, George Jackson, recalled that his mistress used to supervise him as he pulled weeds. "Sometimes I pulled a cabbage stead of weed," for which he would be whipped because "She told me she had to learn me to be careful." "By age ten or twelve," according to one historian, most slave children "were capable of working alongside adults in the field."⁹ They were not yet considered full field hands, but girls and boys were already set on the tasks that most would be expected to do for the rest of their lives. While a few wound up learning a craft or serving in the masters' houses, the fields—whether of tobacco, rice, sugar, wheat, or most of all cotton—became the destination of most children. Thus the future held few surprises or new kinds of ventures for slaves who had hardly reached adolescence.

At a time that motherhood was raised to a sacred status in the United States, the fragile maternity of slaves could be broken at will and reflected the nature of the institution of slavery and the power of masters that lay behind it. And there was nothing sacred about marriage between slaves from the point of view of planters who did not recognize the slave marriage rituals (and did not respect the exclusive sexual rights of the partners) and who could separate partners without compunction. Slave families could be dissolved and all slave children removed from their most intimate contacts at the will of a master, or after he died as his estate was divided or sold for debt. This threat was a constant reminder of the slave family's vulnerability as well as a means to keep mothers and fathers in line.¹⁰

Most stories about slave family separations were evanescent, retold within the slave community as part of the rich oral culture among African American slaves. Some were recorded in 1937 when interviewers for the New Deal's Works Progress Administration (WPA) took down the recollections of surviving freedmen and -women in one of the most remarkable historical recuperations in American history. Most episodes of separation became part of the careful recording of plantation account books. And some appeared in fictionalized narratives like that of Harriet Beecher Stowe. We also have the story of Mary Walker's struggle to save her children from separation and from their inevitable future destiny as slaves that has been assembled recently by a historian.

Mary Walker was a light-skinned slave born on August 18, 1818, on a plantation in North Carolina owned by Duncan Cameron. A favored house slave, Mary was early trained as a fine needle seamstress to serve the women of the household. When her master became president of the State Bank in Raleigh, North Carolina, he took his wife, his six unmarried daughters, and a dozen house servants with him. Then several daughters became ill, and "Judge" Cameron, desperate to save them, sent them for medical care to Philadelphia, where Mary Walker accompanied them. On one of those trips, in July 1848 at the age of thirty, Mary Walker escaped from slavery with the assistance of a well-organized group of blacks and whites eager to assist runaway slaves.

Despite being a valued and well-treated house servant, Mary had acted as she did to avoid separation from her children. She had reason to believe this was about to happen as Cameron's son Paul took charge and changed the routine of the plantation. She subsequently spent the entire period from her initial escape in Pennsylvania until the end of the Civil War trying to buy her children's liberty so they might be reunited with her. As one of the intermediaries who acted on her behalf noted "her heart is slowly breaking. She thinks of nothing but her children, and speaks of nothing else when she speaks of herself."[11] Through hard work, she managed to buy the freedom of some of her children. It was not, however, until the end of the Civil War in 1865 that she succeeded in reuniting with the last of her sons.

Even the most pampered slaves were never sure they could keep their families together. The distance between the power of such a mother and the typical mother in the North, whose growing role within the family we have observed, was enormous. Even privileged adult slaves were without recourse against their masters, treated much more like dependent and incompetent children than were many of the children of the North.

The general wretchedness of the slave condition became especially visible as Union soldiers confronted the large numbers of ragged slave children who began following Northern troops during the war and whose number grew toward war's end. Writing to his parents, one soldier observed, "The nigers are thick as fles a round a barn yard, negrows wenches and childrens they have escape from the rebs, the roads and woods are fool of them."[12] In hopes for freedom, children increasingly became camp followers, offering services of various sorts by attaching themselves to the Army of the Republic. In many cases, men who freed themselves by joining the Union Army tried to find ways to liberate their families. Some northern army commanders set up contraband camps at military bases where children received charitable assistance, medicine, and Bibles.[13] As the army marched through the South, the condition of black slave children could not be ignored.

The nature of slavery as an inherited part of their parents' condition was a profound contradiction of American freedom and an affront to the commitment not to define the child by the status of the parents. But the visible experience of deprived children—nearly all could not read or write—as well as their neediness and earnest desire for help was one of the encounters of war that few had expected or later forgot. Oliver Wilcox Norton wrote about the desire for freedom he found among slaves as well as their abysmal illiteracy. He had brought a Sunday school paper with him and "I read some of the stories to the children and gave them the paper. How their eyes sparkled as they saw the pictures! But the reading was Greek to them." "This is 'the land of the free and the home of the brave,'" he concluded sarcastically.[14] Those in charge of troops who went to Southern states as the Confederacy was defeated often noted in their reports that children urgently needed instruction "in the elements of an English education," and called for teachers and "elementary books, primers, spelling books, etc." to be sent for this purpose.[15]

Slave children never could reach that "higher destiny" that Nathaniel Willis had announced as part of the American promise during the early republic. Just as slavery was a manifest contradiction of American freedom, slave children exposed the underside of American parent-child relations—children whose parents were unable fully to care for them or to protect them. After the war, over a million formerly enslaved children, some newly reunited with parents and kin, opened a brief chapter in the American story of family relations as the possibilities and promises of freedom opened up to black children.[16] Parents, children, and siblings scrambled to reunite, as they looked forward to a time when domesticity, the ability to earn their own living as free men and women, and literacy would become their right.

Newly freed slaves struggled for what one historian has called "the right to maintain the integrity of their families." They did so alone as well as with help. Some of this assistance came from the federal agency known familiarly as the Freedman's Bureau. Not all succeeded, but many families were made whole at the conclusion of the war. In pursuit of real change and with high hopes for success, strongly committed black reformers and Yankees came to save the newly freed young, promising family reunions, education, better clothes, and better food. But within two decades of the war's end, most of the promise went unfulfilled as an older system of discrimination and racism cut off the children of the freedmen from any real betterment, let alone that "higher destiny" which was the supposed reward of American childhood.[17]

That story of forgotten promises remained largely (though never entirely) hidden in the South in the decades after Union soldiers and reformers left the South at the end of the Reconstruction regimes in the 1870s. Instead, the poverty of freedmen and their children and the tightening grip of the Jim Crow system of legal separation between white and black confined young African American children in the Southern states to a netherworld of freedom, with none of the fruits that whites took for granted. The children of freedmen and freedwomen would become old men and old women before real opportunities for equality in the United States became available a century after the conclusion of the Civil War, in the civil rights legislation of the 1960s.

In this Southern world of semi-freedom, African Americans took care of their own orphans as they had in slavery days. Extended family ties, and even strangers, made up for the absence of real opportunity and the hazards of life when children were left without parents. Children whose parents had died, disappeared, or disclaimed responsibility were provided for informally in a process of kin and community adoption and support that African American sociologist Charles Johnson would write about in the 1930s. "The ease with which the adoptions are made is interesting. There are few families, indeed, however poor, that would not attempt to rear a child left with them. Adoption, in a sense, takes the place of social agencies and orphans homes."[18] But the problem of broken families and homeless children were not problems for African Americans only.[19] Fully exposed by the war, these deprivations of care captured the national imagination thereafter.

II

With the wreckage of the nation before them and the growing number of the war's orphans,[20] Americans began to pay much more sustained attention to threatened and isolated children everywhere in the nation. Immigration and urban growth had already made such children familiar figures before the war, but it was in the two decades after the Civil War that children without parents and those neglected by parents held the spotlight. Just as the Revolution made Americans eager to understand how independence could be encouraged in the household, the Civil War exposed the problems of stranded children whose isolation was a result not of nurtured independence but of abandonment and unthinking neglect.

The betrayal of innocence represented by these children soon dominated discussions of parenting. What after all was a child's due, and what were the society's obligations to provide it? When did the interests of children override the authority of parents, and who determined this? What did it mean to be forced into an early adulthood, and how was this related to what Americans understood as a proper childhood? A society committed to independence became deeply troubled by homeless children, who embodied independence in its most extreme and brutal form.

The end of the war had not been the beginning of these questions. In the American colonies and during the early republic, the care of poor, vulnerable children—usually the orphan or bastard child, who had no rights and was bound out or indentured to avoid becoming a charge on the community purse—had been variously addressed through private charities or the public poorhouse. And the problem was a familiar one in Europe for centuries. By the 1850s, as immigrants accumulated in bulging American cities and poverty became visible and stark on dangerous streets, the philanthropic and reformist

"Prayer Time in Five Points Nursery, ca. 1889." Illustration 23 from Jacob Riis, *How the Other Half Lives: Studies among the Tenements of New York*, edited by Sam Bass Warner, Jr. (1890; repr., Cambridge, MA: Harvard University Press, 1970). Note that the Five Points Nursery was one of the institutions established by Charles Loring Brace and the Children's Aid Society in New York.

impulse turned its attention to the problem of the street child. Found-lings were discovered on doorsteps; dirty, ragged children picked over street garbage; young thieves and "guttersnipes" lurked in the dark corners of forbidding neighborhoods; young girls learned the balance sheets of seduction.[21]

The fear regarding these children of the streets and the attempt to provide them with a more orderly existence was a profound prob-lem throughout the Western world by the mid-nineteenth century as a result of extensive rural-to-urban migration and industrialization. In response, European and American cities began to create a vari-ety of institutions to house the children as one way of addressing the problem. Institutions in Hamburg (*Rauhe Haus*) and in Mettray, France, created in the 1830s and '40s became the basis for widespread imitation, and similar institutions began to proliferate rapidly at mid-century in Europe and the United States, and then furiously after the Civil War.[22]

A quaint term with a long history, the word "foundling" described an infant, usually fatherless, abandoned by a mother unable to care for her child. The foundling was well known to European cities since at least the sixteenth century, when institutions were created for its care.[23] Starting in the 1870s, such infants, deserted at a church or a charitable institution, left on the street or at the door of a rich family, began to haunt the conscience of many American communities. Manifestly helpless, such a child became a reminder of urban disorder, family instability, and restless sexuality. Americans became especially alert to these matters after the chaos of the Civil War, when the foundling seemed to be everywhere and foundling asylums sprang up in major cities across the country—in Boston, San Francisco, Chicago, and Washington, DC.[24] New York, which had more foundlings than any other city, erected four such institutions in the decade after the war. As a vulnerable infant, without effective physical and emotional nurture, the foundling rarely survived for long. The asylums attempted to deal with the ruthless mortality statistics indicating that the vast majority of abandoned children could expect to die within weeks or months. The life expectancy of infants who were rescued was rarely much better, but the asylum took the children off the street and helped to give conscientious urban citizens the sense that something had been done, that a child thrown away had been recovered.

The foundling was the most sympathetic expression of innocence betrayed, and elicited the most sentimental response. But the abandoned infant was only one of a parade of missing and misplaced children who became the public face of the parent-child problem in the decades after the Civil War. Before they turned twenty, almost half of American children in the decades from 1860 to 1880 had lost one parent.[25] The displaced child was part of the demographics of broken families, a situation with roots in the war itself. The brutal toll of the Civil War left many children without fathers or with fathers too injured to work and unable to support their families. In the new young republic, the independent child embodied the ideal future citizen, while a loving mother replaced the patriarchal father. In the second half of the century, the familiar image of the loving mother was increasingly shadowed by one of a mother forced to discard her child as war, migration, and industrial dislocation directed concerns toward children left altogether too alone.

The streets of cities were full of children who had run away from abusive or drunken fathers (and mothers), as well as children who found employment or companionship there. New York, especially, was alive with street children, and Charles Loring Brace, whose life and career would become identified with the displaced children of the city, was transfixed by them. "Half-clothed, cold and hungry, sleeping around in boxes, not knowing where he shall get his next meal and utterly without friends, he can hardly imagine that there is someone above him, who truly cares for him and follows and pities him."[26] Brace was thinking that a heavenly father was incomprehensible to such a child, but in his mind was also the much more obvious absence of just and caring earthly fathers. Fathers were almost by definition nonexistent for foundlings, but as Brace discovered, they were also frequently absent from the lives of many of the young boys, ages seven to twelve, he encountered on the streets. These observations led him to establish the New York Children's Aid Society in 1853.

Brace was the son of a well-known and highly regarded Connecticut schoolmaster whom Harriet Beecher Stowe adored as her favorite teacher, and was connected by marriage to the Beecher family. Their observations about families, black and white, and about social conscience and religious obligation were helping to define the culture at midcentury. The Beecher sisters especially were framing how Americans conceived and modeled home life. Brace had also been deeply influenced by Horace Bushnell, the famous Hartford minister whose sermons about parents and children he had attended. Bushnell's view of the parent's vital role in forming the child's life and the child's ability to move toward redemption had left its mark on Brace's vision of children's needs and potentials.

By the 1840s, Brace had been observing the deterioration of family life among the destitute in the Five Points slum in New York City, one of the most insalubrious and dangerous areas anywhere on earth

"Street Arabs in the Area of Mulberry Street, ca. 1889." Illustration 25 from Jacob Riis, *How the Other Half Lives: Studies among the Tenements of New York*, edited by Sam Bass Warner, Jr. (1890; repr., Cambridge, MA: Harvard University Press, 1970).

at the time, and he sought to rescue children from the chaotic conse-quences. The purpose of the Children's Aid Society, according to one of its reports, "is to take from the streets, boys from seven to twelve years of age, who are living in such exposed and neglected circum-stances, as to be likely to fall into vicious habits, or those who have already taken the first steps into crime . . . to place them, if possible, in better circumstances, and to maintain an oversight and influence upon them after they leave."[27] Brace's attention to these children, his excellent connections to important people in the city, and his energy, vision, and fervor led him to found the society in 1853 and to imme-diately set up institutions to implement his vision, among them the Five Points Mission and the Newsboys Lodging House.

The society Brace created has subsequently been mostly remem-bered for initiating the "orphan trains" to the West that became com-mon in the later part of the century and which through their long

life sent about one-quarter of a million children on such expeditions.
In so doing, Brace set the pattern often imitated by other nations like
Britain. But Brace's objectives were much larger and more varied.
In salvaging children from isolation and neglect, Brace and the Children's Aid Society hoped in the long run to save American society
from the criminal consequences of such maltreatment and early training in indecency. But their immediate mission was to address the growing problem of homeless and abandoned children. At the end of the
Civil War, the author of a report from the Children's Aid Society's
Boston affiliate was aware that the war had deeply exacerbated these
conditions. "Some of our boys had fathers or protectors in the service
of the Government. Many children will be left fatherless and uncared
for, after the losses and destruction of the war."[28] The problem was
widespread and urgent. According to police reports, 150 children were
abandoned every month in New York during the decade of the 1870s.
In response, that year, the Children's Aid Society provided 24,000
children in New York alone with a variety of services. This included
6,000 orphans and 15,000 homeless youth.[29]

The common alternatives to the streets were the poorhouse, where
children would be warehoused, and the jails to which those caught
in crimes were sent. Brace hated the regimentation of institutional
life and thought it sapped the independence of children. In his view,
according to one of his biographers, "Compulsory prayer and strict
discipline could not encourage real virtue but only superficial accom-
modations to authority. . . ."[30] This suspicion of subordination to authority for the young was a distinctly American vision, here applied
even to the most marginal children.

Brace genuinely liked the children he met. He described the news-
boy, who was becoming a common sight on city streets, as a "lighthearted youngster." "He is always ready to make fun of his own suf-
ferings, and to 'chaff' others. . . . His morals are, of course, not of a
high order, living as he does, in a fighting, swearing, stealing, and
gambling set. Yet he has his code; he will not get drunk; he pays
his debts to other boys, and thinks it dishonorable to sell papers on
their beat, . . . he is generous to a fault and will always divide his
last sixpence with a poorer boy."[31] In line with his mentor Bushnell's
emphasis on the importance of parental influence, Brace looked to

fulfill the potentials of such young people by placing them in a good family environment that would promote positive growth and result in resilient independence.

As he set out to encourage real virtue and strength among these least fortunate children, Brace and the society he founded turned to a vision of a coherent family as they imagined these to have existed in the early republic, one that provided a strong contrast to the parents whose lack of concern for their children and vicious habits had caused the problems. How then to make families available to those homeless youth without sending them back to homes from which they had escaped or been expelled? Brace thought he found the solution among families in rural areas (and especially in the more western parts of the country), where a healthful locale and hardworking families would care for those who needed both care and the opportunity to learn to work. Among these families, Brace believed that children could develop good habits while contributing to a household where they would be appreciated and valued. Of course, separating children from their families (and many children Brace saved were not fully orphaned, some not orphans at all) was deeply problematic. But Brace believed that children deserved to be brought up to experience responsibility to others while being taken care of by those who could exercise their authority with insight. In his view, such families could still be found in Michigan (the first locale for the expedition of the orphan trains) or in Ohio or in upstate New York.[32]

The successful execution of such a vision is hardly the same thing as its morally inspired intention. And Brace has received his share of blame for breaking up families while allowing the labor of these children to be exploited. The varied and sometimes harsh experiences of "orphans" sent out West, who frequently became a convenient form of free labor, children who were inadequately monitored by his organization, form part of the larger story of the failures of foster care in the United States. Charles Loring Brace was America's great pioneer in this realm. Coming out of the first half of the nineteenth century, influenced by the molders of American ideals of childhood, such as Bushnell and Stowe, Brace's innovations in the care of abused and lost children were entirely consonant with the tradition of responsible children's work in the early republic.

The Children's Aid Society became the first in a long line of organizations that tried to help children whose own families were not up to
the task, children whose numbers and needs for care became an ever
greater challenge to cities during the late nineteenth century. Its influence spread far beyond the United States as the nineteenth century
saw a strong sharing of ideas among Western nations about abused
and abandoned children. Brace's emphasis on foster care within families, and the transportation of children to rural places, was often
imitated where fears about juvenile crime and homelessness were
growing along with industrialization and city life.[33] Over time, foster
families as the ideal solution to the problems of children inadequately
cared for became the preferred alternative to institutions such as orphanages and houses of rescue, and by the twentieth century they
were the reigning orthodoxy for states, municipalities, and charities
that responded to children left adrift. By the end of the nineteenth
century, Catholic organizations in the United States, fearful that the
Children's Aid Society's real intention was to convert the children of
their immigrant communities to Protestant beliefs, followed suit and
set up similar expeditions with similarly unpredictable outcomes.[34]
Throughout the country, and increasingly beyond it by the early twentieth century, children were removed from orphanages and placed in
"foster" or adoptive families wherever possible, and the pattern first
established by the Children's Aid Society continues to dominate our
view of what to do with the children of poverty and misfortune to
this day.

Ironically, one of the results of this concern to remove children
from institutions was that charitable organizations and the state that
empowered them broke up families simply because they were poor.
In the late nineteenth century, reformers feared that poverty itself was
a kind of disease. Brace was deeply anxious about the consequences
for children of such families who seemed to pass their bad habits
forward to the next generation. "The greatest evil that I have experienced in the whole course of twenty years' experience, and the one
that requires the most difficult handling is hereditary pauperism."
In New York, the Children's Act of 1875 sought to remove children
from the poorhouse where they resided with families who were dependent on public charity. By liberating children from such wretched

places, they removed children from the influence of their parents, hoping to stanch the inheritance of pauper habits. Poverty thus became a legitimate reason for breaking up families, much as neglect and abuse had been. As one historian has concluded, "No longer did parents need to commit a crime, act immorally, or abuse their offspring before reformers urged authorities to step in and remove their children." In the view of these reformers, if the children could be "placed early enough in a better environment, even the children of paupers could aspire to independence and self-support."[35]

During the Civil War, President Lincoln had used state power to break up the households of slave owners in order to free the abused slaves. In the late nineteenth century, reformers similarly saved the children of urban poverty from the perceived abuse of their families. In balancing the ideals of family cohesion against those of encouraging children to learn habits of independence, Americans began a long march along a razor's edge.[36]

III

The economic energy released by the war and the postwar recovery turned the reunited nation into an engine of rapid development and expansion, moving people from North to South, as part of troop deployments and postwar reconstruction through the Freedman's Bureau and other agencies eager to bring the South into a more enlightened modern age. Yankee teachers, mostly women, seeking to educate the freed children (and often their parents) followed the trek. As the Northern economy expanded, others moved from Europe across the Atlantic in a dizzying acceleration of migrations that spread beyond older regions of Western Europe toward the east and south of the European continent by 1890. The period also witnessed the rapid opening up of the American West to people who now traveled by rail as well as in old-fashioned wagons to fill up and fill in a nation that now spanned a continent. Orphans sent from New York, Boston, Chicago, and Philadelphia followed. Even freedmen and women and their children moved from the old South[37] to the newer West and Southwest and would soon begin to move northward as well, anticipating a much more numerous migration early in the next century. In addition to farming and industry, the number of mining enterprises and mining towns exploded in the West, as Americans split open the Rockies.

If all this relocation promised renewed opportunities after the bloody carnage of war upon the land, it also meant a new fear for the human wreckage that came with so much change so fast, and in so distended a society. After the Civil War, American literature adopted the image of the lone child in a mining camp as a kind of talisman, as the "Luck of Roaring Camp" first charmed readers of Bret Harte in 1868, and an orphaned Huckleberry Finn determined to move west defined the very substance of the American imagination. While the image of the child might humanize the rough life of miners or express the deepest yearning for freedom, the child could turn savage if not effectively cared for.[38] The dangerous classes that Brace had begun to warn about before the war were now everywhere growing, as social order was disrupted in a newly, but still precariously, united nation. The disorder was often most obvious in the children it produced.

In his *Commentaries on American Law*, James Kent, America's premier legal commentator, observed that "the courts of justice may, in their sound discretion, and when the morals, or safety, or interests of the children strongly require it, withdraw the infants from the custody of the father or mother, and place the care and the custody of them elsewhere."[39] This vision of a society's obligation to protect children had impelled Brace and was the firm basis for most actions to remove children from their parents. Americans took the family very seriously and did not casually disassemble it, but then in the second half of the nineteenth century there seemed to be more and more evidence that removal and oversight by the state or by organizations empowered by the state were becoming necessary.[40] Protecting children might require a partnership between parents and the state.

This was how Mary Ellen Wilson wound up with Francis and Mary Connelly on West Forty-first Street in Manhattan. But Mary Ellen's brutal treatment at the hands of those entrusted with her care created an uproar sufficient to be heard throughout the city, the state, and around the country. In April 1874, almost exactly nine years after the ceremonial conclusion of the Civil War at Appomattox Courthouse,

Mary Ellen came dramatically to the public's attention. Her plaintive story has become the subject of repeated retellings in the history of social welfare. The ability of her story to enter the realm of myth as she was freed from the terrors of her home life tells us much about the period after the Civil War when child mistreatment and cruelty became a domestic analogue to a war fought over the rights of slaves.

Confined and repeatedly whipped and beaten by the couple to whom she was assigned in 1868 by the New York Department of Charities, Mary Ellen's appeals for help were overheard by a visitor to the building on "an errand of mercy to a dying woman," whose last request was that something be done for the cruelly abused child. The kindly visitor, after trying to find aid from various institutions without success, finally contacted Henry Bergh, the founder, in 1866, of the Society for the Prevention of Cruelty to Animals. Bergh alone was prepared to help.

Mary Ellen's subsequent statements about her daily beatings by the woman she called "Mamma," the absolute restrictions on her freedom of movement, and the prohibitions placed on her playing with other children became the occasion for a citywide discussion of what a child could expect from her parents or caretakers. Among the many things missing from Mary Ellen's life, one seemed primary: "I have no recollection of ever having been kissed by any one—have never been kissed by mamma. I have never been taken on my mamma's lap and caressed and petted. . . . I don't want to go back to live with mamma, because she beats me so. I have no recollection of ever being on the street in my life."[41] Today, as stories of children confined to basement rooms by evil caretakers or subjected to sexual slavery by strangers capture broad audiences through newspapers and television, Mary Ellen's story seems like an anticipation of the problems that children face in a world where the cruelty of strangers seems more common than kindness, and where the mass media are primed to feast on the gruesome details.[42]

In its own time, the story became the symbolic moment for the inception of the Society for the Prevention of Cruelty to Children, an offshoot of the older society devoted to the humane treatment of animals. This society and its objectives became the resonant center, as well as the product, of a new public consciousness about children,

"Annie Wolff, aged seven years, as she was driven forth by her cruel step-mother, beaten and starved, with her arms tied upon her back; and as she appeared after six months in the Society's Care." Case No. 25,745 on the Blotter of the Society for the Prevention of Cruelty to Children (SPCC), from Jacob A. Riis, *The Children of the Poor* (1892; repr., New York: Arno Press and New York Times, 1971), p. 146. Note how this case was used to illustrate the kind of treatment that Mary Ellen had experienced and how the SPCC viewed its role as a savior of such children.

while its local branches proceeded to have lives of their own in cities across the country.[43] Throughout the Western world, the problem of mistreated children called upon the newspaper-reading public's emotional response, as the sentimental appeal of children required that strangers offer sympathy and succor to those who were both needy and innocent.[44] Societies to rescue abused children sprang up in cities throughout the Western world in response. The United States set the pattern and the New York Society for the Prevention of Cruelty became the first of these.

Symbolic or not, Mary Ellen's mistreatment and the creation of the society in the United States also marked the emergence of a new chapter in discussions regarding what it meant to be a child and how a child could be expected to be treated physically and emotionally by those who cared for her. In these cases, it became clear that the divinely inspired mother, carefully constructed in the early nineteenth century, who would rear upstanding children, was not the only possibility. In proposing to rescue children from abuse, Americans were exploring issues of children's rights that would become more common in the twentieth century.

Colonial Americans had spoken often of what children were due from their parents. By this they usually meant that they had physical, educational, and spiritual needs that their parents were required to address. Mary Ellen had clearly been deprived of these. Never having left the house, she was not provided with a way to learn about her society. She had been deprived of adequate clothing, of nourishing food, and of the companionship of peers. But Mary Ellen's appeal in 1874 was not based exclusively on her physical deprivation or inadequate education in mind and spirit. Her appeal was for emotional sustenance. She had the right to her mamma's kisses and caresses. These were now seen, by the huge audience that responded to her plight, as equally important and necessary to children.

Social observers such as Alexis de Tocqueville and legal theorist Timothy Walker had used the word "affection" earlier in the century, but its meaning was still ambiguous and not fully transparent when they invoked the term. By the time Mary Ellen makes her court appearance in New York in 1874, affection has been better defined. By then, a new emphasis on sentimental attachments, the tendency to view children as the emotional center of family life, and a childhood as necessarily set apart from other arenas of social life were becoming familiar. Sociologist Viviana Zelizer suggests that this new vision of childhood and its unique emotional value were infusing American culture by the last third of the nineteenth century, strongly influencing public policies as well as private lives.[45]

The new ideal of childhood removed children from the marketplace and separated them from commercial pollution. Innocent and vulnerable, children required protection from just those abuses that were commonly found on the streets, in industry, and in too many homes. This new childhood as a realm of innocence was visible in the illustrations of the period, in the imaginative literature of late Victorian fantasy such as *Peter Pan*, and in the fact that a story like Mary Ellen's could elicit a loud public outcry. In Mary Ellen's story, we witness a moment when private sentiments and public policies meet in the establishment of an organization whose purpose is to monitor the right of children to be treated according to the new definition, and the public's obligation to ensure their protection.

The rights of children were most often championed by people like Brace—well educated, well connected, and well raised. The values began at the top of the social order and reached downward as reformers tried to bring "childhood" to the poor and underprivileged. This would remain true for the rest of the century as charity workers, social settlement workers, and (in the twentieth century) social workers, turned their attention to providing assistance to the less fortunate.[46] Almost none of these people had experienced the streets as the children they hoped to rescue had. But insights into the conditions of the poor sometimes came from those who had glimpsed it, if only fleetingly, in their own experience.

Jacob Riis came to the United States in the 1870s at age nineteen, alone and with few resources. Like many other immigrants, he left behind a small-town existence, in his case in Denmark, to seek his fortune in America. His own father had exercised his authority in the strict patriarchal mold with his twelve sons, all of whom he guided into their professions. Jacob resisted. Apprenticed to be a carpenter, he chose instead to follow his own inclinations and desires by coming to the United States where he imagined he had the best hopes to prosper. This would allow him someday to marry his sweetheart, Elizabeth, whose industrialist father thought Riis's prospects inadequate to his beautiful daughter's station. Like all patriarchs, Elizabeth's father had the first and final say in these matters.[47]

Riis came from a good family and brought $40 and letters of introduction to the Danish consulate. But these proved inadequate in the new land, and so he moved from city to city to find work, as well as digging in a mine and performing menial tasks on a farm. His condition was at best marginal, and he found himself often unemployed and homeless on the streets. As Riis discovered, being poor and without connections, despite having a willingness to work and ambition to succeed, could land people in trouble—and in jail. Riis learned to survive, alone and hungry on the streets of New York, for quite a long time until he almost despaired of any possible improvement. He was frequently on the run from the police, who had little sympathy or understanding for his plight. In an overnight boarding facility at the local police station, often used to shelter the homeless, a fellow occupant stole his most prized possession, a gold locket with Elizabeth's portrait.

As Riis explained in the story of his survival and ultimate success as a journalist whose beat became poor New York immigrant neighborhoods, his experiences allowed him to understand those whose misfortune was inadvertent and whose lives could be salvaged with help from people of good will. At a time when reformers drew a sharp distinction between the vicious poor, who had been bred through generations of pauperism and crime, and the unfortunate poor, Riis's fall from respectability during his migration taught him to seek out those whom ill fortune, not evil character, had dealt a bad hand.

Later in life, as a successful journalist, Riis stayed true to his vision when he turned his attention to the many poor children of the city. These he captured in his sentimental and widely read vignettes and the photographs that gave visible meaning to the texts. In the children and their struggling but devoted parents, Riis found stories that became classic portraits of American urban poverty in the late nineteenth century. We still read *How the Other Half Lives* and the *Children*

"Sweatshop in Ludlow Street Tenement, ca. 1889." Illustration 17 from Jacob Riis, *How the Other Half Lives: Studies among the Tenements of New York*, edited by Sam Bass Warner, Jr. (1890; repr., Cambridge, MA: Harvard University Press, 1970). This is clearly inside someone's home; note the ketubah—Jewish wedding contract—hanging on the wall in upper part of the photo.

of the Poor for insights into the private lives and homes of the tenement dwellers of New York City, as well as the sensibilities of child saving.

Child saving became a kind of minor industry in the last third of the nineteenth century as many concerned citizens followed in the footsteps of Brace or attached themselves to the Society for the Prevention of Cruelty to Children. Poverty grew with the rapid pace of industrial life and the massive immigration from *shtetls*, villages, and cities throughout the southern and eastern perimeters of Europe—Italy, Greece, the Balkans, Russia, Poland, and even the Middle East. At a time when children were increasingly used to tug at the emotional heartstrings, who could resist responding to the appeal of young people fed into slums and sweatshops or found surviving as street hustlers?[48]

Among the children to whom reformers turned their attention were some not on the streets at all, but solidly occupied as workers. Rose Cohen was ten when her father introduced her to his workplace on the Lower East Side. There he was greeted by a coworker who met Rahel (later Rose) for the first time with "Avrom, is this your daughter? Why, she is only a little girl." To which he replied, "but wait till you see her sew." And sew she did, basting pockets from six in the morning until seven in the evening when she and her father trudged home to supper. During the day she sat on a tall backless stool amidst the din of machinery and the salty adult talk of the other workers. Rose tells of the routines, the drudgery, and the desire for even a slight variation in the daily grind. For her, Fridays were best; then she worked only half the day, spending the other half at home preparing the house for the Jewish Sabbath. "All morning I would count the hours and half hours and my heart beat with joy at the thought that I would soon leave the shop. . . . When I came out into the street I had to stand still for a while and look about. I felt dazed by the light and the air and the joy of knowing that I was free."[49] Freedom clearly came in many forms. Rose set her heart on the freedom to work at home.

At home, she turned to washing the floors and the laundry, after stopping momentarily to envy the school girls coming home for lunch in "their white summery dresses and with books under their arms, they appeared to me like wonderful little beings of a world entirely different from mine."[50] The contrast between these girls in white dresses who spent their days in school and Rose, who knew only work, could not be sharper. It was the lives of these privileged girls that became the standard set by child savers in the late nineteenth century. But, hundreds of thousands of Rose Cohens existed in the cities of the United States in the late nineteenth century— young, vulnerable, dreamy, eager to be released from drudgery and envious of those whose childhoods were defined by school, fresh air, and leisure time.

Children helping their parents caught the attention of the women and men who campaigned to stop child labor in the late nineteenth century, probably the most aggressive and widespread of the efforts on behalf of children. It was also a campaign that had a significant international dimension in the Western world. The regulation of child labor became the first of the rights proposed for children internationally.[51] The presence of so many child laborers was an assault on the ideal of a carefully protected childhood adopted by reformers who absorbed the prevailing sentimental vision of childhood of the period. Rose's very existence as a child worker contradicted its basic values, and her hard life could be used to enlist public support for campaigns against child labor. As an adult, Rose used her own story as a means to encourage reform.

In trying to protect these children, reformers overrode the desires of families who put children like Rose to work and insisted on their vital contribution to the well-being of the family. Most immigrant families, struggling to survive in difficult circumstances, could do so only with the help of their children. Many also brought with them to the United States an older perspective on children's obligations and obedience to their family's wishes. It was Rose's father who brought her to work with him, where he continued to supervise and care for her, as he did regularly when he made sure that she got some of the meat from his lunch plate. His caretaking represented a form of parenting increasingly suspect in the eyes of those child savers who were now officially protecting the interests of children.[52]

Rose's contributions to family survival were not unique either to the city or to poor working-class immigrants. We have seen hardworking children in the first half of the nineteenth century performing various household and rural tasks. Several things had changed, however, to make this working child a different and more frightening phenomenon. Urban children like Rose did not work on home grounds, as Ulysses Grant had, and while she worked under the supervision of her father, her work was not defined by him (or by herself) but by the routine of the workshop or factory. Her life was confined both because it was indoors and because it was regulated by the clock. Ulysses had worked at his own pace and then took time for various self-defined leisure activities in the open air. The newness of the urban industrial work routine offended the sensibilities of Americans when it was first introduced earlier in the nineteenth century, and became especially problematic when it was applied to children

Portuguese girl, spinner, Fall River, Massachusetts (1916). Photograph by Lewis Wickes Hine. National Child Labor Committee (US) Collection, Prints & Photographs Division, Library of Congress, Image # LC-DIG-nclc-03040.

later in the century.[53] By the late nineteenth century children by the millions became part of this new form of work.

Other things had also changed. By the time Rose was working on a high stool in a sweatshop, schools had become a common feature of American life. Public schooling, democratically available to all and publicly funded, was introduced into eastern cities and midwestern towns in the 1840s and 1850s. By the end of the Civil War, widespread schooling was an established part of Americans' sense of themselves as a democratic and modern people. Schools thus became an essential part of the project of Reconstruction for the South, whose white citizens, as well as freed people, were viewed as ignorant because of the lack of public schools. Where Ulysses Grant had gone to school irregularly in Ohio in the early century and Daniel Drake had moved from irregular schooling to an apprenticeship to a medical doctor, by the late nineteenth century, school attendance had become much more systematic, sustained, and regularized. In the 1880s, states began to pass compulsory attendance laws and set the age for leaving school between twelve and fourteen. Preparation for careers, while not nearly as clear-cut as they would become in the twentieth century, had also moved toward institutionalized training. Normal schools for teachers and medical schools for doctors became the usual path to the professions. And everywhere, schooling was identified with childhood and youth. Indeed, it was being linked to age in ways that made the association seem almost natural: children from seven to fourteen were more and more believed to belong in school.[54]

Reformers were affronted not only by the conditions of Rose's work, but by the fact that the work kept her from school and from associating with others of her own age. Indeed, factory work respected no social boundaries, mixing men and women, young and old, in ways that by the late nineteenth century threatened the separations between the sexes and between adults and children that respectable middle-class Americans took to be natural. This was what finally may have made reformers most apprehensive. Girls like Rose, young and vulnerable, seemed unprotected in the workplace, and the late nineteenth century was full of stories of girls "led astray" and seduced by older men, who stole their virtue and then abandoned them to the streets. In *Sister Carrie*, Theodore Dreiser, whose naturalistic novels tried to capture the pulse of real life, used the image of the girl adrift in the city to describe the possibilities and moral hazards facing such girls.[55] This was not at all Rose's fate, but it was the fate of many girls like Rose who either chafed at the restrictions on their freedom or were enticed by the allure of the cities in which they were shut up almost every day in dreary conditions. Many sought escape in romantic liaisons and the consumer goods these promised, as Sister Carrie did. In the late nineteenth century, the age of sexual consent was raised everywhere from (to us) an appalling ten to between fourteen and eighteen years of age in order to protect women from just such temptations and from the men who might offer them.[56]

What seems like meddling in the affairs of the poor was thus a response to the changes that had taken place in a society no longer safely rural, and to the many children no longer engaged at home by traditional household routines. Those earlier working habits were now remembered as providing the essentials of character training, as Brace did through the Children's Aid Society's embrace of rural families. Industrial work, immigrant families, disorder, ignorance, and immorality were all problems associated with cities and the loss of childhood among the poor. It was therefore not so much Rose Cohen that reformers were worried about but others in circumstances like hers who might well end up on the street, as loose cogs in a city that threatened innocence.

IV

"How strong is this attachment to home and kindred that makes the Jew cling to the humblest hearth and gather his children and his children's children about it, though grinding poverty leave them only a bare crust to share, I saw in the case of little Jetta Brodzky, who strayed away from her own door, looking for her papa. They were strangers and ignorant and poor, so that weeks went by before they could make their loss known and get a hearing, and meanwhile Jetta, who had been picked up and taken to Police Headquarters, had been hidden away in an asylum, given another name. . . ." Jetta was a well-loved, though poor, immigrant child who had gone to summon her father for supper. Her story, together with many other true stories of poverty, despair and survival that Jacob Riis wrote and gathered together in his books, illustrates the pattern of Riis's sympathies and those of the audience to whom he appealed. Jetta was eventually returned to her family, but only after years of fruitless search and only after Riis himself became involved.[57]

From his own experience, Riis knew that a stranger child could be lost and understood the importance of good luck in making it out of the morass of city institutions. Jetta's plight illustrated how easily a child could disappear in the city of the late nineteenth century and, more troubling still, how easily a child might be presumed to be abandoned when in fact loving parents were waiting to find her. Of course, parents were sometimes not loving, coping as best they could with difficult circumstances as the plight of the poor worsened in cities during the course of the nineteenth century.[58] This potential confusion between discarded children, abused children who ran away, and children who were inadvertently mistaken for these because their parents had the will but not the wherewithal to find them became one of the period's stock in trade. All these losses of childhood protection and preservation became part of the period's ardent speculations about the new requirements of parenthood.

The best-known story of a child in the decades after the Civil War was also a story of disappearance and attempted recovery. In fact, by the time Riis published his story about Jetta in 1892 in the *Children of the Poor*, the oft-told tale of Charley Ross, the "Lost Boy," had permeated the culture to become the emblematic story of a child lost in America. The broad reach of Charley Ross's story, by then a staple of journalism, had likely informed the shape of the story that Riis wrote about Jetta Brodzky.[59]

Neither poor nor an immigrant, Charley had spent his early childhood in the most privileged sector of American society. These characteristics (not usually associated with helplessness), allowed his disappearance to anchor his story in the national psyche, turning him into an emblem of innocence betrayed in the decades from the end of the Civil War to the 1920s. In its time, Charley Ross's story collected the emotional energy of the sentimental appeal of children and the sympathy for abandoned children, gathering these together with the fears generated by the children of the city streets into a composite that was irresistible.

Charles Brewster Ross was abducted by two men from the front lawn of his spacious house in Germantown, Pennsylvania, on July 2, 1874. Before him, the kidnapping of children was not unknown, but it was barely recognized as a crime or separated from the general plight of misplaced children. Kidnapping existed in the laws only as a misdemeanor and the police rarely took note of reported abductions, some of which found their way into the private advertisements of newspapers. A beautiful, curly haired blond boy not yet three years of age, Charley appealed to the contemporary image of innocence, a fitting companion to Stowe's blond and blue-eyed Little Eva. Trusting in the good faith of the men who lured them with candy, Charley and his brother, Walter, went with their abductors, ostensibly to buy firecrackers for the upcoming Fourth of July celebration. They rode off in a wagon on an afternoon when Charley's mother was away from home and the children were in the care of a nursemaid. When Christian Ross, Charley's father, returned in the evening to find his sons missing and then set off to find Charley, the plight of lost children became a national drama.

As a successful businessman, Christian Ross was well connected to the leaders of his community, but even he was told by the police that the children had likely wandered off when he contacted the authorities. But when Charley's brother, Walter, returned alone and Christian received a ransom note demanding $20,000 for the child's safe return, the police responded with alarm and began to blanket the area with officers and inquiries while Christian enlisted the help of family and community members in his quest to find the boy. Although he was shocked by the ransom demanded, not least by the fact that his son's well-being might be equated to cold cash, and by the blood-curdling threats to harm his son in various ways, Christian followed the advice of the police and refused to pay the ransom.

And Christian was initially supported by public opinion. "Here at our very door, and in our crowded streets, a child is stolen and hid away so successfully that neither its parents nor the authorities can find trace of either the stealer or the stolen," the *Philadelphia Inquirer* observed. The conclusion was obvious: "If the child of Mr. Ross can be stolen and hid away for many days together, the children of any other citizen may be stolen and hid away forever. They must find those who stole him, in order that the law may deal with them so rigorously as to make the punishment of the guilty a restraining terror to any who may think to make profit by stealing away children."[60] Christian went through weeks of torment as he received a series of ransom notes with escalating threats while bargaining unsuccessfully for the return of his child. He knew neither Charley's fate nor his whereabouts; like Brodzky's daughter two decades later, little Charley had disappeared into the netherworld of the city where neither police nor private efforts could discover him.

Christian's loss, unlike Brodsky's, did not remain his own. With wealthy friends, the attention of the police in both Philadelphia and New York, the eager ear of newsmen, and prominent citizens ready to raise a subscription to fund the ransom, Christian's plight became a newspaper staple. It generated rumors of all kinds, and was soon well known through press, word of mouth, newly invented missing child posters, theater plays, and traveling circuses, including that of P. T. Barnum who spread the story throughout the United States. The Western Union Company provided Christian with a dedicated line free of charge, as he pursued the leads that came in from various parts of the country where ordinary citizens proved eager to help by reporting sightings of Charley. The lost child posters broadcast Charley's picture and description widely, and people throughout the country (and eventually abroad) began simply to call him "the lost boy." After several attempts to pay the ransom misfired and Christian's ordeal stretched into months, Americans throughout the nation deputized themselves to help. In the process, the story of the lost boy became the occasion to reflect on what parents owed their children.

How could Christian have failed? What kind of father does not get his son back? What should parents do when confronted with such evil? Christian's good intentions as a citizen had resulted in a failure of parenting. Eventually, Christian wrote his own version of the case in a memoir appropriately entitled *The Father's Story* in order to quell the public outcry and the growing condemnation of his behavior. As a public display of Christian's love and grief for his son, it enshrined

After his kidnapping in July 1874, reward posters helped to make Charley Ross famous as the "lost boy." This is a photograph of the poster I found at a small general store in Woodside, California, now a historic site. Photograph by John Lesch.

Charley's story by becoming a monument to a father's love. This memoir, the vast network of missing children's posters, and news accounts became staple subjects of private discussion and popular culture. Parenting, and fatherhood specifically, were now widely defined in deeply emotional terms. Nothing could be worse, Americans concluded than the loss of a child, whose emotional value was immeasurable. A father's obligations to his child were not just related to the child's supervision—to the need to house, clothe, and feed him— or his responsible citizenship. It took a story of extreme loss to bring this into the cultural mainstream, but once there the emotional definition of parenting had taken the field, leaving all other considerations behind.

Alexis de Tocqueville had proposed that American parent-child relations were rooted in affection. This now became, by the second half of the century, the primary and dominant public vision. Christian was not condemned for failing to protect his house, his name, or his estate, or, indeed, others in the community. By the time he wrote publicly about his grief, he did not defend himself in those terms. No amount of money should have stood in the way of Ross's retrieval of his child; no other interest could stand up to the grief over a lost child. He was condemned for not allowing his feelings to overwhelm all other matters—to pay the ransom quickly and get his son back. Ross wrote to demonstrate that he had learned this lesson.

The mystery of Charley Ross, the "lost boy," lasted a long time in the popular imagination and even years later, after the death of Christian Ross and the presumed kidnappers, the story had so pervaded American consciousness that children appeared to claim the mantle of the lost child. And the kidnap story itself became a template for later kidnappers and the parents of kidnap victims who hoped to learn from Christian's mistakes. But the echoes of the story were finally less about loss or kidnapping than about confirming a new standard of parenting, one that brought the father back into the picture without restoring a traditional kind of fatherhood. Instead, like the real Christian Ross who spent the rest of his life searching for his son, the new ideal of fatherhood firmly planted the child's welfare as the central focus of family life. The public now could stand in judgment on the role of parents and evaluate even proper, prosperous, and

well-connected fathers and mothers. They, too, had to meet dominant standards, just as the various new agencies were judging the families of the ghetto and the slum.

v

Charley's story highlights many features of the changes introduced
in the late nineteenth century: the terrible costs to men's abilities to
father in traditional ways by the bloodbath of the Civil War; the acute
awareness of the many children who were fatherless, abandoned, mistreated, and needing care in urban communities; the public reckon-
ing that parents could expect. All of these matters would appear again
in the century to come. But the peculiar meditation on fatherhood
that is embodied in the tale of Charley Ross requires a broader historical reflection on how family life was being reimagined and remade
in the second half of the nineteenth century.

Most of us carry around an image of Victorian fathers, implanted
by books and films such as *Life with Father, The Forsyte Saga,* and
innumerable memoirs of the late nineteenth century. These fathers
seem to emerge from time immemorial. Such a father is knowing,
authoritative, beneficent, and almost always the guiding influence in
the life of important men and women born in the period. Reformers such as Jane Addams, Grace Abbott, and Florence Kelley, and re-
forming journalists and educational leaders such as Freda Kirchwey,
Lucy Sprague Mitchell, and Kate Douglas Wiggin remembered their
fathers in this way, for their combination of moral seriousness and
kindness.[61]

In fact, these roles were hardly remnants of a long ago past. Instead
Anglo Americans in the nineteenth century were actively remaking
the family, redefining motherhood and fatherhood, as they recon-
stituted family life around a new set of rituals centered on children
and private life. Through newly institutionalized holiday routines,
dinner table etiquettes, and other family practices that became "traditions," domestic life became the setting for rituals of loving obligation. In the United States and England, birthdays, Christmases, and
other family events (many still familiar to us today) took on deeply
personal meanings.[62] Journalist Henry Seidel Canby recalled, "In the

American nineties generally home was the most impressive experience of life." He added, "The woman who could not make a home[,] and the man who could not support one, was condemned and not tacitly."[63] This re-anchoring of family can be glimpsed in the story of Christian Ross's ordeal.

During Christian's time, his story also had deeply religious overtones as Charley's loss and Christian's redemption (after he devoted his life to finding the children of strangers) illuminated the sacramental qualities of the new obligations being defined within the family. Unlike the haphazard and loosely regulated relations of parents and children before the Civil War, by the late nineteenth century, family life became both highly ritualized and publicly supervised. Each of the roles in respectable families was carved out and made to appear immutable. Mothers, fathers, and children now had their proper places, acknowledged and defined through popular culture.

There is still more going on in Charley Ross's story than the simple elevation of family life. That story and the others that became part of the public culture of the late nineteenth century were framed in distinctly class terms as the Victorian family was being defined through class distinctions. In the period after the American Revolution all children and parents, regardless of their wealth or position, were assumed to be contributing to a new republican society, just as they engaged in their household economy to which each made some contribution. Neither Tocqueville nor Gurowski distinguished between poor farmers and rich landowners in their evaluations of parent-child relations. This does not mean that no differences existed, only that these differences were not expected to impinge on this basic and common relationship between the generations.

This viewpoint changed after the Civil War. By the end of the century in the United States, the reconstruction of family life took place against a backdrop of abandoned children who were assumed to be the detritus of the new immigrant and working classes' lack of responsibility. Family life in the high Victorian manner was distinctly a middle- and upper-class affair. Private life, let alone the highly ritualized private life that was helping to define the Victorian family, can only happen where houses (or apartments) have suitable places for privacy—separate spaces for sleeping, childrearing, and personal hygiene—dwelling privileges not usually available to the poor as Riis's photographs of slums demonstrated. Most African American families, poor rural families, and urban working families expected obedience, as families depended on their children's help.[64] They might love their children, but they could not let affection get in the way of their realistic appraisals of how the family needed to coordinate its money-gaining activities. The new standards of the family were class standards as the reformers incorporated class ideals into the very notion of family decency. Indeed, the middle classes defined themselves in terms of these distinctions embedded in the very nature of family life. Riis found interesting exceptions, of course, when he played on the sentimental beliefs of the time. But the very success of his stories depended on his readers bringing certain prejudices with them about "the other half," prejudices that Riis could dispel with his touching portrait of the loving Brodzky family and others like them.

After the Civil War, the United States was still in many ways a disjointed society, even a wild and woolly place. Many Americans were fleeing earlier lives and commitments, and were insecurely anchored in their private lives. For every immigrant like Brodzky desperately searching for his child, one could find another who had abandoned wife and children in the old country to restart life in the new. For every Christian Ross protecting his family and its honor, one could find in the newspapers stories of roués like Stanford White exploiting young girls for their erotic pleasures. During this time, the abandonment of Native American or Hispanic wives by men eager for respectability in many parts of the West and Southwest was a common occurrence. Convenient alliances made with nonwhite women before the Civil War, and the offspring of these unions, became burdens by the end of the century as Americans began to institute laws against miscegenation. As men sought respectability after the Civil War, they found it problematic to recognize wives or children across race lines.[65] In the process, many interracial children were lost or forgotten. Even men from respectable homes in the East left families behind them for long periods of time, as they sought their fortunes in the mining towns of the new West. One visitor to Colorado "estimated that the majority of mines in the new state were named after wives and children waiting for the return of their hopeful bonanza kings."[66] In those places, the proportion of children was low, while the proportion of women who were prostitutes was high and family life mostly nonexistent.

In the nineteenth century, common-law marriages were widespread in the United States, usually undertaken without benefit of clergy or state certification. By the end of the century, states began to close down on these various forms of uncertified unions.[67] Before then, families could be conveniently formed and rapidly left behind. Desertion, not divorce, was the way couples parted. In this context, by the end of the nineteenth century, the middle class sought to set itself apart in forming respectable families, as older arrangements became objects of reproof.

In a loosely jointed society where each state set its own rules about matrimony, children could and did become the lost cogs of casual households. The fear that these children might be abandoned was a defining quality of the time. The confidence in secure independence that earlier Americans imagined as part of a new republican child-hood faded as the nineteenth century progressed, so that by the end of the century, few remembered its original democratic nature and that it had once included everyone. As the middle class set itself apart through its new rules, its members elevated certain standards as basic to respectability and proper caretaking, just as they did certain table manners and funeral etiquettes.[68] Toward this end, they created new institutions of public life in cities, including agencies that rescued children, foundling homes, and, of course, schools.

The effect on childhood was profound. The belief in the sturdy independence of children that was a fact of life in the early nineteenth century did not disappear, but confidence that this could apply to all children had diminished. Instead, children who were inadequately cared for were to be pitied and rescued. If possible, they, too, would be put into good homes where they could grow into independence. But many others became inhabitants of various institutions where children were warehoused and regimented.

As the Civil War was ending, when she was just nine years old, Kate Douglas Wiggin could still act in a way that demonstrated her independence of mind as she cared for her younger sister whom she took to school for the first time. "I led her in proudly, her hair polished until it shone like mahogany, while her frock of blue gingham, adorned with white tape trimming, and starched until it stood out like a balloon, was so clearly *le dernier cri* that it almost provoked applause from the school." Later in the day, however, the teacher began to use her sister badly when she "snapped the child's ear with her thimble-finger, one of her ways of registering disapproval." That was, as Wiggin recalled, "too much for me. *I, at the age of nine, was a responsible human being. . . .* I took the weeping infant by the hand, saying, 'I will take my little sister home, please,' and walked majestically from the school, not to come back that day." Her action received her father's approval. While Kate subsequently returned to school, her sister would thereafter be taught at home.[69] Her parents had accepted her responsible judgment that school was not right for her sister. This behavior, firm in its own judgment and one that challenged school authority, would become less possible as schools and other forms of public authority began to define childhood by the end of the century.[70] But the older values remained active and alive. They would serve as a basis for John Dewey's attempt to make American education more democratic.

The drive to supervise children and their parents also continued. In the twentieth century, more forms of oversight and different kinds of advice would become common. As American society became more complex and as its population drew on innumerable new sources, questions regarding the roles of children and their parents occupied more and more public space. The changing conditions, the sense of new problems, and the confrontation with new groups of people never entirely displaced the reliance on defining American culture by the independence of its children, although these new conditions did change what that came to mean and how it could be made available to children.

CHAPTER 3

What Mother Needs to Know

The New Science of Childhood, 1890–1940

The nineteenth century brought more than the disruption and insecurity caused by war. New scientific values, which emphasized careful observation and numerical precision, inspired Americans to imagine a progressive and improved modernity. That modernity found an especially strong expression around matters relating to childhood. Even before the Civil War began, Charles Darwin's challenging ideas erupted to focus a brilliant new light on all matters relating to biological life. His influence would last well past the end of the century. Darwin transformed how modern humans were understood to relate to the past, to the future, to their ancestors, and to their progeny. When Darwin took his own son as his subject, he was perhaps the first scientist to investigate the child seriously as the object of intense observation.[1] He would not be the last.

By the late nineteenth century, the study of children became widespread among scientists, doctors, and educators, who gradually replaced amateur child savers, all of them eager to inform the laymen with their new knowledge. In New York City, between 1888 and 1890, a small group of mothers began to meet with the moral philosopher Felix Adler, to discuss children and how they learned. This group became known as the Society for the Study of Child Nature. Adler adopted the altered vision of fatherhood that surfaced in the late nineteenth century to this purpose. A father's primary duty, Adler declared, was to be "the guardian of the permanent welfare of his child, to respect, to protect, to develop its individuality."[2] The small group he led grew over time into a large organization dedicated to child study. At Clark University in Massachusetts, psychologist G. Stanley Hall, who had been educated in Germany, where scientific values prevailed, was intent on investigating children with seriousness and rigor and was eager to share his knowledge widely. Hall's intense curiosity about human development also led him to invite Sigmund Freud to the United States in 1909. It was to be the founder of psychoanalysis's first and only visit to America. In San Francisco, the educator and children's book author Kate Douglas Wiggin started the first free kindergarten in the midst of a slum, hoping thereby to give children new rights to pleasure balanced by good character development. Americans were not shy about absorbing the insights from other nations' intellectual experiences, from evolution, psychoanalysis, kindergarten pedagogy, or university science. But they usually adapted these to a particular American perspective.

Everywhere by the turn of the century, older ideas about children—their need for play, for schooling, and for good families—found new life in this context. The impulse to reform took off with an invigorated sense of purpose as the tools of inquiry provided hope about the possibilities of a better future. The intersection between science and the home was often catalyzed by those who set out to rescue the children of misfortune, an inheritance from the nineteenth-century child savers; but it eventually grew most abundantly as a means to define what was "normal" and how every American mother could help her children toward this twentieth-century ideal.

Americans believed deeply in their unique modernity, especially when it came to how they raised their children. In 1900, at the cusp of the new century, one writer in the *Ladies' Home Journal* declared that the American's vision regarding children was "absolutely unique in the world. He no longer regards his child as an animal to be tamed by beating, or as a possible saint, but as the heir to all the good things of time. And the boy from his cradle knows his importance. . . . The future is the kingdom of which these young people are taught that they will be the legitimate rulers."[3] What the writer called this "strange . . . attitude toward his child" became an obvious fact of life for the "average American parent" two decades later. In heralding this view for the new century, the *Ladies' Home Journal* and the parents who were its audience inherited their commitment from their nineteenth-century predecessors who looked at children as the "legitimate rulers" of the future. But like so much else from the past, this view in which the child "knows his importance" would be transformed in meaning and in its practices as the twentieth century progressed.

I

It took two decades for the "average American child" to commandeer attention from professionals. At the beginning of the century, the perspective of child savers and their focus on the children of deprivation still predominated. The harsh lives of the working poor and the misfortunes of their children in ghettos and slums were the primary concerns. The reports of reformers could be numbingly repetitive: so many nameless infants dead, so many boys and girls betrayed by their difficult home lives, so many juveniles whose petty crimes became the subject of public knowledge. Gathering accurate and complete statistics became a rallying point of child reformers of the early twentieth century, a celebration of numbers that would alert the public to the problems of childhood and touch their hearts with lost lives. It was all supposed to lead to swift and determined action.

In their epoch-defining book, *The Delinquent Child and the Home* (1912), Sophonisba Breckinridge and Edith Abbott put it succinctly: "Heretofore, the kindly but hurried public never saw as a whole what it cannot now avoid seeing—the sad procession of little children and older brothers and sisters who . . . cannot keep step with the great company of normal, orderly, protected children."[4] By proclaiming that the mission of their progressive generation was to bring the "sad procession" of unprotected children into view, Breckinridge and Abbott set out to make the misfortunes of these children visible to the public, but in so doing, they began to shed an indirect light on what a "normal, orderly, protected childhood" required. During the first three decades of the twentieth century, public concerns about children steadily shifted from the sad procession of the unfortunate toward the normal. The two were bound together by the growing scientific expertise of the observers and by the statistical analysis on which it was based.

Case number 47: A German family with seven children. The mother is American born. The father immigrated at the age of twenty-seven and came directly to Chicago, where he has lived for thirty-three years. The family were at one time fairly prosperous, but the father was ruined by drink. . . . The father has rheumatism badly and cannot work regularly. The mother takes in washing, but does not earn very much. One son has been paralyzed since he was seven months old. At the age of nine *this boy* was brought to court as a truant and was sent to the Chicago Parental School. A year later he was brought into court for violating his parole and was again sent to the Parental School. At the age of eleven he was again brought into court for using vile language and encouraging boys to stay away from school. This time he was committed to the John Worthy School. At the age of twelve he was arrested for running away from home and attending school irregularly. . . .[5]

Case number 56: A Polish family with five children. The father has been dead eighteen years. The mother died three years ago and the home was then broken up. After her husband's death she had married a man who was an iron-worker, who proved to be a very brutal and disreputable man. The mother owned the home and he "married her for what she had." The neighbors think he killed her by beating her. She is said to have been a drinking woman, and she and the stepfather were very cruel to *the boy* who went hungry and half clad. When he was fourteen he was brought into court, charged with stealing a pail of mincemeat valued at $2.40 from a moving car, and he was put on probation. When he was fifteen he was brought into court, charged with stealing seven pounds of scrap copper wire from a freight car, and he was again put on probation under the care of a police officer. . . .[6]

The cases went on and on. Most portrayed the desperate and unruly lives of urban immigrant families, but these two sad "cases" were neither special nor representative. Breckinridge and Abbott knew well that the sources for troubled children's lives were varied and complex and could not easily be reduced to a single cause, a view that defined the progressive approach to delinquency during the first half of the twentieth century. Breckinridge and Abbott brought case numbers 47 and 56, and almost 15,000 others, to the attention of the public because they were now available from the records of the

Chicago Juvenile Court, the first juvenile court in the United States and long a source of progressive pride. The Chicago court became the model for similar courts in the rest of the nation and throughout the Western world. Aiming to protect children from the full force of the law by emphasizing their age and lack of adult responsibility, the juvenile court engaged social service workers whose job was to investigate and remediate the situation that had produced the problems in the first place. Each of these files defined the child by his or her family environment and its difficulties. Case files like these eventually became the basis for the social work method. To us, they expose the pitiable reasons that youths came to the attention of the court and the police—truancy, vile language, petty theft—mostly banal behaviors that could lead to probation or institutional commitment for juveniles in the early twentieth century.[7] They also allow us to grasp the ease with which children could be labeled delinquent.[8] The youth's namelessness (juvenile records were kept sealed and offenders not publicly named) offers the reader only the shallowest purchase on his life. But the drumbeat of family ills made readers and the larger public conscious of the importance of *normal* family life. And the demands for regularity could be more frequently enforced because families came to the attention of public authorities.[9]

The attention to family harms continued the exposure that had begun in the nineteenth century, when a sentimental attachment to a well-kept home was a standby of women's magazines and of Victorian domesticity. What was then a soft-focus ideal became a public requirement in the new century and an increasingly enforceable standard. In one of its midcentury issues (1855), the *Ladies' Repository*, one of those journals that sentimentalized mother, home, and childhood, ran an article "How to Make Home Intolerable." Among these factors were "a smoky chimney," "a scolding wife," "a dirty wife," drink and drunkenness, ill-trained children, and ill-cooked meals. Children brought up in such an atmosphere were "unfortunate children—how our heart pities them! Brought into the midst of the world helpless, they are left amidst the gloomy associations of depravity, dirt, and disease; and they hang about the sordid dwelling an infant brood, imparting no joy to the home—only so many gaping mouths to be fed—increasing its squalor and discomfort."[10] By the end of the nineteenth century, pity had led to the empowerment of agencies whose purpose was exposure and reform.

These three "ds"–depravity, dirt, and disease—threaded the nineteenth-century evangelical sensibility into the twentieth-century scientific approach to reform, social work, and childrearing advice.[11] That these scourges would become part of the new scientific case-work process should not surprise us, since the Victorian underpin-nings of early-twentieth-century reform are visible once one scratches the statistics-soaked surface. Early-twentieth-century female reform-ers were nurtured in the thick morality of nineteenth-century homes.[12] So, too, had public sensibilities been primed by women's reading and the emphasis on their influence as the caretakers of children. By the late nineteenth century women had moved outside the home into various reform efforts, such as temperance and child labor, as they set about making home life and childhood safer and more tolerable. Very soon thereafter, the normal functioning of the family became the subject of twentieth-century social science paradigms.

Initially, dirt and disease were the bêtes noires of women's work as the nineteenth-century sentimental hearth gave way to the twentieth-century's educated household.[13] This was the first and, for some time, the dominant entry point for all kinds of childrearing advice. To-day's parenting manuals often advise parents in matters related to a child's emotional and cognitive well-being and, most recently, about successful schooling. But the origin of this advice literature lay not in aspirations for psychological adjustment or cognitive enrichment but in a much simpler goal—keeping the child alive.

In the nineteenth century, parents yearned for this seemingly sim-ple objective. Many of them had experienced the painful death of infants and children. No one was immune. These included power-ful politicians like Abraham Lincoln, who lost three of his four sons; wildly popular writers like Mark Twain, whose son died in infancy and who had two daughters predecease him; and even the great Charles Darwin, who grieved all his life over the loss of three of his children. Both parents, publicly endowed with deep emotional responses to their young by the late Victorian period, were believed to experience the loss keenly, but it was mothers who were viewed as potential allies in a campaign to alter children's destiny.

Portrait of Slater baby in coffin (1902). Photograph from Joseph Judd Pennell Photographs Collection (1888–1923), Kansas Collection, Kenneth Spencer Research Library, University of Kansas. This is one of many photographs taken and saved of dead infants. Photography made the keeping of such mementos common in the late nineteenth and early twentieth centuries.

The most popular and most widely used turn-of-the-century child-care manual was written by Dr. L. Emmett Holt (first published in 1894 and then republished regularly into the 1920s). Like all its contemporary successors, it was a how-to book that focused on how to diaper and breast feed (and prepare hygienic formula if breast feeding was not possible); how to take the infant's temperature and read the results; how and when to bathe and at what temperature; how to interpret an infant's cry; what was the best ambient temperature for the nursery; and how to encourage good health habits of all kinds. Above all, it was concerned with feeding. The book included suggestions for feeding schedules and sample menus, as well as weight charts, which by their very nature emphasized what was normal.

Although it dealt with mothers from the high perch of professional expertise, *The Care and Feeding of Children* was a clear, simple, and didactic manual for child survival. It was by no means the first of its kind. In the middle of the eighteenth century, the great British physician William Cadogan had written a similar manual (with much similar advice).[14] But by the twentieth century not only was the reading public vastly larger, but the advice might actually make a significant difference. Child survival through the difficult infant stage especially became a matter to which mothers could hope to make a genuine contribution.[15]

Nineteenth-century women's magazines, with their religious and moralizing sensibility, were full of advice literature; they were also full of poems and tales of consolation. The expected death of infants and children, of all ages, made it imperative that mothers be prepared for their loss. Much of their treacly quality, with children being turned into angels, was meant to provide comfort to mothers who could do nothing to stop the diseases and death that took their children away. The articles could moralize about dirt as distasteful and problematic, but not until the last third of the nineteenth century and the early twentieth century did a new understanding of how disease spread, how it could be contained, and the advance of disinfectants and public sanitation usher in a real "science" of public health based on hygiene. A good part of that new optimism came from the growing emphasis on cleanliness and its role in preventing disease. The campaign to eliminate dirt inside the house and create more sanitary conditions in cities was a widespread aim of reform. It was now clear why and how combatting dirt and germs in the house, as well as the larger public household, mattered to the survival of infants and children. What Dr. Cadogan had suspected and Dr. Holt had proposed as a part of his standard pitch to mothers—that they could be enlisted as allies in the survival of infants and young children—the Children's Bureau would prove, starting in the second decade of the twentieth century in its closely controlled surveys of differential infant death statistics.[16]

The origin of the United States Children's Bureau (1912) lay in the quest for that knowledge, in the accompanying drive to improve the chances for infant survival, and in promoting a more equal distribution of the benefits of this knowledge. In fact, during the first two years of the bureau's existence the subject of infant and child mortality "absorbed almost the entire force of the bureau."[17] As female reformers, newly schooled in colleges and universities, discovered how infant life could be preserved and how the waste of child life could be stanched, this knowledge became ammunition in the crusade of women who took their public roles as defenders of the home seriously and set out to make it a necessary part of the armory of private life. American women were by no means singular in this devotion to reform; women throughout the Western world were enlisted to make the twentieth the "Century of the Child," in the words of Swedish reformer Ellen Key. The bureau's work had been anticipated in several European countries where a commitment to reducing infant mortality and providing for pure milk was already in place. In 1905 and 1907, those committed to infant welfare were brought together at international conferences.[18] The work of the Children's Bureau was thus part of a much wider modern effort in behalf of children, although its prominent position as a branch of the federal government was probably unique as was its powerful sense of the potential that the United States had in leading the world.

Reformers and professionals were not alone in seeking a means to ensure infant survival. The long line of childrearing experts to which American parents turned throughout the twentieth century had been well prepared at the end of the nineteenth century by the appearance of an alert audience, eager for advice and ready for instruction. In

1889, Louis Starr, in his pamphlet *Hygiene of the Nursery* proclaimed that "intelligent parents are ever ready to be instructed and willing to cooperate in the great work of preventing disease—the highest aim of scientific medicine." Careful to protect the increasingly well patrolled boundary between lay knowledge and medical expertise, Starr noted that mothers "should recognize that years of training and experience are necessary to acquire the ability to put the full values upon symptoms, and to handle the tools of medicine." At the same time, "every woman of ordinary brain-power can do much to keep her baby alive."[19]

At almost exactly the same time, pioneering psychologist G. Stanley Hall was enlisting the help of mothers in his efforts to study children's growth scientifically, and Hall's charts of child development were deeply indebted to the careful observations by mothers of their own children. Many of these mothers had been recruited from the Association of Collegiate Alumnae that formed a section on the study of children in the last decade of the nineteenth century. College-educated women were making a variety of contributions to the study of child life, both as laypersons and, increasingly, as experts. Women of "ordinary brain-power" were also beginning to organize into the National Congress of Mothers, starting in 1897. That organization brought parents of all races and social classes together to learn about children by gathering the best scientific information and sharing that knowledge with one another. Their proclaimed goal, according to Alice Birney, its first president, was that each mother "must take into her heart all homes, all children, all motherhood."[20] Helping one's own child was thus deeply connected to the larger purpose of helping all children as a single goal. Soon, teachers joined mothers as the National Congress of Mothers become the Parent and Teachers Association of America. Doctors, too, were newly committed to children. Pediatrics had been institutionalized as a specialty in 1891 as a section of the American Medical Association through the strenuous efforts of Dr. Abraham Jacobi. By the twentieth century, women and experts were combining their efforts in the United States in hopes of keeping babies alive.

Holt was not the first late-nineteenth-century physician intent on arming mothers with knowledge, but he became its most prominent figure and an early president of the American Pediatric Society (1898). It was Holt's genius to propose his book in the form of "A *Catechism* for the Use of Mothers and Children's Nurses," thereby grasping the gospel behind the movement and bridging the gap between the religiously informed motherhood of the nineteenth century and the scientifically informed motherhood of the twentieth. What could be simpler and what could better display the overlap between science and an earlier evangelical fervor? Despite Holt's obvious authority, his book was not intimidating in tone, and it was accessible to even the simplest "normal" brain. By merely answering a series of very basic questions regarding infants and young children and the conditions by which their health could be ensured, Holt enlisted legions of mothers to his side as armies of a new scientific religion.

Unlike some later experts, Holt understood that mothers could make a positive contribution, as few could resist the possibility of saving their child's life. "Why should mothers nurse their children? First, because there is no perfect substitute for good breast-feeding. Secondly, statistics show that the mortality of bottle fed infants during the first year is fully three times as great as that of those who were breast-fed."[21] This statistic, used in the 1923 edition of his manual, had been developed by the first and only agency in American history that was ever entirely devoted to the welfare of children.

From its inception, the United States Children's Bureau sent out survey teams to study differential infant mortality rates, and to find ways to explain why some children died. Its very first reports as an agency under the leadership of Julia Lathrop were on this subject. Starting in Johnstown, Pennsylvania, the bureau subsequently followed up on its initial findings by sending teams of researchers to Montclair, New Jersey; Baltimore, Maryland; and Manchester, New Hampshire, hoping to capture the variety of environments and the complexity of the urbanizing population of the nation. And wherever the researchers went, the published statistics soon followed. By visiting every possible household (they were only infrequently turned away), the census takers discovered that in 1912 in suburban Montclair, the poorest and most foreign fourth ward had a far higher incidence of infant mortality than other, wealthier quarters. But this high rate was not permanent. "In 1913, however, the infant mortality rate for the fourth ward was lower," as a result of the founding of a baby clinic and "the follow-

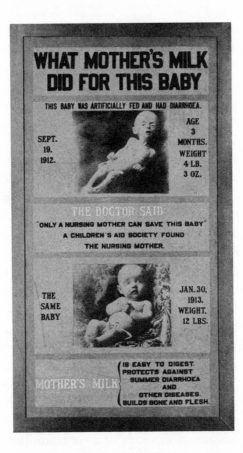

"What Mother's Milk Did." Wall panel from the exhibit of the Children's Bureau showing an arrangement of photographs and statements pasted on a larger background. Illustration from Anna Louis Strong, *Child-Welfare Exhibits: Types and Preparation*, US Department of Labor, Children's Bureau, Miscellaneous Series, no. 4 (Washington, DC, 1915).

up visits of the nurse to the mothers in their homes and the careful supervision of the board of health of the housing and sanitation of this section."[22] The careful supervision of infant care paid off, and, with a little help, mothers could save their babies. This real alteration in differential child mortality is something to remember as Americans a century later contemplate their lackluster performance among Western nations in infant mortality statistics.[23]

One of the bureau's main objectives was to make sure that all children had their births properly registered. Its early pamphlets on infant

care, sent out by the hundreds of thousands and then by the millions, instructed mothers of the nation to provide this for their own
children. By assuring an accurate recording of their children's births,
mothers became part of the campaign for national knowledge as well
as standard-bearers of the well-being of their children. The three objectives that went hand in hand for progressive women who started
and ran the Children's Bureau in the teens and twenties—child survival, birth registration, accurate statistics—became a holy trinity of
the early federal campaigns on behalf of children. More accurate *public* knowledge could be used to inform mothers who became part of
the *private* campaign to keep children alive, a success that would be
registered in improving *national* statistics on child survival.

In the twenty-first century, after more than one hundred years of
childrearing advice and harangues, during which mothers (and also
fathers) have been given so many, often conflicting, forms of advice
regarding their children's proper nurture, it is difficult to realize that
originally there was a simple goal about which there was no confusion and no conflict. That goal was child survival.[24] Intended for
the population at large, immigrant and native, rich and poor, educated and unschooled, rural, suburban, and urban, that goal was a
basic democratic ideal. As Julia Lathrop announced, "Work for infant
welfare . . . is a profoundly important public concern which tests
the public spirit and democracy of a community."[25] The progressive
women of the early twentieth century wanted American children to
survive because they saw themselves as the guardians of childhood
and of national welfare. They were embarrassed by how badly the
United States, the richest country in the world and the most admired,
did in comparison with other societies. Statistics that showed American mortality rates in a world context were prominently displayed
in the findings about suburban Montclair. The United States lagged
well behind Finland, France, the Netherlands, Denmark, Sweden,
Norway, New Zealand, and Scotland in infant mortality rates (much
as they lag behind these countries today) and was just barely ahead
of Italy and Serbia, places scarcely viewed as enlightened and advanced.[26] American infant mortality statistics were the telling stig-
mata of the social neglect of children's well-being—a very public
matter, and a national scandal.

Psychiatrist William Alanson White, from whom American parents in the 1920s and 1930s often learned about their children's emotional problems, shrewdly observed in 1919, "We must first have a *live child* if we are to have any problem at all."[27] The success of advisors like Dr. Holt, of Mrs. Max West (the original author of the Children's Bureau's wildly popular *Infant Care* pamphlet), of the Children's Bureau's many campaigns to collect statistics on children's nutrition and hygiene, of its sponsorship of local clinics, visiting nurses, instructional posters, and the initiative that led to the first piece of federal health care legislation for children in 1922 (the Sheppard-Towner Act) helped to bring down the rates of American infant and child mortality.[28] Only after that success, as mothers began to expect their children to survive, could parents direct their attention to other concerns regarding young children.

Lawrence K. Frank, one of the most important spokesmen for the creation and implementation of a new science of childhood, understood this connection well. "Up until very recent years, our attitude toward children has been a more or less fatalistic one. . . . Within less than a generation the whole picture of infant mortality has been completely changed and the former fatalistic attitude that nothing could be done to protect children from infections has been replaced by a confident expectation that continued research and experimentation will provide still more protection for childhood." Frank explained that this fundamental change was the basis for the new commitment to the study of child development. That revolution took place quickly because the changes in health expectations had taken place "within less than a generation." Shedding ancient folklore and traditions that obstructed change, parents could become modern as their children became the objects of observation, measurement, and "enlightened control."[29]

II

The stage had been set for the dramatic spike of interest in childrearing advice aimed at emotional health and sound personality development that came in the decade of the 1920s. In this delicate area, mothers' instincts to protect their children became more problematic as their careful supervision could, and often did, lead to excessive oversight. John Watson articulated the most extreme version of this concern. Watson used the science of behaviorism to urge mothers to step back, control their emotional inclinations, and not coddle their children. "Do not kiss and hug them," he advised, because such emotionally charged behavior undermined habit training.

Others, too, drew upon science to understand children's emotional life and behavior and to instruct parents in how these could develop normally. During the twenties, the Laura Spelman Rockefeller Foundation sponsored new "scientific" laboratories and centers for the study of children across the country, including an important one in the strategic American heartland—Ames, Iowa.[30] Sigmund Freud's acolytes in the new science of psychoanalysis offered advice in popular magazines and newspapers, and the first parenting magazine, which frequently focused on emotional health, was published in 1926, and quickly enlisted thousands of subscribers. This same jazz decade produced the first full science of "child development," a perspective that would dominate popular views on childrearing for the next century, when Yale psychologist Arnold Gesell provided a set of guidelines to a "normal" childhood. By the end of the decade, Gesell, who had a medical degree as well as research training in educational psychology, announced that "Development, quite as much as disease[,] falls within the theory and practice of pediatrics."[31]

With this fourth D—development—twentieth-century experts had a basis for measuring babies' progress through various childhood milestones. Now that babies were expected to survive, mothers would begin bringing their physically healthy babies for exacting observations regarding progress in mental, psychological, and cognitive areas as they wondered whether their language, emotions, and social interactions were age-appropriate. Age distinctions became more and more of a yardstick in the period, affecting ideas about learning as well as development.[32] Where Emmett Holt provided weight charts, Arnold Gesell provided measuring sticks for the first months and then years of a healthy, surviving child's life. It was a brave new world.

In this world, it was almost as if parents and experts had made a pact, financed by new foundation money, to create a modern childhood at just the time when the century-long decline in births was making families much smaller. I have suggested that the late nineteenth century saw a reinvigorated emphasis on family life. But instead of increasing the number of children it raised, this renewed family emphasis did the opposite. The middle class, especially (and others to a lesser degree), significantly reduced the number of children in the household, from the average of four or five before the Civil War to two or three by the early twentieth century. This was a dramatic demographic change inscribing a change in behavior that alerts us to several important matters closely related to the turn to expert advice. First, some of the ability to change birth patterns resulted from the reliance on medical devices and expertise, made available to middle-class women by doctors.[33] Second, the desire to have fewer children was not simply a desire to cut down on the cost of childrearing. Instead, the cost of rearing *each surviving child more effectively* became a powerful incentive both to reduce the number of children and to turn to whatever had become available to ensure that children survived and prospered. Thus child survival and child nurture reinforced each other as expressions of reduced fertility and reduced mortality. Both were responses to the heightened commitment to childhood and to family life. More carefully reared children, better child survival, and more effective use of birth control all point toward a new emphasis on control within families. This also had significant consequences for how Americans' traditional commitment to children's independence was understood and refashioned.

Many fine studies are available on the history of twentieth-century childrearing advice. These all agree that the 1920s witnessed an earthquake of advice that spoke to and elevated parental anxieties about how best to raise children in newly "modern" and scientific ways. The Holt approach and the one adopted by the Children's Bureau pamphlet, *Infant Care*, had emphasized regularity of practices and encouraged mothers to approach their tasks with a certain dispassion. John Watson, the best known of the 1920s advisors, took this perspective to a whole new level. Watson's quirky and iconoclastic attack on American mothers as unfit to raise their children was just one of the many kinds of advice available and probably the most insulting. His perversity was to some degree a matter of personal style,[34] as he adopted a "modern" form of attack that defied conventional and traditional values. But all the experts now lined up to provide parenting

instruction that became a fusillade against the Victorian way of motherhood, with its sticky sentimentality, repression of sexuality, and cloying
moralism. The image of the good mother that had been built up over a
century was clearly in the line of fire as experts began to imagine what
"modern" children needed.

The growth of attention to children in the nineteenth century, accompanied by a broad new awareness of the special characteristics of
childhood, had emerged out of the increasingly central role accorded
to women in the home and to their innate maternity. This perspective now came around full circle as male experts attacked women's
knowledge and made them suspects in the mismanagement of their
children. Experts attacked old wives' tales that served as the false basis
for knowledge; they excoriated information passed on from mothers to their daughters as full of superstitions and unhygienic; they
abused women as both too soft on their children and too punitive.
Part of the problem resulted from the fact that experts were trying
to salvage the independent child at a time when having fewer children
allowed for more concentrated maternal attention. The once active
role of children in the household regime had shrunk as fewer children turned the household into a very different place for parents and
children. At the same time, the aura of science gave advisors a cudgel
to punish old-fashioned mothering, which is why the attack became
so intense so quickly.

Mrs. Max West, an educated amateur and a good writer, with
a deep commitment to children and their well-being, had used, in
the words of Children's Bureau chief Julia Lathrop, "exhaustive study
of the standard literature on the hygiene of infancy as well as other
specialists in this field" to put together the pamphlet *Infant Care*, distributed broadly and free of charge by the bureau. She was its author
and so acknowledged on the front cover of the early editions. An ad-
visory committee of doctors appointed by the bureau initially fully
approved of the pamphlet that was soon distributed by the bushel-full
to congressmen eager to respond to the requests of their constituents
for information about child care. In its letter of transmittal, Lathrop
noted that the pamphlet was "addressed to the average mother of this
country. . . . It endeavors to present the accepted view of the best authorities of the present time."[35]

By 1919, these best authorities could no longer provide their expert certification to such an important source of public information written by an amateur. "Physicians will be much more apt to recommend it" if the author were not identified as Mrs. West. The writer, hitherto freely acknowledged, was indignant at having her authorial voice questioned: "I think there is a slight injustice in this attitude, for, after all, I had borne five children, and as I am not a hopelessly feebleminded woman I must have learned a few things for myself by that process. Also, everyone learns from others. Even doctors themselves. So I do not think it quite just to exclude me entirely from the pale of the educated!"[36] Indeed, in the late nineteenth century, many doctors had learned from mothers who were enlisted in the campaign to investigate children. But the tide had now turned, and the expert was in the saddle. West's name no longer appeared on any subsequent edition as the author of *Infant Care*.

One of the many ironies of the changes introduced during the third decade of the twentieth century was surely that the new scientific campaign by experts was founded on the success of battles fought on behalf of American children by the old-fashioned (even spinsterish) women of the turn of the twentieth century, women who still had one foot firmly planted in the nineteenth century. In helping to make it possible for children to survive and for mothers to take that survival for granted, these women were succeeded by male advisors who took over the public voice of childrearing leadership. Increasingly these experts spoke to the private concerns of twentieth-century women eager to make sure that little Johnny or Jane "developed" properly and become "normal" and "well-adjusted."[37] The twentieth-century child was supposed to be a marvelous product of private solicitude and well-instructed attention. Where women reformers had fought for the nation's children, the new experts— psychologists, pediatricians, psychiatrists, and others—would become each mother's personal trainer.[38]

III

John B. Watson is remembered as the epitome of 1920s childrearing advice. In assaulting emotional mothering, with his admonition to treat children as "little adults" and his strict regimen of feeding, toilet training, and other behavioral monitoring, his book, *Psychological Care of Infant and Child*, has been a favorite subject of historical analysis. It is also a confounding challenge to anyone who tries to make sense of twentieth-century parenting advice, since it flies in the face of the long-term American emphasis on encouraging the individual development of children in a context of maternal affection and parental tolerance.[39] Although he has had followers ever since, Watson's extraordinary popularity in fact was largely a flash in the pan, more interesting as a sign that parents were eager to learn from the best "scientific" formulas in the new century than a signal of where parenting was actually going. That does not mean that parents did not turn to Watson's manual for advice or heed its harsh schedules, only that his strict behaviorism petered out by the late 1930s, to leave only some small traces behind. It was both a last gasp of an older vision of children as budding adults, a brutal rejection of sentimental views of children, and a single strand in a much more varied seam of developing views on childrearing and child welfare.

Watson came from a Southern family that could not afford sentimentality. Like many children after the Civil War, he grew up without a father, but in his case not because of wartime casualties. His father ran away twice from his family, first when he left his family of origin to join the Confederate Army, and then when he deserted Watson's mother, Emma, and their children. Raised in South Carolina by his strict Southern Baptist mother, Watson attended evangelical Furman University. His strong-willed mother had kept her son on track despite the material deprivations that resulted from the father's absence. After he graduated, Watson re-created himself at the University of Chicago, where he studied philosophy and psychology.

Never a stickler for convention, Watson would eventually leave his own wife when he took up with his research assistant, a transgression for which he lost his job at Johns Hopkins University. After that he never returned to academia. Rather than offering his advice from the perch of a medical practice or university podium, he subsequently preached as an advertising executive, where, in the spirit of the 1920s, he turned his energies toward self-promotion.[40] Watson both saw himself as self-made and encouraged a traditional view of children as sturdy, needing training in habits without coddling. He refused to believe that an indulgent childhood, in which children were carefully tended, was a good thing.

The decade of the 1920s ushered in a new kind of childhood, but it was still partially connected to an earlier America. And many prominent Americans depended on the memory of that earlier America in order to make their own rebellion clear. Watson's antics from the time he was an adolescent through his adulthood made him a perfect fit for a time when Jazz Age writers gained attention by being naughty and by challenging old-fashioned kinds of respectability. Having come from a lineage of family instability, it was not completely a surprise that Watson took aim at Victorian conventions of family life, where wholesome children surrounded an upstanding father and a warmly embracing mother. As one of Watson's friends, sociologist W. I. Thomas, noted about him, Watson remained "more childish than I imagined," and seemed never to have really grown up.[41] In this respect, he was able to capture some of the revolt that necessarily accompanied the ascent of "scientific" childrearing in the 1920s. Watson's behaviorism impressed itself on childrearing advice in many places beyond the United States, especially in places like Germany, where science, health, and restraint were important components of family culture.[42] In the United States, his advice remained a small current in a larger, more heterogeneous mix of perspectives, most of which stressed love and affection in family relationships. What was lasting was his emphasis on the importance of the early years of child life for psychological well-being. His warnings against excessive mothering would also linger and cling to the general wariness about excessive maternal control, occasionally to be resurrected as the source of the ills of children. In capturing the spirit of the time and exploiting it for his own aggrandizement, Watson helped to push the idea that mothers had a lot to learn.

Many parents were quite eager to learn, as they turned not just to Holt, the Children's Bureau, and Watson, but to a proliferating array of experts. Many of these were influenced by psychoanalytic theories derived from the work of Freud and his disciples, then making its way into American intellectual and psychiatric circles.[43] By the 1920s, several of Freud's books had been translated for American audiences by A. A. Brill. In 1926, the first popular magazine devoted entirely to parenting appeared as *Childhood*, later to change its name more accurately to *Parents' Magazine* in 1929. Its circulation quickly grew and its often psychoanalytically inflected advice reached hundreds of thousands of readers by the 1930s.

Parents' Magazine was not the only journal to carry childrearing advice. Even before its appearance, the *Ladies' Home Journal* published advice about parenting roles, discipline, and matters relating to schooling.[44] Newspapers, and even the radio, also carried advice regarding children. At a time when newspapers were filled with stories of young people gone astray, these often became occasions to instruct parents who feared that their children might become the next Nathan Leopold and Richard Loeb, the two most notorious among the young criminals whose sensational stories filled the papers of the 1920s. In newspapers across the country, psychiatrists and psychologists took turns with ministers and criminologists to offer their thoughts on these matters.[45]

So, too, the decade saw the publication of volumes whose aim was to gather together the new expertise about children and effective childrearing. In one of these, subtitled "A Survey of Present-Day Knowledge Concerning Child Nature and the Promotion of the Well-Being and Education of the Young," psychiatrist William Alanson White observed, "The most important single factor for the child is the quality of the love of his parents. Parents need to have that rare quality of love which is single-minded in its desire for the welfare of the beloved."[46] Not only was White echoing Lydia Maria Child's vision of the self-sacrificing parent, but he went on to denounce the parent who had a "sense of ownership, or the desire to have the child take up a certain career as a matter of parental pride, or later to make a certain type of match that will further the social ambitions of the parent." In a wholly different manner than Watson and set in a very different psychological framework, White was also adapting a distinctly American set of values about the child's rights to define its own future to the new "scientific" childrearing methods.

Parents' Magazine, above all, brought the newer child-centered spirit of twentieth-century family life into American conversation. Its articles rejected harsh or "tyrannical" styles of parenting, and encouraged emotional and democratic connections between parents and children. In one article, Dr. Lawson G. Lowry advised parents to express their emotions toward their children and not fear spoiling them. Mothers should tell children explicitly that they were loved. Dr. Lowry argued that affection and tolerance between family members defined a "family melting pot," to which all members should contribute. The magazine published a host of articles emphasizing democracy in parent-child interactions. Reject tyranny in the home, James Lee Ellenwood advised, "Never impose authority except as a last resort," since "[e]ducation is a two-way street." This view of family equality was, like White's vision, connected to nineteenth-century experiences in which children were given a place at the table of decision making. Helen Van Pelt Wilson declared, parents should allow themselves to be helped by their children. Good parents encouraged their children to live on a more equal plane and would reject the role of authority figures for themselves.[47]

The advice literature of the 1920s through the 1940s often sought a means to encourage the kind of democracy in families that had once resulted from the contribution children made to the life and living of the household. In a democratically organized family, they would be *psychologically* incorporated into their families as equals, rather than earn that role through their economic contributions. On the eve of Dr. Spock's ascendance as the most revered of advisors on childrearing, American parents had already been introduced to the superiority of a "new" kind of household, based on trust, friendship, and a common understanding of family concerns. As their actual tasks shrank, it was important to find an alternative way for children to maintain their shared space in the family. "We don't keep our children in the dark about family problems," according to Ruth Heller Freund.[48] The nursery was to become what the household had once been, the site of democratic interaction, as parenting advisors initiated childrearing strategies to re-create a democratic spirit between generations that had once flowed from the circumstances of early-nineteenth-century life. Rather than treating children as adults the way Watson advised, this emphasis on democracy turned all family members into active learners.

Within a decade of its appearance, *Parents' Magazine* also registered escalating parental anxieties, anxieties that grew as advice about proper parenting increased. The magazine had been at the forefront of the parent education movement, which embraced advice as a salutary byproduct of expertise and scientific knowledge, but the results could be mixed. In 1941, Marion LeBron, anticipating Benjamin Spock's very language a few years later, told parents to "relax and enjoy your children," as she concluded that one of the downsides of increased emphasis on child study and childrearing advice was that parents were beginning to be tense and nervous.[49]

Other articles in the magazine had registered the growing bewilderment of mothers regarding "expert advice." In 1932, psychoanalyst Lorine Pruette warned, "[N]ot all advice of baby doctors, not all the textbooks of psychology, not all the theories of childcare and training are one-tenth as important to the child as *the kind of woman the mother really is.*" The article may have been a direct slap at Watson, suggesting that his views were being vocally rejected just years after his famous book was published. But this article and others also registered the confusion that could result as expert advice tumbled out from all directions into mothers' consciousness. In 1933, *Parents' Magazine* ran a lighthearted poem expressing anti-expert sentiment and poking fun at the idea that "science reigns."

> Sages, your efforts are causing us pain,
> Mothers are frenzied and children few.
> Really your labors are all in vain.
> They *never* behave as you think they do.[50]

Historian Julia Grant has shown that what mothers actually did with the advice experts offered was complicated. Their behavior included large doses of common sense. They combined earlier childrearing methods passed down through generations with newer expert-driven directives. Women of all educational levels were eager to learn, but most did not allow themselves to be bullied into submission. During the 1920s and 1930s, as parents learned that there was ample "expert" advice available, they sought it out, but advice and behavior were neither uniform nor coextensive.[51] And despite a growing emphasis on normative household structure, successful families varied quite a lot.

Born at the beginning of the twentieth century, Margaret Mead grew up in a household of educated women. Her mother had been among the early college pioneers, attending the coeducational University of Chicago, where she met her future husband. Before Margaret's birth, "my mother kept a little notebook in which she jotted down, among other things[,] quotations from William James about developing all of a child's senses." Thus, even before the 1920s, Mead's mother was aware of the significance of psychological advice and knew where to find it. She had also jotted down that "when I knew baby was coming I was anxious to do the best for it," picking up a theme that would become louder and more widespread. Mead's mother read and sometimes followed Holt's advice. "She accepted the admonition about never picking up a crying child unless it was in pain. But she said her babies were good babies who cry only if something is wrong, and so she picked them up." Despite Emily Mead's education, "she had no real gift for play," so Margaret, who was full of playfulness and imagination, filled in. So, too, since her mother's household skills were limited, Margaret learned early to do things that were needed, like cooking. Household work was still expected of children, girls especially, even in the most advanced families.[52]

In fact, the most important influence in Margaret's life was neither her idealistic mother nor her father, a University of Pennsylvania professor, but her paternal grandmother, who "sat at the center of the household. Grandma never threatened. She never raised her voice. She simply commanded respect and obedience by her complete expectation that she would be obeyed." Grandma Mead was a direct connection to the Victorian mothers of the nineteenth century. Margaret Mead would herself become a scientist and an expert on many cultural matters regarding children, beginning in the 1920s when she shocked American readers with descriptions of the looser family ties and sexual mores of adolescent girls in Samoa. Mead, like Watson, contributed to the iconoclastic spirit of the decade. And while her mother was clearly a modern woman, the actual household environment in which Margaret grew up was much more complex and interesting than those imagined as ideal by childrearing experts.

Grandma Mead had been a schoolteacher and, with just a few exceptional periods when Margaret attended school, she also oversaw Margaret's formal education. An innately progressive thinker, Grandma "understood many things that are barely recognizable in the wider educational world even today. . . . She thought that memorizing mere facts was not very important and that drill was stultifying." Martha Mead was a talented storyteller who inspired Margaret's imagination with tales and historical vignettes.

By the 1920s, experts were increasingly disturbed by the kind of presence that Margaret Mead's grandmother represented—the ghost of a pre-scientific past, strong-willed and opinionated, someone who took over her grandchildren's education. People like Grandma Mead, many believed, could only interfere with the carefully laid out "scientific" instructions being offered. It is well to keep in mind that Margaret's mother was eager for expert advice and read both William James, a pioneering psychologist, and Dr. Emmett Holt, a pioneering pediatrician, but in the end, these two august authorities had to keep company with a grandmother drawn from the middle of the Victorian period. Together these different models lay behind Margaret's modern personality and her future influence over how Americans thought about childhood, motherhood, womanhood, and American culture. "I think it was my grandmother who gave me my ease in being a woman. . . . The two women I knew best were mothers and had professional training. So I had no reason to doubt that brains were suitable for a woman."[53]

Margaret Mead, a towering figure in modern academic life and a cultural force in the middle of the twentieth century, was not the only early twentieth-century female intellectual to be strongly influenced by a household relation who was not a parent. Lucy Sprague Mitchell was somewhat older than Mead, but her Chicago home was also enriched by the presence of a female relation, Aunt Mealy, her father's spinster sister, who lived with the family for half of each year (spending the other half with another brother). And once, when Lucy's parents left on an eleven- month trip to the Middle East, Scandinavia and the Mediterranean countries, Aunt Mealy was fully in charge.[54] Not quite the focal figure that Mead's grandmother represented, Aunt Mealy was an important influence during Lucy's childhood, and her complicated family left its mark on her forward-looking, innovative character as a leader of progressive education.

These two women, themselves born just before the high tide of professional childrearing advice, both affected how Americans thought about children, although their views would come not from psychology, per se, but from allied areas like cultural anthropology and education. Psychology was influencing both in the 1920s, a period when the nascent social sciences were still exchanging knowledge with one another rather than clinging to sharp disciplinary boundaries. While Mead studied young people in Samoa and lectured Americans about their own families based on her growing knowledge of primitive peoples, Mitchell at Berkeley and then at the progressive Bank Street School of Education in New York, which she helped to found, observed young Americans in action. Both contributed to the brew of views on children in the twentieth century.

John Watson had famously placed children under intense observation to test his behaviorist theories, although his laboratory work was limited in scope and had few actual subjects. Much more significant to the future of childrearing advice proper in the twentieth century than Watson's quirky conclusions was the research on children sponsored by the Rockefeller Foundation in New York. Under the direction of Lawrence K. Frank (a good friend of Mead's), the foundation was strongly committed to encouraging the science of child development at university locations. Frank and the Rockefeller Foundation provided funding for observational studies that helped to define "normal" child life at places like Ames, Iowa; Berkeley, California; and New Haven, Connecticut. These university-based programs would transform advice.[55] Like Watson early in his career, but much more consistently and on a much more extensive scale, experts now centered their careers on the newly flourishing scientific investigations of children in laboratory research settings. The number of scholars so engaged grew from a mere handful at the end of World War I in 1918 to 600 in 1930, creating a flourishing industry that fed national appetites for knowledge about children.[56]

Probably the single most important of the scientific experts supported by the foundation was Arnold Gesell, who was both a doctor of medicine and a research scientist. Gesell's child study center at Yale University quickly became an influential locale for mid-twentieth-century expertise on child development. At a time that Freudian theories, based on sexual drive and the emotional attachments of children, often found expression in *Parents' Magazine*, and while Watson's manual emphasized strictly monitored habit training drained of demonstrative emotions, Gesell offered a far more comfortable view of how children develop through stages. These stages were built into the natural rhythms of the organism's growth. Just as the fetus developed in the uterus, gradually acquiring recognizable physical features that are in place at a normal birth, the infant subsequently develops through cognitive and mental stages after birth in a social environment. Gesell's task in the laboratory was to observe these stages, link them to a finely graduated hierarchy of age (especially during the first few years), and to define what could be expected of normal children and how these could be monitored. The mother would be encouraged to observe and gently guide this natural evolution as her child grew. By the 1920s, Gesell could count on mothers eagerly bringing in their children for his observation. These quite "normal" children became the subjects of his scientific analysis and the basis for guidelines offered to other mothers.[57]

In 1930, Gesell published the *Guidance of Mental Growth in Infant and Child*, following up on his earlier *The Mental Growth of the Pre-School Child* (1925)—"the *first* systematic piece of work in the developmental psychology and developmental diagnosis of infancy."[58] Together, they laid out a new framework for providing expertise in the field of early childhood. He then wrote a series of books (with Frances Ilg and others) that became classics in the childrearing industry of the twentieth century: *The First Five Years of Life, Infant and Child in the Culture of Today, The Child From Five to Ten*. Through them, mothers learned what was reliably normal in children. Neither psychoanalytic nor behaviorist, the Gesell workshop produced a uniquely American product in which the normal became the standard criterion for raising children. Now that children could be expected to survive, what should mothers expect as they watched their children grow? And what should they become concerned about? In addressing these matters, Gesell's laboratory work was distinctly, though unexpectedly, connected to the earlier work of progressive reformers.

IV

In their statistical studies, the early-twentieth-century reformers aimed to tally the personal and social costs of bad home environments. If child survival was their first concern, delinquency was a close second. The proliferating studies of delinquency began in the early twentieth century and did not end until well into the middle of the century. These studies engaged a variety of social scientific experts—psychologists, sociologists, and criminologists—all of them eager to understand deviant juvenile behavior. Delinquency also became a subject for lawyers, psychiatrists, social workers, and educators, all eager to prevent it. These experts now had access to the records of juvenile courts, school truancy reports, and prison records as well as the materials gathered by various organizations such as the Judge Baker Foundation in Boston. The new public institutions of childhood provided a vast array of new data for study. The field of juvenile criminology became a byproduct of these institutions and generated names that became famous during the half-century from the 1910s through the '50s— William Healy, Sheldon Glueck, W. I. Thomas, and Clifford Shaw.[59] Many other famous social analysts also touched on questions of delinquency, Margaret Mead and William Alanson White among them, as Americans turned to experts to understand why some children went wrong and how to prevent their own children from doing so.

Margaret Mead's observation could be found in popular culture media such as the *Reader's Digest*, while White was often quoted in newspaper accounts of juvenile crime, such as the famous case of Leopold and Loeb. Americans also brought their children for examination and specific mental health advice to clinics and counseling offices that opened across the country in the 1920s and 1930s. According to one close study, "by the end of the decade, more than three hundred psychiatric clinics for children had been founded."[60] Most of the children brought to these were not delinquents.

Experts never did find an effective solution to delinquent behavior in children and adolescents. Indeed, one of the great failings of twentieth-century social science is the continuing inability to predict and solve the problem of juvenile delinquency and gang behavior, or to meet the challenges of juvenile justice.[61] What began as a way to help troubled adolescents and to protect society against predators became another means to help parents cope with growing anxieties about their children's development, in this case fear about their potential for social deviance and emotional maladjustment. An emphasis on the normal child and how normal "adjustment" could be assured, rather than on the slum child and the delinquent from a poor home, quickly consumed the time and effort of many social commentators as childrearing advice and psychological clinics swallowed the energy that had once gone into efforts to find, heal, and control those most likely to go wrong.

The best gauge of this reshuffling of attention can be found in the changing concerns of the White House Conferences on Children and Youth, the most high level and conspicuous place in which public policy about children was expressed. The first conference, organized in 1909 by Theodore Roosevelt at the height of national progressivism, was a response to reformers who sought to aid dependent children (the orphaned, the handicapped, the poor, and the abused) who were most likely to manifest antisocial behavior. It was overseen by the heads of various charitable organizations devoted to what we today call "at risk" children. Although deviant behavior remained a concern, in the conference organized twenty years later in 1929, the subject had largely shifted to ordinary young children and their health, habits, and home environments.

The volume on the young child that emerged from the conference was dedicated to "The Children of America" and drawn from the section chaired by John E. Anderson, a psychologist at Yale where Gesell was defining norms to be reached by well-adjusted children. Its many experts investigated what normal children were like at various ages, the practices of normal families, and what experts knew about discipline, emotional life, and personal habits. The last third of the volume had several separate chapters on the Negro child, thereby acknowledging the minority status of these children and differences that existed between norms for them and for white children. *The Young Child in the Home* was eventually published in 1936 in the midst of the abnormal conditions of the Great Depression. It highlighted the degree to which the emphasis on how to measure normal patterns of child development had become the defining standard of expertise.[62]

William White, the influential Progressive Era journalist and shrewd observer of American life, always presented himself as a rather normal human being with a commonsense view of what was appropriate for American politics. The son of a doctor who gave up medicine to run a pharmacy and then a farm, William was born in 1868 and grew up in Emporia, Kansas, at the edge of the open plains. "I had the prairies, the wide illimitable stretches of green in their spring and summer verdure, stretching westward from my front door." His life was connected to the nineteenth century and to its belief in children's right to grow up by roaming freely and in doing so learning independence of mind. "As a little child, before they caught and bound me to a school desk, I remember spring, summer, and golden autumn as though I had lived always out of doors." He also recalled the work he did. "I cannot remember when I did not have to fill up the wood box back of the kitchen stove. And there were chips to rake up around the woodpile and bring in for kindling, and cobs to gather." He added that these were hardly work. "I am ashamed to admit that the machinations of grown-ups at first concealed from me the fact that they were evil and onerous. I did chores cheerfully in the primitive, savage simplicity of childhood."[63] A nineteenth-century child, the adult White saw his childhood in early twentieth-century terms, using "savage" in a way that G. Stanley Hall would have understood as he adopted an evolutionary perspective on children; like many of Darwin's early heirs, Hall believed that childhood repeated early stages in human evolution.

Born after the Civil War in the middle of the country, William White's experience of chores and the outdoors made his childhood quite unexceptional, even though, unlike most American children at that time and place, he was an only child (his younger brother had died). By the time he was ten or eleven, his mother read to him from Charles Dickens, James Fenimore Cooper, George Eliot, and even George Sand, an intellectual exposure that was probably more adventuresome than other children's early reading, but like others he was also expected to know his Mother Goose rhymes and many verses of the "Golden Text." He did not like school, but that, too, would not have differentiated William from most boys of his time, since the outdoors was much more alluring than the inside of a classroom. "The school," White asserted, "only taught him superficial things—to read, write, and figure, and to take care of himself on the playground."[64]

According to the White House Conference study on young children, by the first third of the twentieth century, White's childhood might have been exemplary, but it was no longer "normal." The investigators were acutely aware that there were important differences within the population. "When the population is divided on the basis of socio-economic status and the practices of the resulting groups are studied in detail, a picture is obtained of a society composed of a series of cultures. . . . The differences in practice between these groups begins at birth."[65] Shrewdly aware that American families existed within different kinds of environments that mattered, the conference report did not propose a single standard. Still the volume was not shy in defining the normal height, weight, development, and experiences of the average child in the United States. By the late 1920s and 1930s that child was an urban child, went to school by the age of 5 or 6, and would have played in his own or a neighbor's yard, not much further afield. She would have gone to the movies once a week with her parents. While there were considerable differences in the equipment available in homes of different socioeconomic classes, including books, toys, and play apparatus in the yards, each of these different classes/cultures had a range that was normal within the group.

Among the measures of family life investigated and depicted in the volume, one was the number of childrearing advice publications and radio programs devoted to this subject taken by the family. Of course, these varied by social class, but in no class, even the lowest (unskilled laborers), did fewer than one-third of all mothers read at least an article on child care. This self-reporting may have exaggerated a bit, but probably not by much. And of the survey participants overall "more than one-half of the mothers and one-fourth of the fathers listen to talks on child care over the radio at least irregularly."[66] The new exposure to advice literature on children was pervasive, even for those who did not read much or often.

While investigators did not ask how many children collected wood chips for the kitchen stove, they determined that the vast majority of all children in the survey ran errands; this did not vary at all by social class and very little by age. "It can be concluded that the great majority of children between the ages of six and twelve are called upon to run errands." Thus, even urban children continued to make some

small contribution to the well-being of the family, though the elaborate work routines of the earlier farming-dominated nineteenth century had disappeared, and William White's tasks as a child were hardly
normal. Many parents in the first half of the twentieth century clung
to simple chores as a way to maintain a sense that children learned the
importance of work and made some contribution to the welfare of
others. But Sidonie Gruenberg, an influential adviser to parents, was
quoted in *Time* magazine telling parents that children should begin
receiving spending money "between the ages of 5 and 7, because one
'must learn to spend before he can earn.' The allowance should be
given as something due the child, not as something for which he
must work." She was thus suggesting that children's participation in
the family was enough in itself—no work was required, at least for
young children.[67] She also made clear that a consumer economy was
changing what children might expect. Most of the predominantly
urban children in the White House Conference study dressed and
fed themselves—hardly an onerous duty, but by this point in time a
measure of the autonomy of young children (as suggested by ads in
Parents' Magazine). By age five, one-half of girls and the same proportion of boys dressed themselves; 97 percent fed themselves.[68] The demands made on children had shrunk significantly.

In their elaborate and extensive investigations of three thousand
American families, the White House Conference never asked how
many grandparents, aunts, or other kin (or strangers) lived with the
family. By 1932, the assumption was that families, whether of high or
low status, were what sociologists call "nuclear": composed of parents
and children only. In fact, however, recent demographers have concluded that the proportion of households that still contained others
living in the family remained fairly stable (among whites and blacks)
from the 1880s through the 1940s at about 20 percent (with a bit of
a decline by 1940 to 17 percent). The proportion of homes that contained grandparents and aunts and were therefore "extended" did not
decline markedly until after World War II.[69] But they were no longer
seen in the White House study as relevant to the home environment
of ordinary children and not included in the inquiry. In the view of
these sociologists, Grandma Mead and Aunt Mealy were no longer
significant to the raising of normal children.

Remarkable
New Type Garments

teach Children to Dress Themselves!

Your child's first lesson in *self-reliance* is *self-dressing*. You can teach him quickly, easily, this simple way —

IF you keep on dressing your child when he should be learning to dress himself, you may be forming a habit of dependence upon others that he will never quite overcome. So say leading child psychologists and educators.

Vanta will help you. Originated by Vanta, SELF-HELP undergarments are designed to teach children to dress themselves when only two years old. They make a happy game of dressing — a game that the child looks forward to each day. But an *important* game that teaches him to *think* for himself, *act* for himself, *do* for himself. A self-reliant, resourceful, independent character in the making.

In exactly the same place on the *outside* and *front* of each Vanta SELF-HELP Garment is an attractive Red Heart label. This bright red label catches the child's eye and he quickly learns when his garments are *right side out*, and which is *front*, and *back*.

Fastenings are always in front. Buttons are in plain sight and buttonholes are large enough for chubby little fingers. In brief, every SELF-HELP Garment is designed to *encourage* and *help* your child to help himself.

See Vanta SELF-HELP Garments in the Infants' Department of your favorite store, or write us immediately if you fail to find the garments you desire. Look for Vanta's Red Heart label — "The Sign of the Heart." This famous label is your child's first guiding mark to independence . . . your own key to precious hours saved for recreation!

"Teach Children to Dress Themselves." Advertisement for Vanta Baby Garments from *Parents' Magazine* 11 (September 1936), 69.

Give your Child the Priceless Gift of
Self-Reliance
by Teaching Him to
Dress Himself this Simple Vanta Way

YOU can give that precious growing child of yours a gift that will stand him in good stead all the days of his life—the gift of a sturdy, self-reliant, resourceful character.

Child psychologists and modern educators place great emphasis on the character-building qualities that result from early training in self-dressing. Self-reliance and confidence are sure to result, they say.

Let Vanta help you. Originated by Vanta, SELF-HELP undergarments are designed to teach children to dress themselves when only two years old. They make a happy game of dressing—a game that the child looks forward to each day. But an *important game* that teaches him to *think* for himself, *act* for himself, *do* for himself. A self-reliant, resourceful, independent character in the making. You want that.

How Vanta helps

In exactly the same place on the *outside* and *front* of each Vanta *SELF-HELP* Garment is an attractive Red Heart label. This bright red label catches the child's eye and he quickly learns when his garments are *right side out*, and which is *front*, and *back*.

Fastenings are always in front. Buttons are in plain sight and buttonholes are large enough for chubby little fingers. In brief, every SELF-HELP Garment is designed to *encourage* and *help* your child to help himself.

Other garments often make a complex and difficult task of self-dressing, discouraging the child. Vanta, the first authentic SELF-HELP Garments, are made as a result of long study to make dressing so simple that with comparatively little instruction, the child develops naturally without discouragement, and constantly grows in capacity and confidence to assume more difficult tasks.

See Vanta SELF-HELP Garments in the Infants' Department of your favorite store, or write us immediately if you fail to find the garments you desire. Look for Vanta's Red Heart label—"The Sign of the Heart". This famous label is your child's first guiding mark to independence . . . your own key to precious hours saved for rest and recreation!

Send 10c for "The Toddler," 34 pages of training, feeding and health helps for mothers of children from 2 to 12. Send coupon today.

**Vanta
QUALITY**

Vanta
Baby Garments

EARNSHAW KNITTING CO., Dept. P-1036, Newton, Mass.
Enclosed find 10c. Please send me copy "THE TODDLER"

Name..

Address...

"Give Your Children the Priceless Gift of Self-Reliance." Advertisement for Vanta Baby Garments, *Parents' Magazine* II (October 1936), 96. Note the emphasis on self-reliance to be encouraged among even very young children.

In fact, however, there were more grandparents around. The perception of the declining significance of grandparents was just that, a perception based on the fact that most grandparents now usually lived apart from the family. Longer life expectancy affected Americans at both ends of the life cycle. In effect, by the time of the White House survey, the phenomenon of grandparents at home seemed no longer worthy of a place in carefully defined normal household practices. The full standardization of what twentieth-century families consisted of and how children were expected to be raised did not become fully visible until the middle third of the twentieth century. These standards were not fully enshrined until the 1940s and 1950s as sociological theory.[70]

In the early twentieth century, many of the female social scientists who brought family life to public attention and addressed concerns about appropriate household order were themselves raised in families that did not conform to the two-generation norm. This was true for Margaret Mead, Lucy Sprague Mitchell, and Grace and Edith Abbott[71] whose grandmothers or maiden aunts were deeply involved in their childhoods. It was also true for Elsie Clews Parsons, a pioneering anthropologist, whose wealthy and socially prominent New York family employed a range of servants who resided in the household.[72] These women, who made important careers in the first part of the twentieth century, all had mothers whose childrearing tasks were shared in significant ways with what evolutionary psychologist Sarah Hrdy calls allomothers—women who were not biological mothers but shared in rearing and supervising the welfare of children.[73] Some of these allomothers were no doubt aware of the newest scientific theories about children; others were not. In any event, they no longer fit a social norm. Many childrearing experts were suspicious of the influence of grandmothers and maiden aunts, and they sought to create a modern generation of parents who were not in thrall to old-fashioned views about children and old wives' tales they associated with these other women in the household.

The childhoods of people like White or Mead, who influenced how Americans thought and behaved in the first part of the twentieth century, were forgotten as social scientists began to define what was normal for childrearing by the time the United States entered World

War II. What had started as a drive to save infants from an early grave was transformed into a new set of standards about how parents could and should manage childhood and what an American family should look like.[74] The Rockefeller Foundation's Lawrence Frank said it well: "Only very slowly has it been discovered that the health of the child can be protected and his development fostered by enlightened control of his hygiene, food, and other aspects of his nurture. . . . It is probable that all existing agencies and practices of childrearing and child care will be reorganized in the light" of the new knowledge of "the life sciences." All this "represents a very large and significant break with the past. " It was all newly possible because parents had learned that their children could survive.[75]

Over the course of three decades, an emphatic shift had taken place from the generation of progressive women, many of them spinsters, who hoped to assist in the protection of America's most unfortunate and vulnerable children to the new generation of mothers who were to be guided by scientific authorities about how best to raise their own children at home. By the time Frank made his observation in 1939, the emphasis was on the private household where mothers and fathers would be encouraged to believe that they could determine the fate of their children under the careful supervision of experts.

V

Lucy Sprague became a leader of progressive education in New York in the 1920s and 1930s. Born in Chicago in 1878 in a bustling Victorian household, Lucy was one of six children; only four survived. Her mother, "had never been her old self since Otho's death, [and] now lay on her bed, silent and without tears." Despite her distinctly nineteenth-century upbringing, Lucy helped to define schooling for young children in the twentieth century. Lucy's father and his friends had helped to make the city of Chicago into a prosperous hub of finance and industry and she deeply identified with the city: "The young city, almost as a personality itself struggling to grow up, had a profound influence on my development." For Lucy, the Chicago of her childhood was the big enterprising city, which she associated with her father's circle, "the men who made Chicago and at the same time made fortunes for themselves."[76] It was a class-based Chicago in which her successful family occupied the upper rung.

A failure whenever she went to school, which made her twitch and feel "terrible pains in her legs," Lucy began to educate herself using her father's extensive library. Embarrassed by the large house in which she lived and the fact that her father divided people along class lines and had one attitude toward those who had money and another toward those who did not, Lucy found herself going to Hull House, where she fell "under the spell of Jane Addams."[77] Hull House was a social settlement that aimed to provide help and instruction to new immigrants to the city, a place to which mothers could bring their children while they learned to become Americans. Lucy had also been deeply influenced by the Haymarket riot and by the Pullman strike, important events in the nineteenth-century history of labor that reflected the sharp antagonisms generated by the rampant capitalist development of the time. Chicago embodied and unleashed both the capitalist vigor and the responses to it. Lucy's Chicago milieu helps us to understand not only her own roots as an educational reformer but also the basis for many of the reforms and changes that Chicago activists and academics helped to institute.

Despite Lucy's ambivalent attitude toward her father and his wealth, it was he who helped her to define herself. He introduced her to the world contained in the many books he collected and, though he was himself without a college degree, facilitated her contact to the professors and students who flocked to the city after the University of Chicago opened its doors in 1892. "The opening of the University was to Father a climax of his pride for the city he loved almost as a personal possession. . . . He regarded professors with a kind of reverence once accorded the clergy. He felt it a personal opportunity as well as a civic responsibility to open his home to the faculty members who were strangers in his city."[78]

As a result of her father's contacts, Lucy met the first dean of women at the university, Alice Freeman Palmer, previously president of Wellesley College, who lived at their house for a while, and the reformer Sophonisba Breckinridge. She also met her future husband Wesley Clair Mitchell, then a graduate student in economics and later an important influence in developing the statistical base for our knowledge of the American economy. During the First World War, Wesley Mitchell worked to create a clearinghouse of statistical activities for the War Industries Board, the War Trade Board, and the Shipping Board. After the war, he went on to organize the Bureau of Economic Statistics in the nation's capital. In the 1930s, he was influential in creating the New School for Social Research as well as the Social Science Research Council. Committed to empirical research based on statistical measures, Mitchell also admired Thorstein Veblen and John Dewey; he studied with both in Chicago. The broth of the new university was rich in relationships and in personalities who crisscrossed disciplines and absorbed the diverse flavors of the great city.

Chicago, the young city on the edge of the plains and the lake, was both the hub of the progressive drive to guard infant life and to understand delinquency, and the site for the emergence of the new university-based expertise of the social sciences. It was a place in which the drive to collect statistics emerged as a vital part of how we learn about social life and social relations. Chicago brought people from many parts of the country, distinguished professors from the East, and aspiring students from the Midwest, many like Wesley Mitchell born in small towns. And it brought a very large array of immigrants from other parts of the world who often became the subjects of investigation. It was here that reformers and young scholars found their subjects, their purpose, and each other.

In 1889, Jane Addams established the first American settlement at Hull House and it became the portal for many of the women and men who were committed to finding a way to assist children toward a better life. Addams was a guiding spirit in founding the juvenile court in Cook County (Chicago), the first in the nation, in 1899. Many of the social reformers came through the doors of these institutions. Julia Lathrop, the first director of the Children's Bureau, was one of them. And many of the most influential researchers on children received degrees from the social science departments and professional schools of the University of Chicago. Grace Abbott, who took the reins of the Children's Bureau after Lathrop left, received a master's degree from the university in political science; her sister Edith Abbott earned a doctoral degree in economics, as did Sophonisba Breckinridge, who also had the distinction of being the first woman to earn a law degree from the University of Chicago.

William Healy, born in England, came to Chicago to get his medical degree at the university and stayed to establish the first child guidance clinic, which became the center of pioneering research on juvenile crime. Well known later for creating the Judge Baker Foundation in Boston, he began by founding the Chicago Juvenile Psychopathic Institute. It was renamed the Institute for Juvenile Research in the 1920s when the sociologist Clifford Shaw (from the rural Midwest) took over. Shaw and his colleague, Henry McKay (also a midwestern farm boy), whom he met when they were graduate students at the university, became the most important and innovative researchers on gangs and youth crime in the 1930s. Their studies all centered on Chicago.[79] W. I. Thomas had begun his studies in Tennessee and had focused on English literature, but he brought a passionate interest in social organization to the University in Chicago, where he studied sociology and anthropology, in the late nineteenth century. The university was also the place to which the subsequently notorious John Watson came to do graduate work in psychology, because he knew that John Dewey was there and because he wanted to escape from the stifling provincialism of his Southern Baptist childhood.[80]

The city together with its university, which was quickly becoming a world-class place to pursue social science research, were thus the strategic center for the initial interest in and commitment to children, childrearing, and delinquency. In the late nineteenth century, the University of Chicago was also the setting for John Dewey's critical observations and insights into how children learn, and his radical efforts to reframe, reform, and revitalize American schools. Dewey was a magnet for other scholars, but he had also been influenced by the city. Dewey absorbed Chicago's passion for reform and its focus on children, as well as its proximity to the older values of rural and small-town midwestern America, to institute the most influential movement in education of the twentieth century. As America's premier philosopher of active knowledge, he affected many at the University of Chicago, including the educational ideals of Lucy

Sprague Mitchell and the economics of her husband Wesley Clair Mitchell. And Dewey's spirit also inspired many others in the surrounding community of Chicago activists.[81]

Dewey's ideas about children and education and their centrality to democracy would affect the fundamental principles not only of American pedagogy but also of modern educational beliefs around the world. And Dewey's influence was hardly limited to education. His first truly important interest was in how Darwin's ideas were refashioning philosophy and forcing the reorientation of knowledge toward the future and the unknown. Dewey sought to bring to the schooling of young Americans some of the vitality and independence that had once been part of an active life in the family economy and small-town America. He wanted knowledge to be grounded in physical experience and tied to work. Dewey believed that much of this essential spirit was being lost in rote learning and the bureaucratic system of education in which the young were bound to their texts and their desks. They had lost touch with what work meant and no longer had the resources to provide themselves with basics of life; they hardly knew where their food came from. Dewey had no illusions about returning to an earlier American household in which children learned habits of work and independence through experience (he had absorbed Darwin's lessons about the inexorable quality of change). But he hoped to have the schools compensate for that loss. Toward this end, he set up a laboratory school at the University of Chicago, where he and his wife, Alice Chipman, studied children and how they learned, and implemented their visions of the reformed classroom.

Chicago went on to feed many other places and universities with its people and the energy of its research. By the 1920s and 1930s, the area between Washington, DC, and Boston was as likely to contain centers for innovative research on children as Chicago had a generation earlier: Healy left for Boston, Abbott for Washington, DC, and Dewey for New York. Lucy Sprague Mitchell went initially to California to nurse her parents, as a good Victorian daughter was expected to do, and then to become the first dean of women at the University of California at Berkeley. Finally she moved with her husband to New York, where each of them did the work for which they are best remembered. And New Haven, not Chicago, became the prime location for laboratory observations that underlay ideas of childhood development. But all of these places had connections to Chicago, just as Chicago was part of the nationalizing of ideas about children and the agitations on their behalf.

By the twentieth century, older patterns—rural, local, and small-town—had given way to a society organized around university-based expertise and a scientific outlook that transcended the boundaries of place. The private concerns of family life had become the subject of research and national purpose. As Americans moved from the country to the city, as industry took over from farming, as new immigrants became a visible presence, and as professionals went to school to pursue advanced degrees and set about changing the society around them, the nation became the focus of interest and the nation's children the subject of dedicated inquiry and promotion. Where progressive women, full of a new confidence that came from statistics, had looked to remedy the conditions of the children of the poor, the new professionals looked to the ordinary child and her normal home life as the object of measurement and control. The nursery was one of the institutions to which professionals directed their inquiries and prescriptions; the school was another. Parents now had advisors of all kinds. They were also forced to compete with other institutions for their children's attention as the fundamental economic, social, and cultural reorganization of the United States transformed how children were raised in the twentieth century.

CHAPTER 4

A Wider World

Adolescence, Immigration, and Schooling, 1920–1960

Between 1900 and 1930, the United States began to assume much greater visibility on the world's stage. While the early republic had not been shy about proclaiming its world-changing importance as a form of government, the actual role played by the United States in the nineteenth century was modest compared with the imperial ambitions and behaviors of other Western states like Britain, France, or Germany, as well as Japan in the Pacific. That began to change in the late nineteenth century, and by the early twentieth, America's presence in world affairs was palpable. Presidents Theodore Roosevelt and Woodrow Wilson both insisted that the nation play a part in international diplomacy based on the new stature of a nation enlarged physically and in population, with a powerfully competitive economy.

While Roosevelt acted as an intermediary in other people's wars through diplomacy in the Russo-Japanese War, in 1917 Wilson took the United States directly into the vast and stymied World War being fought in Europe since 1914 that was destroying a generation of youth and redrawing the map of Europe. The entry of the United States was crucial to bringing the gaping wound of war to a close. The United States' entanglements on the world stage were a new experience for a nation that had tried for almost a century to remain largely separate from and protected from the machinations of alliances and their diplomatic commitments. Even in the 1920s, some American politicians acted as if they could remain ensconced on an isolated continent protected by two oceans. In reality, this was no longer useful even as an illusion, either economically or politically. And Herbert Hoover, who would eventually round out the decade as president, was already feeding millions of Europe's starving children in the early 1920s, an expression of America's largesse and its newfound position in the world.

As the United States emerged as an international power, symbol-ized by President Wilson's prominent role in the peace negotiations at Versailles, the nation's new self-confidence affected how children grew up. The high school especially embodied America's new stature. This uniquely American institution with its unusual investment in youth development and its extension of childhood dependency into adolescence answered several needs associated with the growth of the American economy and the power that went with it. While changing how young Americans prepared for adulthood, the high school also became the best means to manage the enormous immigration that fueled economic development. The vibrant engine of America's econ-omy antedated and prepared for the new role that the United States was beginning to play internationally and brought immigration in its wake. Immigrants brought many things to American shores—an ea-gerness for hard work, aspirations for improvement, varied habits of life, and their children. These required public responses that would motivate the second generation and augment, without overwhelming, the delicate strategies that immigrants needed to survive. Extended schooling also had to be aligned with older democratic commit-ments if it was to remain the basis for a better future for the nation's citizens.

The invention of the high school sat solidly on the bounty of wealth created by the American economy and a long history of imagining what kind of education was required to serve and harness a diverse population. Since the early republic, educational theorists had also understood how crucial education was in preparing America's prog-eny for an indeterminate future. That solid footing for the American faith in schooling was not destabilized even when the Great Depres-sion hit.[1] Instead, the goal of education for America's adolescents was confirmed by the Depression and subsequently by New Deal policies as young people, left jobless, were coaxed to remain in high school, often through federal relief programs.[2] The Second World War tem-porarily stopped that steady march toward higher schooling—but not for long. That trend continued for most of the rest of the century as high school became the defining experience of American adolescence. And the American pattern set the standard for most European na-tions and their youth by the end of the century.

Leonard Covello, an immigrant child from Italy in the early twentieth century, who became first a schoolteacher and then an influential high school principal, captured this American attachment to schooling well when he dedicated his memoir, *The Heart Is the Teacher,* "To those who believe that the struggle for a better world will be won or lost in our schools." Covello understood that the American vision of an improved world was linked to its commitments to schooling. This belief in the power of education still guides American social thought, although today we no longer place our faith in the high school, which one hundred years ago seemed the beacon in that struggle.[3] Still, the high school—and the youth culture that emerged as its adolescent inhabitants used its institutional base for their own purposes—was for a long time the envy of the world, part of what America stood for as it became a world power.

I

Families in the United States had always been diverse. Even in the early republican period, Northern and Southern families, black and white families, rural and urban families, and rich and poor families raised their children in different settings and with varied objectives. That was one of the reasons that publicly supported schools first appeared under the banner of common schools for all. Their aim was to make sure that "all classes of society are blended," in the words of one of their early promoters, educational reformer James Carter. "The principle, upon which our free schools are established," Carter argued in 1826, "is in itself, a stern leveler of factitious distinctions." To create an "effective check against an aristocracy of wealth," one purpose of democratic common schools was to encourage talented children, regardless of their birth or circumstances, to rise in society and contribute to the well-being of the nation. By leveling and blending, school would make a variety of distinctions less prominent.[4]

Regular and repeated immigrations made the need to blend more urgent in the United States than in other Western societies, although these were also promoting public elementary schools by the middle of the nineteenth century. The American effort to establish free public schools was not very different from similar efforts in France,

England, Sweden, and Germany. All these nations had moderniz-
ing economies and were eager to confirm strong national identities
among their populations. In creating broad-based literacy, schools
made populations legible to the administrative apparatus of the state
while they gave citizens a sense of national belonging and helped
them to become better workers.

If the United States was not unique, it was different in several re-
spects. One difference resulted from the fact that its many schools
grew in a fragmentary way in a society not centrally administered.
American schools originated from and were organized and financed
at the local level—by counties, townships, and cities. As a result,
urban schools and rural schools remained quite different for a long
time, while Southern schools lagged behind Northern and Western
schools in their pace of development. In the South, public schools had
barely taken root before the Civil War, and education was officially
prohibited for those who were slaves. After the war, Reconstruction
regimes finally set up schools for former slaves under the auspices of
the Freedman's Bureau (a unique, though short-lived, federal under-
taking), and public schools under local auspices began to appear for
the population in Southern states generally.

More variegated from the beginning, American schools also had
an additional agenda. Americans who directed their attention to
schooling explicitly imagined that it would provide a lever for social
mobility. "Every generation, while the system is executed according
to the true spirit of it," James Carter declared, "will bring its quota
of *new men* to fill the public places of distinction—men who owe
nothing to the fortunes or the crimes of their fathers." Without such
schools, which were "the very life blood" of free institutions and republican government, American principles could not survive.[5]

Carter looked back to the Puritan fathers for the origin of this
ideal. In fact, Thomas Jefferson, hardly a New England Puritan, had
envisaged a similar plan for public education in his *Notes on the State
of Virginia* (1786).[6] Jefferson proposed a process of selection based on
broad initial participation by all children. As students proceeded up
the ranks of schooling, those with talent would continue to the next
level, while those who did not display such talent would drop away.
This systematic selection process would lead finally to attendance

at a state university where Jefferson hoped the future public leaders would be educated to the highest cultural levels. Neither wealth nor influence but only the free play of talent promoted for the public good would serve as the basis for success in this system. The impulse to promote education as a form of selective mobility as well as a means toward citizen solidarity expressed an American perspective on schooling that remains vital to this day. Public schools were to provide a diverse and complex population with the means to become effective citizens as well as an avenue toward individual advancement beyond the limitations of birth.

From the middle of the nineteenth century to the beginning of the twentieth, public schools grew like undisciplined plants throughout the expanding landscape from Maine to Florida, Rhode Island to the Pacific Coast. By the early twentieth century, urban school reformers tried to bring some order into the growth by exercising systematic new administrative perspectives in city schools, but nationally school districts remained diverse.[7] Some schools were no more than one-room establishments, and these have left us with images of the little red schoolhouse as a fabled part of US history.[8] Not long after the end of the Civil War, Bernard Baruch attended his first school in a private home: "The 'classroom' was in the kitchen. . . . I learned my letters lying on my stomach on the floor," as the lady of the house nursed her children. This son of South Carolina went on to become a great financier and an important adviser to presidents.[9]

In Montana, decades later, Chet Huntley, a future journalist and television anchor, went to school in the early twentieth century in a multipurpose building where "funerals . . . christenings, marriages, and elections" were also held. "It was, indeed, a community center, in that it housed the collective joys and sorrows of the neighborhood." The "student body included about a dozen pupils, ranging from the first to the eighth grades, all in one room." Indeed, in many ways, farm or ranch life and its associated schooling had not changed that much since Ulysses Grant was a boy in Ohio a century earlier. Huntley's first childhood chores, for example, required that he "take a team and wagon, drive through the range land," and gather "cow chips" for the fire at the family ranch. Other tasks soon followed and resulted, as Huntley noted, in "years of 'learning by doing,' " especially in "the

Sod school, District 62, two miles west of Merna, Custer County, Nebraska (1889). Photograph by Solomon D. Butcher. Prairie Settlement: Nebraska Photographs and Family Letters Collection, Nebraska State Historical Society, Image # RG2608. PH:000000–001774.

ways and care of ranch animals." But however heavy the demands of farming, the school had been "one of the initial undertakings of our new outpost society," according to Huntley."[10]

By the time Chet Huntley attended his simple schoolroom in Saco, Montana, students in cities throughout the United States were gathering in much larger and far more crowded buildings and in classrooms sharply differentiated by age. Urban schooling had become a complex enterprise and its administration and pedagogy the subject of dispute and controversy. The large, multi-classroom school arranged carefully by grades was usually the setting for immigrants who lived in large industrial cities, as most immigrant children or children of recent immigrants did. But even immigrant children, especially those of Scandinavian or German background, were to be found in rural schools where the school year was often interrupted by farm calendars and student learning not fully determined by pedagogically defined age-grade standards. It was not until the 1930s that many rural schools were "consolidated" in ways that allowed them to become more like their urban counterparts in organization and curriculum because they were attended by more pupils.

Neither the schools American children attended nor their experiences were exactly the same, but for most, this did not matter very much. Whatever the initial goals of education, students often attended erratically and only for a few years, until the end of the nineteenth century when states began to impose school attendance requirements. The lives of most American young people combined duties at home or work outside the home with some school attendance, which might span different locations in a highly mobile population. The United States had an unusually literate citizenry compared with other nations but, for most Americans, this had been acquired through a few years of scattered schooling. Hardly the significant or defining experience of childhood, school life was remembered in most memoirs briefly, if at all, in the context of much fuller descriptions of free play and work with siblings and friends, under the supervision of parents, grandparents, and other relatives.[11] Born in midcentury, Kate Douglas Wiggin was a voracious reader but admitted, "School days play an extraordinarily small part in my life." And when she brought her younger sister home after a bad first-day experience at school with a punitive teacher, Wiggin's father happily kept the sister home thereafter and taught her himself.[12]

An occasional vivid recollection of a teacher or a special school-based experience was all that most people recorded of their years in elementary school. Even Edna Ferber, who claimed to love school as she grew up in Wisconsin, remembered very little about it. Neither did Bernard Baruch even though he admired his teacher, Mr. Wallace, despite the fact that he frequently brought students back from their daydreams with a sharp rap on their knuckles. Immigrant children often had more vivid but not necessarily positive recollections. The future philosopher Sidney Hook, growing up in desperately poor, immigrant Williamsburg, Brooklyn, mostly remembered the discipline and the boredom. "Our teachers were proud that 'one could hear a pin drop' in their class as the lively little bodies sat in petrified silence." These teachers also did not spare the rod. Schooling became part of the rhythm of life but hardly central to childhood. As Gertrude Berg, a radio and early television star, described her New York City school days, "I should probably say that I liked school—it sounds better. But the whole truth is, I didn't. I wasn't interested and there was always something I would rather be doing than sitting in a classroom, like, for instance, sitting at home." For Berg, as for Mark Twain, schooling was good for a laugh but other things created childhood memories.[13]

II

That attitude changed when the history of American schools pulled away quickly and decisively from schools in other Western nations. The American faith in education was nowhere more pointedly advertised than in the creation of the high school. The White House Conference on Child Health and Protection put this faith in ringing terms in 1934: "The school is the embodiment of the most profound faith of the American people, a faith that if the rising generation can be sufficiently educated, the ills of society will disappear. The constantly lengthening period of school attendance, the constantly enlarging contributions of money for the maintenance of the school, the rising standards of preparation of the teachers . . . these and many other evidences attest the faith of the people in their schools."[14] It was one thing to invest in this faith by expanding facilities and another to ensure that the young took advantage of it. The United States succeeded on both counts. The "wider world"[15] of the high school vested American childhood more and more deeply in schooling in the twentieth century as it occupied a longer period of life and was extended at a strategic juncture in personal development. School now offered memorable experiences and altered the nature of growing up.

Unlike the equivalents of high schools elsewhere in the West such as the *lycée* or *gymnasium*—places of exclusive higher learning attended by only a tiny fragment of the population—American high schools became democratic almost as soon as they became an important part of the educational system. In thirty years between 1890 and 1920, Americans built an average of one high school per day, according to education historian William Reese. The expansion was so rapid and extensive that the journal *School Life* boasted that "New York has more secondary schools than all of France, Los Angeles more than all of Austria, and Detroit more than London, though its population is only one-tenth as great." Reese notes that "from 1890 to 1930, the high school population doubled every decade."[16]

And this growth continued deep into the twentieth century. Economic historian Claudia Goldin found that the "high school enrollment rate rose from 18 percent to 73 percent and the graduation rate increased from 9 to 51 percent during the three decades after 1910. The rate of increase was nothing short of spectacular and the levels attained were unequaled by any other country until much later in the century."[17] American education was truly revolutionary in this regard, since it succeeded in enticing the majority of adolescents into a longer school regime and created a uniquely American institution to contain them. Nothing better expressed America's new prominence in the world or Americans' elevated expectations regarding the future. By the middle decades of the twentieth century, the vast majority of adolescents, regardless of where they or their parents were born, were drawn into the ambit of the high school. By then, most students not only attended for a year or two but were also likely to graduate. By the mid-1930s, 50 percent of high school students in non-Southern states were graduating. In the South, many African American students did not have access to full high school curricula from which they could graduate. But Goldin makes clear, "even though the South lagged the rest of the nation in educational attainment, its rates of secondary school enrollment and graduation were still higher than were those of many nations at the time." This was the case for white as well as black youth.[18]

The comprehensive public high school transformed the aims of education from being a limited period directed toward making the young literate and reliable citizens into a training institution for variously defined social and economic purposes. Rather than a short transition period of personal uncertainty and discovery, adolescence became a prolonged sojourn of development spent among other youth. Across the American landscape, new high schools often became the most visible and prominent buildings in the public square, providing a

Watsonville High School, designed by William H. Weeks in 1917, at a cost of over $90,000. Photographer unknown. SCPL Local History Photograph Collection, Santa Cruz Public Libraries, California, Image # 0200. As this photo shows, even small towns could have a grand high school building, a demonstration of the importance placed on the high school in communities of all kinds.

crucial source for community identification and hosting sports teams with recognizable local insignia. In the process, the high school became one of the dominant sites for the creation of twentieth-century American culture. The extended education provided to the majority of American youth also gave the United States a significant economic edge in a world that, over the course of the century, became more dependent on advanced literacy and other skills.

From then on, for better or for worse, school played a large role in the memories of Americans. At its best, it provided what Edna Ferber remembered as "four miraculous years of the most exhilarating and heartening fun." This was not merely because it was "the place in which I and my classmates spent four years grubbing away at algebra, geometry, economics, English and physics. . . . It was, for us, a clubhouse, a forum, a social center, playground, a second home."[19] For many adolescents, the image of the high school as a second home captures the significance and primacy of the institution on a personal level. It substituted for family and displaced parents.

But high schools also captured an important political and social reality. Starting in the twentieth century, the prominence of high school accompanied the ascent of the United States as it assumed a new and visible place in world affairs. America's new visibility was the result of policy decisions that created a powerful navy to challenge the once dominant British and the emerging might of Japan. It resulted from the political assertiveness of newly confident presidents, like Roosevelt and Wilson. Much of it grew from the enormous engine of the American economy—an economy whose surpluses of agricultural products from vast midwestern farms and minerals from Western mines were carried on an extraordinary network of railroads (the United States had two-thirds of all the world's railroad tracks). It was also an economy that increasingly grew from the belching factories of a huge, sophisticated, and integrated axis of heavy industries that came to dominate the landscape of the East and Midwest. It came, too, from the financial power that New York was beginning to exercise in the world.

The high school would take its place among the factors that made the United States a world power in the first half of the twentieth century. The new extensive system of high schools reflected a willingness to invest in young people that was unequaled anywhere else. By the First World War, the American economic powerhouse had made the United States a world presence and a potential international player, a part that it would then exercise as a victor in the war and in the negotiations that followed. That power would then be demonstrated by the critical role the United States played in World War II and the postwar world.

The driving economy had also brought to American shores a huge array of immigrant families eager to participate in its success. In the late nineteenth century, the immigrants who initially built the railroads, dug the mines, fueled the factories, and plowed the fields—from Germany, Ireland, Sweden, China, England, and Norway—were overwhelmed in sheer volume by those from Italy, Poland, Russia, and the Austro-Hungarian Empire as well as from Mexico, Greece, and the

Steamer class in Hancock School, Boston, Massachusetts (1909). Photograph by Lewis Wickes Hine. National Child Labor Committee (US) Collection, Prints & Photographs Division, Library of Congress, Image # LC-DIG-nclc-04529. This steamer class was designed for immigrant children to enable them to learn English as quickly as possible and then join others of their grade.

Middle East. These new arrivals added to the complexity of cultures and religions and the cacophony of family forms and parental styles. Little wonder then that the White House Conference on Child and Health Protection in 1934 concluded, "To describe a typical American home at the present time is almost impossible."[20]

Always multiform, the domestic life of Americans now began to incorporate styles, manners, and beliefs from parts of the world that had often provided little or no schooling to their population and where nationalism was sometimes an irritant in a polyglot empire. Common schooling at the elementary level had, from the start, been about enforcing some uniformity in language, and often in belief, as well as providing literacy. But what kind of uniformity or nationality could the Austro-Hungarian or the Ottoman Empire expect or require of their many diverse people, and how did Sicilian or Calabrian peasants regard the efforts at centralization through education from a recently united Italian state led by distant Northern Italians? Not only could the United States not expect its new immigrants to be well schooled, many brought little experience of modern forms of national identity. Instead, many newcomers linked their identities to villages or regions, often defined by special dialects.[21] These were matters that American cities would have to confront as they welcomed new people into their neighborhoods and schools.

The new immigration provided the evolving schools across the country with a challenge and a stimulus. They had to educate the children of peasants and city dwellers who lacked experience with schools, and the schools themselves had to be transformed to make them truly effective. Enforcing attendance requirements was one response; extending schooling for longer periods of a child's life was another. But the most innovative of America's responses concerned the nature of the longer schooling it offered to the various peoples it began to serve. Forced to address that issue, the "comprehensive" high school became a radical innovation in education. In Claudia Goldin's words, "the secondary school as we know it today was a uniquely-American invention." The American comprehensive high school managed to retain the equalitarian emphasis that had underwritten common schools and promoted the idea of mobility while providing for an enormously diverse and variously motivated population. Part of its innovation required a diversified curriculum that moved in many directions away from the former classical model. In the late nineteenth century, public secondary schools had already introduced scientific courses of studies as an alternative to the classics, and then in the twentieth century, schools moved to offer commercial, vocational, and other forms of curricula, such as home economics. By World War I, there was general agreement among educators that high schools should provide practical curricula.[22]

The innovation did not stop there. American high schools opened their doors to non-academic or only marginally academic offerings, including an enormous range of clubs, artistic performances, sports, newspapers and literary magazines, and purely recreational events. For many educators, this arena was where students were supposed to exercise self-government and self-determination. It was here, in the extracurricular realm, that young people could claim their rights to self-expression while learning about democratic values in action. Whatever effect Dewey had on American schooling in the long run, in this expansion of what schools were and how students operated within them, he and his followers had established the critical importance of students' self-activity. The American high school was thus meant to provide, in this realm at least, the independence and self-direction that it was sidelining as it kept older children and youth in school and under adult control for longer periods of time. As one educational leader observed, the extracurricular arena was "[t]he one place where democratic ideals and objectives may function in a natural matrix. . . ."[23] Dewey had emphasized experience, rather than merely anticipatory study, and the extracurricular arena provided just that. Based in real activity and connected to the affairs of the larger community, the extracurricular world was the proxy for what Ulysses Grant had learned through real work and the independence he was given to pursue it. The tiny community center that occupied the same school building in Chet Huntley's childhood Montana was reimagined for adolescents in high schools as they spread across the country in the 1920s.

Not all American schoolchildren were immigrants and initially, at least, those who attended high school were drawn disproportionately from the established population who more readily grasped its advantages. But it was often the problems associated with its newest citizens, most conspicuous in the roiling immigrant cities of the nation, that were the source of many of the innovations in schools and the way these could be best deployed to harness the human resources of the young. This was surely one of the potential "ills of society" noted by the White House Conference convened in 1929 by President Herbert Hoover, and toward which Americans directed their faith in education. In the new American vision, high schools could educate many more students to a new level of literacy adequate to a growing corporate nation and an international power while keeping children, brought here from places where neither literacy nor national identity could be assumed, in school much longer. High school enforced time in school away from the influence of parents, and it did so in ways that were meant to appeal to the boisterous population of adolescents it was now seeking to house. As Edna Ferber, herself a member of the third generation of Jewish immigrants (her grandparents were born in Hungary and Germany), so incisively suggested, the high school could be "a second home."

The special contribution that Americans made to schooling—the invention and expansion of the democratic high school—was under-written by American economic might, and it brought adolescence, immigration, and education together in a powerful mixture that helped to define culture through much of the twentieth century as students attended common institutions well past their early child-hood years. Since American youth did not go into the army, except as wartime conscripts, they went to school instead. In this wider world, beyond the family and the locally derived and often ethnically defined neighborhood, immigrant youth were brought into conversation with an array of influences that were "educational" in the broadest sense of that term. It exposed them to things that were "grown up" and unfa-miliar and gave them a vantage on their families and neighborhoods.

The high school also gave American adolescents an institutional platform and visibility. Without the high school, youth would have otherwise been lost sight of in a welter of adult milieus. Although schooling did not invent adolescence, whose creaky entry into public consciousness had already been charted in the nineteenth century and whose physical transformation and strange yearnings G. Stan-ley Hall had enshrined in two volumes in 1904, adolescents became prominent with the growth of high school.[24] As a result, adolescents and their culture were far more visible in the United States than else-where in the world until well into the second half of the twentieth century.

American youth in the twentieth century embodied American culture and American power because they attended high school. Else-where in the West—in Germany, France, England, Italy, and the Scan-dinavian countries—adolescents envied American youth and the leisure afforded by their extended schooling. And they began to copy their fashions, music, and mannerisms, hoping thereby to also assim-ilate their privileges, privileges that included freedom of expression as well as wealth.[25] By the time European nations began to catch up by extending schools to older youths, the scripts had already been written by Americans. By 1970, the novelist Kurt Vonnegut would claim, "High school is closer to the core of the American experience than anything else I can think of."[26] Nowhere else were adolescents

so favored and nowhere else did they seem to be so important as sym-
bols of a free and prosperous nation.

III

Born in Warsaw, Poland, in the second decade of the twentieth
century, Kate Simon came to the United States as a four-year-old.
Like other immigrants, her father had preceded the rest of the family members and was not altogether delighted when they arrived.
Simon remembered her parents as mismatched in temperament and
ambition and she chafed at her father's overweening control and at
being burdened with the care of her sickly younger brother. Briefly
the object of her father's solicitous attention because he hoped she
would become a concert pianist and that, as her manager, he could
thereby transcend the narrow vistas of his unsatisfactory life, Kate
refused the gift and turned away from music. Intelligent, observant,
and rebellious, she rejected the path he laid out for her and suffered
the consequences. She never forgave him for trying to use her future
for his own ends, and accused him of cruelty, niggardliness, and self-
importance in the two memoirs she wrote about her childhood and
youth. As a child she could not really escape him, but that changed
when she went to high school. Her father initially did not want her
to continue at school at all, but then insisted that she could go for just
one year. But she discovered a world beyond home that offered a stark
choice.[27] It was, in her own words, "a wider world."

At James Monroe High School in the Bronx, Kate's drive and independence began to flower as teachers and fellow students supported
her decision to leave home and assisted her in finding places to live
and the means to support herself through school. "James Monroe was
the first stage on which I created of myself a distinctive, conspicuous
character," she recalled. This character had been suppressed in the
narrow confines of her first-generation household. As a new school
in a city that was adapting to its diverse population, James Monroe
allowed its students to graduate without completing some of the standard course work in mathematics and science, subjects that Kate could
not master. But at school they were far less concerned with what she
could not do than with finding a way for Kate to succeed and grad-

uate. According to Leonard Covello, who used his own long tenure as principal of Benjamin Franklin High School in the Bronx to adapt to the needs of its ethnic population, this was not so unusual. In the brief acknowledgments to his memoir, he thanked "the High School Division of the New York City Board of Education, which gives to its principals of high schools great latitude in developing special educational programs to meet the needs of the communities in which their schools are located."[28]

This latitude made it possible for Kate to graduate. Members of the English Department recognized Kate's potential as a writer and found her chosen Bohemian style charming. "The English Department loved all of its promising children with a springtime faith, to the point of freeing them from ordinary rigidities. . . . Mr. Brandon [the department chairman], whom I loved as I should have loved my father, also invited us to after-school lectures on several subjects."[29] These included exotic topics such as oriental rugs that would never otherwise have become known to someone of Kate's background. Kate took personal trips as well as shared meals with faculty. In fact, the school, its teachers, and students opened her up to new experiences and freed her from her family and its limited horizons. Although Kate never entirely broke off her contacts with her family and continued to value seeing her mother and siblings, she never lived at home again.

The deeply patriarchal household Simon described is often associated with many traditional European families, among them Eastern European Jews like the Simons. It was a pattern almost impossible to sustain in the American context, as early-twentieth-century social workers and sociologists who studied it understood. Louis Wirth was especially perceptive about its transitory nature. In his widely influential master's thesis, written in 1925, at precisely the time Kate Simon was attending high school in the Bronx, and later in his influential and appropriately titled *The Ghetto* based on its research, Wirth described the trials of Jewish families in Chicago, another important immigrant city. "Jewish parents are more apt to regard disobedience and disrespect on the part of their children as a problem and family crises as calamities than the other groups. Deviations from the customs, the traditions and norms of conduct of the group often constitute a serious problem."[30] Wirth exaggerated the difference between Jewish families and other recent immigrants, in part because he focused on the travails of very observant Jews who watched their children discard the orthodox customs and rituals that once held the Jewish community together in Eastern Europe. But even non-religious families, less bound to these traditions, found it difficult to understand their children's disrespect and disobedience.

The Simons were far from orthodox, and Kate's mother even gave up the sacred ritual of lighting Sabbath candles, but Wirth's sense of the expectation of obedience and the resulting tendency toward discord defined the atmosphere in first-generation families like theirs. Parents were confused about how they could preserve their standing in the ethnic community and among their kin, as well as their own self-respect, as they watched their children adapt to the requirements of the new world to which they had brought them. Immigrants had crossed the ocean to survive and, if possible, to succeed, but not necessarily to change. Their ethnic lives in the United States, including newspapers, food stores, theaters, clubs and burial societies (often linked to their hometowns), were a buffer meant to shield them from the overwhelming threat of change. Above all the family itself was meant to shield immigrants by providing them with the economic and emotional support of their primary attachments.

Their children brought change straight into the heart of the family. Immigrants tried to maintain the common good of the family as a governing principle and a means for cultural continuity, but changing their personal habits, their language, and "individualizing" their goals was what America was all about for the young. Schools were deeply implicated in creating this conflict in perspectives.[31] The high school, especially, because it emboldened older children, difficult enough to control in the best of circumstances and on whom parents were often dependent economically, was especially potent in this regard. Exposed all day long to others, many of whom were unlike themselves, to American ideas and values, and peers and teachers who approved of their transformation, second-generation high school students made conflict a poignant part of the experience of almost all migrant groups. According to sociologists W. Lloyd Warner and Leo Srole, who studied a range of different groups including Greeks, Italians, French Canadians, Poles, and Jews, the threat to parenting authority in the United States strained first generation immigrant households especially because fathers lost the brace of institutional supports that once undergirded their authority. "Does he capitulate to the incontestable logic of the situation and assume the father role after the American mode, converting himself from the patriarch to something more like 'first among equals?' The evidence from the newer ethnic groups . . . is that the father reasserts his authority through direct controls with even greater vigor than before."[32] They were reinforcing Sigmund Freud's similar observations about turn-of-the-century Vienna: "Even in our middle class families, fathers as a rule inclined to refuse their sons independence and the means necessary to secure it, . . . foster the germ of the growth of hostility which is inherent in the relation. . . . In our society today fathers are apt to cling desperately to what is left of a now sadly antiquated *potestas patris familias.*"[33] Even European patriarchy was beginning to erode. The American challenge to what was left of it was a further irritant in a difficult situation; all the more so when the resistance to authority came from daughters. The challenge to paternal authority thus often resulted in more rigid attempts at enforcement, as appears to have been the case in Simon's family.

Italian parents were quite as sensitive as Jewish families to the ways in which schooling in the United States undermined their authority, and they resented how American children upended their once unquestioned expectations about obedience and quiet subordination.[34] "Children listened to their elders," Leonard Covello remembered about his own childhood in Avigliano, Italy. "We rarely ventured even a question and never offered a comment." Covello devoted himself to finding ways of educating second-generation high school students without causing disrespect to their immigrant parents, but he knew that this attitude was impossible to sustain in America. Louis Wirth summarized the views of settlement and social workers: " 'Obedience to parents seems to be dying out among Jews,' says a Boston charity worker. 'The children feel it isn't necessary to obey a mother who wears a shawl or a father who wears a full beard.' 'Sometimes it is the young daughter who rules the Jewish family,' observes a Pittsburgh settlement head, 'because she alone knows what is 'American.' "[35] The inversion of generational hierarchies in America that had given children unusual status in the nineteenth-century United States was here repeated in another, more painful guise.

Language, the fundamental basis for communication and understanding, was a primary source of conflict as children learned English while their parents clung to their old tongue, out of both necessity and conviction. And parents became dependent on the English language skills of their children. Wirth concluded that "the use of the new language may actually make him [the child] the most important personage in the household." One father reported, "He was getting away from me and I could do nothing to stop it. He could talk English and I couldn't. . . . Sometimes I was boiling mad when he would talk English at the table, when all the rest talked Yiddish. But I knew what a hot-head he was and in America you can never tell what children might do. He might even run away."[36] It was not always clear which was more of a threat—losing familial authority or losing one's children.

The dissonance in generational expectations also focused on material things. The Simons fought over almost everything that related to expenditures that could have made the children's lives more comfortable and more conformably American. This was one of the chief sources of Kate's discontent. Poor, fearful of complete destitution in a strange land, and accustomed to strict self-denial, immigrant parents were shocked by American indulgences. Kate's father begrudged the nickel for candy at the movies. "Our lives were meager enough. Did he ever think of buying us even the cheapest toy, like the other fathers did, instead of stashing every spare penny in the bank and taking out only for his relatives?" As another child of an immigrant home, Robert Merrill, who would eventually become a star at the Metropolitan Opera, recalled about his impecunious father (a sewing machine operator), "He was always counting pennies, and when he had to spend them it was physically painful to him, like losing part of himself."[37]

At a time of expanding consumption, as children were learning, like their parents, to buy and enjoy a world of new goods and leisure activities, the differences between American kids and those from immigrant households could cut the latter like a sharp knife.[38] Leonard Covello learned about the importance of sports to American boys when he went to high school, so he was "spurred on to make one of the school teams so that I could proudly display the school emblem, a huge maroon 'M' on a white sweater." His father was not pleased: "There is hardly enough to eat in the house. We kill ourselves. We work so that he can have some future—and he spends his time at school playing." Hard work, sacrifice of material things, and an emphasis on self-denial were immigrant values, and these values were often suffocating to the children. Covello concluded, "It was no use. I should have known better. It was one of those times when ordinarily I would have resorted to the old standby, 'You will never understand.' Instead, I said nothing, simply grabbed my school books and walked out of the flat." Not long afterward, Leonard quit school so that he could work full time to help at home.[39]

An inevitable source of contention in immigrant homes concerned what girls could and could not do outside the house, and how much leeway they had for independent action. Fears about lost honor often haunted these families as they faced new contexts and dangers and the rapidly changing mores of American youths in the early twentieth century. Kate Simon's father regularly held out the image of the streetwalker (embodied by a local second-generation Polish girl of abandoned virtue) to keep his daughter in line, threatening to throw her out of the house if she went out with boys. But Kate longed for some of the mystery that beckoned in the guise of sex and, with it, the sense of liberation from home. On the cusp of adolescence, she found herself obsessed with a handsome Italian boy. Secretly observing the goings on at the porch of his house on Friday and Saturday nights, she remembered "the high-heeled girls, undoubtedly wearing brassieres under their light-weight flouncy dresses, bouncing around on the couches, allowing a boy's arm to rest on their shoulders for a moment. . . . It was painful, the bright liveliness; it made me an outcast, cut off from all pleasures forever and ever."[40] Restrictions imposed on immigrant girls in traditional families could be experienced as extreme exclusion from the society of peers, from everything that was modern, as well as a sign of parental tyranny. For some, such as Kate Simon, it led to total withdrawal from the control of parents.

The desire for things, for play, for pleasures was often centered in sexual yearning as adolescents discovered this as a physical ache, but its power was also cultural, part of growing up and growing away. Always full of taboos, sex was a threat to respectability and a special sticking point in intergenerational relations. The fear of sexual misbehavior by their adolescent daughters brought immigrant parents to various social agencies for assistance. For American authorities, sexuality was the very substance of fears about girls' delinquency.[41] In the most extreme cases, this resulted in a girl being sent to a home for wayward girls and exposed her to numerous humiliations. Often, families who had hoped to find some means to keep control over their daughters lost it entirely to state agencies and the police at a time when age-of-consent legislation became a potent form of social control over female adolescents. These laws protected girls but also made sexual experimentation by young people more visible to the courts and its officers.

Sex was probably the most powerful symbol for the disobedience of second-generation children. The *Jewish Daily Forward*'s letters-to-the-editor column, "A Bintel Brief," was full of lamentations about fallen daughters that resulted from this fundamental tension between the generations. In his own studies of three thousand juvenile court cases, sociologist W. I. Thomas concluded that "sexual passion does not play an important role," in the sexual delinquency of girls. Instead, it resulted from "an impulse to get amusement, adventure, pretty clothes, favorable notice, distinction, freedom in the larger world which presents so many allurements and comparisons."[42] Second-generation girls felt all of these things acutely, both the allurements and the comparisons to those American girls they assumed had a more privileged life.

Caught between desire for the new worlds of "pleasure" and parental strictures to hold them back from making irremediable mistakes in a culture with strange rules, young women like Kate Simon often rebelled. In Kate's case, with the encouragement and support of her high school contacts, this did not stop her from succeeding as a travel writer and an independent woman. But not all women had Kate's talent, her luck, or her insightful mother who refused to give up on her even after she moved out. Although she had plenty of sexually enticing escapades in high school during the 1920s, sex itself was hardly the defining quality of her rebellion or of her desire for American pleasures.

Girls were not alone in experiencing difficulties in sexual matters. Irving Louis Horowitz spent most of his childhood in a first-generation Jewish household in Harlem (one of the few remaining in that increasingly African American neighborhood). Then the family moved to Brooklyn. Newly arrived at his new school, P. S. 193, while serving as stairwell monitor, this future sociologist attacked a girl to whom he was keenly attracted. He had observed similar activities in his old neighborhood. As his own desires emerged and his infatuation for the nameless girl grew, he felt he could assert himself and imitate what he had once barely understood in a setting that was much more casual and expressive about sexual matters. "I grabbed the poor girl and slammed her against the wall, just as I remembered from Harlem. I tore at her clothes, tried mightily to kiss her, at the same time yelling profanities. . . . Naturally she was terrified. . . . I didn't mean her harm. But neither did I know what to do. I had no idea of what an erect penis was to do."[43] Irving had misread the cultural signals entirely, taking as a mark of mainstream American culture the behaviors he had seen in the African American area where he grew up, and through whose guidance he sought to satisfy his nascent lusts. The attempt landed him and his parents at the principal's office where they had to confront the girl's parents, and it became the basis for a two-week suspension.

Sex for adolescents in immigrant households could be especially bewildering in neighborhoods where different groups of newcomers came together, each with different pasts and practices. High schools brought together students from many local neighborhoods in a cross-cultural mix. The painfulness of sex could be especially acute to parents because it signaled new maturity in their children, and its satisfaction touched all the tender places in cultures under assault—the juncture between the past and the future, the possible crushing of ancient taboos, the seductions of the new, and the real possibilities of a mixing of heritages in the future generation of children and grandchildren. As one first-generation Jewish father told Warner and Srole, investigating social life in a town they called Yankee City, "Do you think in Europe you would leave a girl alone with a boy? Never, on your life! . . . I like them when they are small" but soon "they get ideas and they don't respect you any more. . . . What good would it do for me to say to them, 'Don't do so-and-so?' None! They would say everybody does it and so can they."[44] Everybody does it became an often invoked refrain.

In some immigrant neighborhoods, traditions such as the Mediterranean practice of males in the family guarding the virtue of daughters remained alive, if only transitionally, even for the second generation. In an interview with Leonard Covello, one second-generation Italian American brother recorded: "I have two sisters, one is twelve, the other sixteen and a half. Being girls they belong to the women's department of the family, and I don't stick my nose into their business. That is, as long as they are in the house. When they go out in the street or somewhere else, it is my business to see to it that they keep up the good name of my family."[45] This emphasis on the brother's role in chaperoning unmarried adolescent sisters and even cousins remained vital, at least for a time.

If sex stood at the juncture between tradition and change, so did the high school. Schooling offered European immigrants a setting that promised social improvement, a promise that was much more important to some than to other groups. It threatened their control over their children's future as well as their sense of the security offered by conformity to the past. And while high school peer society had rules, this could seem quite otherwise to immigrants not accustomed to seeing young men and women go off to school together and mixing in classrooms, cafeterias, and the expanding number of after-school clubs and social events. For Southern Italian migrants, schooling for adolescents signaled great danger as their daughters associated with boys of their own age apart from the careful oversight of kin. When they sent their youth off to school, they gave over control to strangers who might not have the same concern about supervision that had kept Southern Italian families respectable through careful chaperonage. First-generation families often kept their older children out of school completely, fearful not only that they would break away from the duties to help at home but that the promiscuous life of high schools would encourage sexual misbehavior among daughters.

In a city like New York, the vast school system offered many possibilities for single-sex high schools, especially among the vocational schools that grew with the rising enrollment of immigrant youth. Irving Louis Horowitz's sister, Paula, for example, went to Wadleigh High School in the Bronx in the 1930s, a girls' commercial school. New York even had special separate academic schools, like Bay Ridge High School in Brooklyn, because the city recognized this as an important matter for families. Schools like these made it easier to bridge the gap of understanding and encouraged attendance. But in smaller cities where only one or two schools served the entire population, the choice could be problematic. In New Haven, a large, bustling industrial city in the late nineteenth and early twentieth century, but hardly on the scale of New York, most Italian families did not trust their older children to the public schools. This inhibited social and economic mobility for the second generation. Not until the 1930s, in the context of the extreme limitations of the economy, did Italians compromise and send their adolescent children to high school in response to their understanding of what seemed economically necessary, not just a state requirement.[46]

Recognizing the hesitations of immigrant parents, urban school districts all over the country in the 1920s began to adapt the junior high schools, once seen as a transition to high school, in an effort to at least keep the second generation in school through the ninth grade. The junior high school, while more local than the high school, also accomplished some of the widening of horizons. In New Haven, as historian Stephen Lassonde observed, "continuing to ninth grade made a real difference in young people's spatial experience of the city and to the variety of teens they encountered as they came of age."[47]

The broadening experience was even greater as second-generation youth went to high schools. Leonard Covello recalled that his first "American" friend, Harold Zoller, took him to his home where he learned to delicately balance a teacup on his knee. Zoller, in turn, came to Leonard's house where he was often treated to mounds of spaghetti. The friendship continued into Columbia College. Leonard had never considered the elite school on Morningside Heights even when he began to dream of college for himself. It was Zoller who first mentioned this possibility and suggested that Leonard was eligible for a Pulitzer scholarship that would pay his way. At Columbia, Zoller helped Leonard to receive "a bid to join the Alpha Chi Rho Fraternity," where he was for years "the only Italo-American to belong to the Columbia Chapter."[48]

Today, we have a difficult time imagining that high school could be a broadening experience. Often viewed simply as holding cells dominated by bullies and controlled by the in-crowd, high schools can be highly segregated institutions.[49] When not segregated completely, they serve as battlegrounds between racial or ethnic groups. There was plenty of conflict between ethnic groups as high schools expanded in the early twentieth century, and some students were alarmed by the diversity and hated it. Robert Merrill, a fat kid mercilessly teased by his peers, recalled, "Public Schools 19 and 210 had been bad enough for me, but at least I had known most of the kids in the neighborhood and felt at home in my misery. But New Utrecht [High School] was the international set, and kids streamed in every morning from every direction and by every device. I myself traveled half an hour by train. It was an immense place, and I felt as if I would be swallowed up alive." But that was only part of the picture. Despite fears like those of Robert Merrill about the "international set," the high school in the first half of the twentieth century was still an aspirational institution that made the children of immigrants feel that they had achieved something of importance and they had an aura of the larger world of learning and of society.[50]

In the mid-1930s, at Wadleigh High School in the Bronx, Irving Louis Horowitz's sister Paula became friendly with African American girls and invited them to her home. From a socially liberal home, she viewed this as a natural continuation of her association with these girls at school. Despite her family's left-leaning sentiments, this did not go over well. "At that point, the New Deal was left at the door, and explosions that ended in physical violence of my father against my sister became the norm," Horowitz recalled. But Paula persisted in "her crime of implementing equality at the grass roots level."[51] She had crossed a racial border, but the borders among immigrant groups or between immigrant and native might have been just as threatening to some parents. High school facilitated contacts away from home, and, at its most effective, could even encourage serious (sometimes romantic) friendships across these borders. This was often part of the most important memories of members of the second generation.

The high school thus became far more than a place where students learned subjects at a higher level, or gained skills for the marketplace. It was an Americanizing institution in ways that fulfilled some of the visions of the planners of the original common schools. At the same time, it was far different from the top-down assimilation that many of the initial founders had expected. Responding to signals from others, students learned to incorporate patterns from different groups into a mixed culture that was increasingly their own, absorbing and translating influences that did indeed transform American culture at the grass roots. In providing an anchor for the distinctive youth culture of twentieth-century America, high schools and junior high schools also allowed for the diffusion of popular culture among young people at a critical point in their own development. American high school students, many of them second-generation immigrants, used what they learned from advertising, the movies, and popular music to develop their own mixed culture of youth. That culture also drew upon the practices of outsiders like blacks and immigrants. The cruelty of the young to "outsiders" who might be despised and ostracized is often enough observed. We less often notice how the blotter paper that is adolescence can incorporate difference into approved youth forms.

On the surface, schools were officially rigid in imposing Americanization. "At elementary school I was thrilled with everything that was taught about America; its history, geography, and what it stands for," one student told Leonard Covello. "But when I came home . . . I felt a painful contrast between what I saw at home and what had been taught during the day. . . . I felt so ashamed, so inferior when I realized that my parents do not exemplify such things at home." In this case, the conflict between parents and teachers became intense and the student's mother exclaimed, "These teachers of yours are driving us crazy."[52] As an adult, Covello realized that the young often bridged the gap between their parents and their new homes as some immigrant youth became conscious of serving at the crossroads between generations. His own story was an especially good example.

In his early years at school, Leonard had permitted the spelling of his last name to be changed by a teacher, became a Protestant convert under the influence of a local evangelical settlement, and went through an Anglicizing process at college. Then, he turned around and began to alter the very institutions that had transformed him. At some point while at Columbia College, Leonard and a small group of other Italian American students began to challenge the process of Americanization—from their changed names to their disdain for the Italian language to shame about food. One of his friends questioned, "Why should we have to prove anything? I'm sick and tired of making excuses for myself." Then, Leonard observed, "we began to delve into the past for what was part of our heritage. . . . What at one time we were ashamed of, must now be brought into the open."[53] Rediscovering the Italian language, not then highly regarded or offered as a foreign language option at school, was one such move; inviting strangers into their homes was another.

Covello eventually became a new kind of educator who worked hard to make a connection between the school and the real lives of its many second-generation immigrant students, long before the idea of multiculturalism became prominent much later in the twentieth century.[54] He found himself in revolt against the mechanical use of intelligence or IQ tests, the craze for which was taking over in schools in the 1920s and in which Italian youth scored well below the norm. He fought against the easy stigmatizing and categorization of inferiority associated with the tests. He became involved in various boys clubs, helped to organize parents' organizations at school, learned from and resorted to the disciplinary regimes of the George Junior Republics, where "problem" boys were sent. He became involved in interethnic group organizations to facilitate understanding between hostile groups. And he was deeply embroiled in trying to heal growing racial tensions in Harlem that came to the surface during World War II. He was hoping to place the school in the larger context of the history, the family life, the community experience, and the work needs of the students it served. He did not run away from home as Kate Simon had.

While Leonard Covello was not alone in understanding what students needed, he was also unusual. One of the students made that clear. "Our teachers made us feel that we came from a different world. We felt the same toward them. We watched them as they came to school in the morning from 'somewhere' outside, from what was to us a different world. . . . We felt that they were perfect and come from a perfect world."[55] Kate Simon had a similar reaction to her teachers. She escaped from her own home to be closer to that world. Covello, more than most commentators, articulated the complicated role of schools for the second generation. His understanding affected his drive to encourage adolescents to move forward into America without completely losing their roots in other cultures. He also understood that most second-generation students, even in high school, stayed with others like themselves, learning from the wider world, adapting to the youth-brewed culture, but associating with those most like themselves, because they could share their hurts, fears, and dreams. As the brilliant sociologist of youth Allison Davis concluded, "As a learning environment for children and adolescents who wish to 'rise in the world' . . . the social clique is an even more important training context than the family."[56] Most students engaged in a wider world while also remaining under the influence of peers and cultures that came from an older one. Those cultures would contribute to and be transformed by the generations that were part of America's high school and junior high school revolution.[57]

IV

By the middle of the twentieth century, high school life defined and normalized adolescence as it set out to tame what was once viewed as an unsettling period of transition from childhood to adulthood. Franklin Roosevelt's New Deal helped to make this possible when its programs provided work opportunities for students so they could stay at school. In 1938, during Roosevelt's second term in office, the US Congress passed the first national anti-child-labor legislation, which prohibited the employment of children in industries that engaged in interstate commerce. While this did not stop children below sixteen from working, it established a standard by which such work became not only less frequent but viewed as socially inappropriate.[58] This enforced the belief that school was the proper site for child life well into the teen years. It became the dominant value for all youth after World War II when America's renewed prosperity brought another period of major school expansion.

Second-generation immigrant youth were not alone in finding the wider world of the high school newly pivotal to their lives. For James Conant, who became president of Harvard University in the middle of the twentieth century and an important science policy maker, his "teachers of physics and chemistry" at the Roxbury Latin School in Boston helped to turn him toward science as a vocation. Conant's experience was not quite like those of others in this chapter, because he attended an elite private school, but as it did with the others, his secondary schooling strongly influenced how he imagined his future.[59]

Edna Ferber, who would make a major career writing plays and Broadway shows, became an avid theatrical performer in her local public high school in Appleton, Wisconsin. Although it was hardly a wealthy or well-equipped school (in fact, it was "the shabbiest and most archaic," in her words), it was a liberating experience for the bubbly, energetic Jewish girl from an assimilated middle-class family. The Ferbers were more observant than the Simons, as they regularly attended a reformed synagogue and were proudly Jewish, but the family had effectively left the "ghetto" mentality behind.[60]

By the 1950s, African American youth even in the segregated South were becoming high school students and having their horizons widened. In Anne Moody's case, a high school teacher in Mississippi told her about the NAACP (which at the time was trying to get a conviction in the Emmett Till case). Mrs. Rice, her teacher, invited Anne to dinner, where she was fed her first knowledge of her people's condition. "Mrs. Rice got to be something like a mother to me. She told me anything I wanted to know." Anne's extremely narrow childhood, burdened by work, had kept her ignorant of things many of her peers had already come to understand. Through her peers and Mrs. Rice, she learned about the dangers to blacks who stepped out of their assigned roles. White immigrants and blacks discovered that high-school teachers could open up their lives. Even Robert Merrill, who hated his high school, admired "Mrs. Miranello, our music teacher, who began my lifelong love affair with the Italian language and Italians."[61]

In the nineteenth century, when it was observed at all, adolescence was often seen in terms of the spiritual transformation young people experienced through the conversions central to evangelical Protestantism.[62] This spiritual turmoil and striving was still deeply embedded in G. Stanley Hall's vision of adolescence in his landmark book on the subject in 1904.[63] The inner state of questioning and questing had older romantic sources as young men sought to make the leap into adulthood. Many of the youth-serving organizations founded in the nineteenth century, like the Young Men's Christian Association, were strongly rooted in this religious dimension.

In the twentieth century, as adolescence became much more noticeable in the context of extended schooling and organizations, like the juvenile court, that broadened the reach of childhood dependency into the teen years, it became an important subject of investigation. Previously understood as an individual transformation accompanying physical maturation, by the second and third decades of the twentieth century, adolescence was recognized as a social phenomenon and a phase marked by friendships, learning and preparation, and the invention of new practices. The emphasis on adolescence as a group phenomenon that affected young people from age thirteen to eighteen (designated "teenagers" in the 1930s) was most visible in school. What was once individual questing began to be institutionally contained and overseen by teachers, and the questioning took place among groups of age peers. High schools and junior high schools provided answers to some of the chaos contained in the state of becoming that defined adolescence, which belongs to neither childhood nor adulthood. Initially a means to contain and direct this process, the high school extended and intensified adolescence into a formal stage of life.

It was no surprise therefore that physicians and psychologists who had earlier guided parents about the needs and development of their infants and young children turned a few decades later toward the problem of adolescence. By the third decade of the twentieth century, adolescent development became a natural extension of the desire to inform parents about what to expect as their children grew. This was only in part the result of the considerable impact of Hall's book. It was also a response to the growing social phenomenon as adolescents found an expanding home at school. Louis Starr, for example, whose *The Hygiene of the Nursery* was a hit in the 1890s, sought to repeat his success in 1915 with his *The Adolescent Period*, with its suggestive subtitle "Its Features and Management."[64] By the mid-twentieth century, as we shall see, this attention and advice blossomed and came to fruition in psychological theories like those of Erik Erikson and a host of advice books.

In the 1830s, Alexis de Tocqueville had claimed that American youth of the time had no adolescence. What he meant was that the transition to adulthood seemed to go smoothly and to require little special attention. One hundred years later, this had changed completely. When in 1928 Margaret Mead published her widely influential observations about young people in Samoa, her provocative description of easygoing sexual initiations and the relaxed relations between youth and their parents in the distant South Seas island was also a commentary about contemporary American adolescence. And Mead used the opportunity to offer a sharp contrast between the subjects of her study and adolescent-parent relations in the contemporary United States that were fraught with tension.[65] Adolescence had become prolonged, problematic, and visible enough to require extended comment. While Mead hoped to use her observations to show how the relations between the generations could be less of a struggle, her book contributed to growing concerns about this newly popularized stage of life.

Youth misbehavior figured prominently in the literature of the Progressive period when reformers and sociologists turned their attention to what became known as juvenile delinquency. This resulted in classic studies such as *The Delinquent Child and the Home*, by Sophonisba Breckenridge and Edith Abbott (1912), and *The Unadjusted Girl*, by W. I. Thomas (1924). Studies of juvenile delinquency continued as a strong current in American social science into the 1930s and 1940s as established investigators like William Healy and younger scholars like Sheldon Gluck (together with his wife Eleanor), became pioneers in delinquency diagnosis and prevention. At the same time, American sociologists such as Clifford Shaw and Henry McKay studied the ecology of delinquent gangs. While delinquency could be a problem for children of any age, it had become connected especially to an unsuccessful transition from childhood as institutions failed to contain the usual strains associated with moving into adulthood. It also became identified as a special problem in immigrant communities where institutions were weakened in the transition to the United States and families struggled with many forces that destabilized family authority.[66] Some of this concern continued as the chaotic and troubling conditions associated with the Great Depression renewed the focus on deviancy, during a time when young people sometimes took to the roads and unemployment undermined stable family lives.[67]

As significant as the continuing concern with delinquency was the new direction in the 1930s and 1940s, as social investigators turned from troubled youths toward studying normal adolescents. Many institutions such as the National Society for the Study of Education turned their sights on the newly visible social phenomenon. In its volume on *Adolescence* (1939), the society noted that it was following in the footsteps of "the numerous studies of adolescent development recently completed or . . . in progress at such institutions as Harvard, Yale, Western Reserve, the Catholic University of America, the University of Chicago, and the University of California, and the related investigations growing out of the work of such agencies as the American Youth Commission and the committees of the Progressive Education Association."[68]

The most prominent expression of this new direction was the influential volume sponsored and published by the White House Conference on Child Health and Protection convened by President Hoover on the eve of the economic collapse. Highlighting the findings of a range of experts and supervised by renowned sociologist Ernest Burgess, the volume issued a wide range of statistics to portray normal adolescent behavior. Only one chapter was concerned with the delinquent. Like the parallel studies of delinquency, the findings directed readers toward a range of influential factors rather than one single basis for understanding why some adolescents became better "adjusted" than others. Not surprisingly in America's vast and polyglot society, family and adolescent experiences varied widely, but the volume's authors were unanimous in using "adjustment" as the measure of an effective adolescent experience.

Adjustment is by definition a socially dependent state of well-being. As it was applied, it measured how well individuals from variously defined social groups conformed to expected patterns and behavioral practices. Adjustment became the opposite of delinquency. Where delinquents broke social norms, the well adjusted supported them. The experts who contributed to the volume were generous in the kinds of social factors they included as important to adjustment—poverty and class, native/foreign and rural/urban status, even sibling order. They were not naive about the social components of adolescent life. But with their tables and statistics, they increasingly committed themselves to a measurement of behavior that emphasized what could be expected of a normal adolescence. They thus confirmed that in the twentieth century, age norms (as was the case in the normalizing of IQ measurements of mental competence) would prevail to define the stages of the life course and specifically the now multiple parts of childhood.[69]

The schools were fundamental to the primacy of this form of evaluation. They provided institutional settings that emphasized both age and the group behaviors of successfully adjusted, ordinary students. Unlike reformatories, the juvenile court, or other kinds of institutions devoted to deviancy or delinquency, the schools emphasized wholesome and desirable qualities, and they embodied America's "faith" in the future. As the century progressed, high school life defined normality for adolescents. During the early twentieth century educators, citing John Dewey, often hoped that schooling would individualize instruction and respond to the personal goals of its population, but the nature of schooling would make the group and the average adolescent, not the unique individual, the primary standard of measurement and evaluation.

When social psychologist David Riesman and his colleagues published *The Lonely Crowd* in 1950,[70] their understanding of the development of the modern "other directed" personality, one that conformed to external signals in judging what was right and wrong, drew on the kind of experience that high schools were already providing to American youth. As a high school–based adolescence became standard and dominated expectations, it was ever more difficult for parents to resist sending their children to school well past the age at which children in other Western countries had long begun to work and earn. It was also becoming very difficult for parents to resist the influence that high school peers were now exerting on their own children. Unlike delinquent peers, high school peers assisted adolescents in adjusting to what was assumed to be normal behavior. For all parents, this represented a new understanding of the limits of their authority. But for immigrants especially, it was a sharp break from the past. As one father told Louis Wirth, "To think that a father should not be able to tell a child what to do and what not to do. I would never have acted that way to my father.'"[71]

What immigrant parents experienced in the extreme, others knew as well. Sociologists Robert and Helen Lynd studied an average midwestern American community in the 1920s that they called "Middletown." Here, as in many other places by the mid-1920s, it was natural to study the life of adolescents at school. As was the case for the White House Study, they divided the population into subgroups in order more accurately to portray average lives. The Lynds, not surprisingly, found that the high school courses in Middletown had become far more diverse than they had been in the previous generation as secondary schooling adapted to a broader range of students. When they turned to the matter of "school life," they concluded that students at high school had a "much better time" than previous generations as they actively selected from the many activities, most of them unrelated to classroom work, that were available. For many, school had become life, defining its rhythms and demanding active loyalty. School life also spilled over into evenings that were absorbed by peer activities. "Approximately half of the boys and girls answering the question say that they are at home less than four evenings out of the week." And parents found themselves on the defensive. One mother observed, "I've never been criticized by my children until these last couple of years since they have been in high school . . . but now both my daughter and older son keep saying, 'But, Mother, you're so old-fashioned.'" When they reminded children that staying out late at dances until "after eleven" was unheard of a generation before, mothers were properly put in their place: "Yes, Mother, but that was fifty years ago."[72]

"Fifty years" or another country, high school had changed generational understandings about the past. In the United States, unlike other Western nations, the school had become a much longer, more normal, and more influential part of the life of youth. It made being an adolescent and then a "teenager" a fundamental experience. It was where adolescents developed a different perspective on themselves, on their parents, and on their futures. Parents now shared control over their "adolescent" children not only with the children's teachers but with their teen peers and with their newly created commercially influenced culture.

v

Among the part-time jobs that Kate Simon held while in high school, one of the most important was as a babysitter for the children of a self-consciously modern professional couple. Because the parents were progressive, intellectually venturesome, and left wing, Kate learned about some of the most recent approaches to childrearing in the 1920s. Laura Bergson, the mother, liked to have her children eat heavy whole-grain breads, honey, and natural products and was quite rigid in enforcing rules about food and bowel movements. Her children were not to eat refined sugars or "poisonous" foods like hot dogs. She was intensely concerned about their physical health, but she was quite relaxed about other matters. Play was an important part of the children's lives; chores were not. The children were provided with few toys but many books and were urged to be imaginative in the use of ordinary household objects and to invest them with potentials for play.[73] This mother's tastes, despite some personal oddities, describe the progressive approach to childrearing—health conscious, devoted to play, suspicious of commercialism. In the 1920s and 1930s, these values often defined progressive views of how children should be treated and how they learn.[74] Such views would be refurbished and given new life at the end of World War II.[75]

In this same household, the father, a doctor, was imperious and tyrannical, thundering at his small daughter, who quaked in his presence. Kate was extremely sensitive to fathers who were abusive to their daughters and her portrait of Dr. Ivan Bergson, with his "superior baronial manner,"[76] drew upon her resentments toward her patriarchal European father, but it may also have reflected the continuing allocation of roles in even the most progressive and well-educated families in the early twentieth century. While mothers were becoming attuned to various childrearing theories and motifs, even professional, well-educated fathers were rarely similarly attentive. Or if they were the targets of advice—and *Parents' Magazine* often advised them even in its earliest years not to indulge their habits of exerting strict discipline—they were not reading this advice, or not following it as mothers were more likely to do.[77] They treated their children according to their own temperaments and personal inclinations rather than theories about how children should best be reared. Advice was for mothers; fathers were on their own. Parenting advice to which fathers could expect to listen with some attention would have to wait until much later in the century.[78]

It is possible that the father's continuing emphasis on discipline in even progressive households reflected the narrowing sphere in which fathers operated, as their roles in family affairs continued to shrink. "Father has not been as much of a parent as mother," an editorial in *Parents' Magazine* in 1935 noted, as it sought ways to make parent-teacher organizations more attractive for dads. Having mounted an effort to survey why this should be the case, the editorial concluded that "women have taken the chief responsibility in parent organizations because they have been traditionally thought to be entrusted with the care of children and because women had more time."[79] *Parents' Magazine* continued to seek a place for fathers, especially in the lives of older children.

As immigrant fathers were forced to see, and native-born fathers understood clearly, the father's place in the family was not certain. Mothers continued to care for young children, with their critical importance confirmed by psychologists and pediatricians. But fathers, who had once supervised older children, now had to compete with the extended reach of the school into later life and especially in the important transition of adolescence. They could stop children from staying out "too late" as one father cited by the White House Conference did, and they might withhold financial assistance, but as educators and instructors in spiritual and vocational matters, their influence had long gone. They were relegated more and more to the realm of children's leisure, and even their physical spaces in middle-class households were increasingly confined to the "den" or the garage. Concerned that fathers might not be able to compete for their children's attention by acting as their pals, one *Parents' Magazine* article concluded, somewhat hesitantly, that "[c]hildren frankly recognize their equals and their superiors in school. . . . They just as honestly respect the real superiority of their fathers." This did not reassure one father, who worried that he could not even keep up with the things his son was learning at school, especially in arithmetic. While his humor regarding this deficiency was part of the appeal of the article, it also seriously exposed the problems fathers were facing as their instructional authority receded as schooling expanded: "Depression haunts me; apprehension dogs my steps. I am about to be weighed in the balance of modern education and found wanting."[80]

In light of their diminished authority, fathers may well have tried to maintain an uncompromising emphasis on discipline as the only clear function left them, jealously guarding this small space in family affairs. Like immigrant fathers who were challenged by their children's superior knowledge, non-immigrant fathers, too, may have taken a strong stand to protect what remained of their roles. Refusing to lose control altogether, they may have been harsher when asserting disciplinary power. As one middle-class informer (a banker) told Robert and Helen Lynd in their Middletown study, there occurred "once in every child's life a brisk passage at arms that 'will teach them where authority lies in the family. You have to teach them to respect parental authority. Once you've done this you can go ahead and get on the best possible relations with them.' "[81] In one confession made in *Parents' Magazine*, an anonymous father admitted the mistakes he had made as a temperamental young man "convinced from the tradition of my own childhood that children should be taught to yield prompt and unquestioned obedience 'because I say so.' It was easy to come down on a young child like a ton of brick[s], and there were times when I did it." Over time, he realized that this was not the best way to handle his son, and one day he observed another father who adopted a quite different technique. "He talked very plainly and simply, but he talked as if the child were another adult. . . . No question of obedience was involved. It was wholly a matter of being reasonable. . . ."[82] The appearance of the article suggested that the instinctive way the remorseful father handled his child was not uncommon, while the magazine used it as an object lesson to teach men a better way to handle discipline.

When the White House Conference interviewed college students about their home lives, they discovered just how varied family nurture could be, but this emphasis on paternal discipline predominated. Some families showed little affection, others were much more demonstrative; some married couples got along well, others fought all the time; some parents were pals with their children and engaged in activities with them, others never did. In general, almost all the personal narratives describe a rather strictly enforced discipline with an emphasis on paternal authority. One young man's views were especially revealing, showing how families balanced their beliefs in the democratic treatment of children with the maintenance of strict discipline: "My parents regarded me on a plane of equality with them and seemed to give me all the consideration they would have given me had I been an adult. They showed their affection for me, but never once did I disobey without being punished. . . . There were two methods of disciplining used on me. In most cases my folks would reason with me and show me wherein I was wrong, in others I would receive a paddling. Sometimes it was a combination of both."[83]

This shrewd narrative portrays the complex nature of the relationships in modern, child-centric households during the middle decades of the twentieth century. By then, both childrearing advice and extended schooling were influencing the experience of childhood. The child was taken seriously and loved, but discipline remained firmly part of the parents' and, especially, the father's domain. Parents took seriously the need to bring up children into a productive adulthood that would promote their welfare but still encourage their independence. As another student noted, "At present my parents' attitude toward me is just what anyone would want. When I came away to college, father forgot all the restrictions of high school days, and left things up to me. He always says 'You're old enough to judge and take care of yourself.' . . . Somehow this compensates for all the earlier rules and regulations." By the time he went off to college, this young man was ready for his independence, but this followed a much longer period of overt regulation than Ulysses Grant had experienced a century earlier. Prolonged schooling now extended into the teen years, and parental authority stayed firmly in place. In summarizing the narratives they collected, the authors of the White House study concluded: "In the entire series of college student narratives there were only a few which showed that students felt that their parents had deliberately or maliciously neglected them. . . . Only a few students thought their parents had punished them severely in hate. The parents sincerely believed the severe punishments were the best way to develop their children into honest and responsible adults."[84] American parents believed that they had their children's best interests in mind as they oversaw them for longer periods of their lives.

The memoir of John Muir, who immigrated to the United States and grew up in the second half of the nineteenth century, introduces us to a father whose extremely harsh disciplinary methods represented a very different kind of paternal control—old-fashioned, hate-filled, and physically abusive. In the real venom to which he exposed his son, the elder Muir helps us to understand the range of meanings for the word "discipline" and to evaluate the dominant patterns in the twentieth century. Unlike many of the late nineteenth-century immigrants, John Muir's family settled immediately on the land, gravitating to the abundant spaces in the middle of the country. Of the various British immigrants who came at the time, Muir noted about his own Scots ancestry, "here their craving land hunger was satisfied."[85]

John's father was religiously devout and followed old-world Calvinist principles in regard to raising his sons. He was like the patriarchs of old, familiar to colonial Americans. The sons worked together with the father even when they suffered from severe bouts of sickness, since the tasks of farming were urgent and unforgiving. "No matter what the weather, there was always something to do," Muir remembered. And in the summer, there were "hard, sweaty days of about sixteen or seventeen hours" in duration. "We were all made slaves through the vice of over-industry."[86] A mean and angry man, the elder Muir not only thrashed John regularly, often without cause, but prohibited him from doing things for which he had an inclination or talent.

John was an apt student and inventive, creating various gadgets and machines that his father took pleasure in destroying. His grandfather had taught him his letters "from shop signs" before he went to school, but he stopped attending school by the time he was eleven because the farm required his full time presence when he became a strong youth. Despite the lack of extended schooling, John was forced by his sternly Protestant father to learn the Bible by heart and, in his words, "by sore flesh." Through regular whippings, by the time he was eleven, he could recite three-fourths of the Old Testament and "all of the New by heart . . . from the beginning of Matthew to the end of Revelation without a single stop." "I can't conceive of anything that would now enable me to concentrate my attention more fully than when I was a mere stripling boy, and it was all done by whipping." Throughout childhood and youth, the thrashings were regular and certain, "unless father happened to be away." Although his brothers eventually left when they came of age, joining other second-generation immigrants in their rejection of their father's tyranny, John as the eldest did not. When he finally did leave to fulfill his ambition and attend the University of Wisconsin at Madison, his father told him not to expect any help from home and to "depend entirely on yourself."[87] It was the teachers at school, not his father at home, who encouraged him in the inclinations that would later define his unique adulthood.

In the nineteenth century, both the demands of religion and the requirements of farming could define a young man's life, although not necessarily his future. That future, in Muir's case, was propelled by schooling (in this instance the university, not high school) that valued what his father had suppressed and punished. Nineteenth-century fathers, especially immigrant fathers, could be like this, and so, too, could some in the twentieth century, as was the case in Kate Simon's household. But the pattern became less prominent in the United States generally and receded earlier than in most European societies, and it declined quite markedly by the mid-twentieth century. American children could move from home more easily, as sons in the Muir household did, and they could find alternative futures for themselves through school. Eventually, even European fathers in the twentieth century could not sustain this posture and were forced to adapt to changing circumstances that discouraged overt and aggressive paternal control.

The most significant of those changing circumstances was related to schooling. Some students did not continue in school beyond eleven or twelve years of age, but this became far less common and acceptable, even among farmers and even among immigrants who resisted schooling as the Italians had, as the twentieth century progressed. In the United States it became illegal to keep children out of school before age fourteen at the earliest, and beyond that in many states. It was also no longer seen as a legitimate choice. The acceptance of school as a regular part of adolescence—indeed as a defining part of adolescence—became a cultural habit, and a habit that tempered paternal authority. By the 1930s, schooling competed with parents for the time and attention of all children; after the Second World War, it became the dominant experience. It also redefined the goals of children. While American children had never been strictly bound by the dictates of their families, the avenues to alternative goals were often fluid in the free-for-all nature of the economy. In the nineteenth century, the paths to careers were still undefined, and even professional lives could develop without much formal schooling. By the twentieth century, high schools became almost the only road toward professions and toward a variety of corporate paths that depended on literacy. Many high school students continued to work part-time and in the summers, as Kate Simon did. Many did not complete high school. Schooling never entirely replaced work, but it became the primary site for adolescence and the strongest force to prepare the young for adult life and livelihood.[88]

For immigrant children, the high school could be much more. It provided an alternative vision to the constricted and difficult lives their parents led and a way out of the restrictions their parents imposed. In some cases, it provided almost an alternative home. Many second-generation memoirs describe home lives as bleak and without love. This led to conflict and it led to pain. The kindness and affection that encouraged self-expression was often absent and was rarely actively encouraged in first-generation households. Many immigrant memoirs attest to this. Most of these lives were not quite as grim as John Muir's experience at home, but they could be deadening. "For as long as I can remember," Irving Louis Horowitz recalled, "the central aspect of the Horowitz family was the absence of love." "Punishment came much more readily than rewards. Anger became the common household denominator." As Horowitz concluded, "The deterioration of family ties proved a blessing in disguise. Individual needs and wants displaced the authoritarian collective." Other memoirs came to similar conclusions describing the relations between husbands and wives and between fathers and their children as cold and punitive, and showing that escape into individual desires and away from the collective was experienced as a real liberation. Kate Simon observed that her parents never hugged or touched each other and rarely the children. "I never saw my mother and father kiss or stroke each other as people did in the movies."[89] Arranged or merely convenient, many European families were formed by couples who had not experienced or expected "romance," which in the United States, at least since the mid-nineteenth century, was assumed to be necessary to a good marriage. The contrast that children saw between the increasingly companionable couples among their American friends' parents (a middle-class ideal by the 1920s), as well as in the movies, and their own parents was often wrenching. Young immigrants realized that family relationships could be different from what they witnessed at home and that knowledge, too, was a spur to their own change and became a kind of education in Americanization.

School could offer the children of immigrants alternative visions of what family life could be like and what interpersonal relations could offer. This might result from their own romances, encouraged by a school environment in which social life was as important as academics. During the 1920s and 1930s, a new version of family life was also promoted in the many new courses on the family in the curriculum, courses that emphasized democracy and affection in households and pointed young people toward ideals of marital companionship.[90] An extension of the new cult of informed childrearing, the courses on family life were meant to create stronger and more durable relations between parents. Regardless of the effect of such programs, school itself was often a site where teachers extended themselves to become almost second parents.

The many different families by the middle of the twentieth century may not have been very much like the ideals proposed either in family education classes or in childrearing and adolescent-rearing manuals, and the numerous immigrant variations certainly meant that no one pattern could define actual family life in the middle of the century. The typical American home, as the White House Conference clearly proclaimed, was "almost impossible" to describe. But other institutions—pediatrics, childrearing advice, and especially schooling—were transforming how American children and youth grew up and, in the process, transforming generational interactions, whether these were immigrants in cities or third- and fourth-generation families on the farm.

CHAPTER 5

All Our Children

Race, Rebellion, and Social Change, 1950–1990

When the United States emerged victorious after World War II, the clear winners were the children of the nation. To this day, we remember this time as the apogee of modern American child-centeredness, and although the reality was more complex, there is some justice to the memory. Americans produced more children per family, housed them better than ever before, turned their attention to the education of all the nation's children in unprecedented ways, and offered a sense of stability even in a frightening Cold War environment. Child-rearing was regarded almost as a profession by mothers of the time. New amusement parks, like Disneyland in California, redefined family vacations. Toy makers and school designers aimed to release the creativity of children and the future seemed a sure thing.[1] Like the young boy in the Uncle Sam hat advertising building products, this American generation seemed to be on top of the world as the United States became its dominant power.

This postwar generation would experience many lows as well as highs. If the sense of security was never entirely firm, it was very much destabilized by the assassination of President John F. Kennedy in 1963, after a short administration full of promises offered with youthful élan. It was even more deeply shaken by the Vietnam War, which questioned the virtue and triumph of American arms, and by the revolt that the war stirred on the nation's campuses. The young people who turned against the war and against their parents' visions more generally were an enormously expanded generation of college students who had once appeared to be perfectly situated for their own triumphs. Racial difference and its consequences remained close to the surface during much of the period, as Americans struggled with the blatant inequality for African Americans in all walks of life, but that was especially problematic at the schools that were supposed

"What's ahead for Me?"

Plenty, little feller. Plenty. For you're a young American . . . and America itself is *young*. Young in years! Young in vigor! Young and strong in determinations! It's going places. And so are *you!*

That's why, in this land of yours, there's a great future for you. But we mustn't waste time! Once we've won the war—*and the* peace—we've got to start building!

Yes, sir . . . *building!* You know, that's the way our forefathers started this country. They *built homes!* That's the way they began to make America grow.

And we've been building and growing ever since. But along side what we're going to build in *your* day we've hardly begun!

In the years ahead we'll build millions of *new* homes! Beautiful, livable, economical homes—the kind Mummy and Daddy dream of for *you!* There's work to do—young man! Millions of homes to be repaired, remodeled, made new! Millions of wonderful *new* homes to be built!

And why do we Americans believe so in building? Because we want every youngster in our democracy to grow up in the healthy environment of a home of his own! But that's not all! We want you—our children—to know the blessings of American progress and prosperity. And both depend so much upon the building of these homes.

All over our land home building can be the sparkplug of our peacetime prosperity . . . the foundation of our country's growth.

Young America—that is what's ahead for you! A greater country, a greater future, a greater opportunity—because yours is the land of "Home, Sweet Home!" Certain-teed Products Corporation, Chicago 3, Illinois.

CERTAIN-TEED

BUILDING   PRODUCTS

"What's Ahead for Me?" Advertisement for Certain-Teed Building Products, from *American Home* 33–34 (March 1945), 77. This ad nicely brings together the sense of children and building the nation's future that defined the postwar years.

to open doors to the future. Since the Second World War had been fought and won in terms of the language of democracy, its denial among the nation's own citizens became an urgent call to action for those who were most dispossessed and for those young people who chafed at the unmet goals.

By the last decades of the twentieth century, young Americans and their parents seemed to be living in a different age entirely than those in the two postwar decades that had welcomed the baby boom. The nation's children were enveloped in a cloud of anxieties, as preparations for the new millennium encouraged self-reflection and self-doubt. But, the origins of deep changes in the family, in the economy, and in national self-confidence also lay in some of the ambiguities, not initially obvious, that began as Americans took up the banner of leadership in a world that in 1945 had been utterly transformed by war. Where Europe had once been at the West's center, the global focus shifted to the United States, and a once simple republic became the West's most visible representative.[2] By the 1960s, the United States was defining that world not only because it had the strongest military and the largest economy but because its cultural practices, including those regarding children and childrearing, schooling, and its vibrant youth culture, were a model for emulation.

I

Dorothy Height and Lewis Killian knew that the decision issued by the Supreme Court on May 17, 1954, was a historical landmark. Both grew up in the first half of the twentieth century when, by law or custom, blacks and whites existed in separate worlds. Height was born in Richmond, Virginia, in 1912 into what we would today describe as a large blended family with children from prior marriages on each side. Richmond, once the capital of the Confederacy, was very much a Jim Crow place, governed by explicit laws that separated the races, but Dorothy spent only a few years there. Like many families fleeing segregation, hers soon moved out of the South to Rankin, Pennsylvania, a small industrial city along the Monongahela River. Height remembered Rankin as "a lucky choice," a place where working conditions were much better than in bigger cities such as Philadelphia and New York, and the "largely foreign born" population of Italians, Croatians, and Germans got along with each other. Dorothy's father was a construction contractor. As a young black girl, Dorothy was very much in the minority at school but she excelled academically, made friends, and became secretary of her class. She also made a name for herself in the Pennsylvania world of debating while she was in school and subsequently as an important figure in the national Young Women's Christian Association.[3]

Lewis Killian, born in Macon, Georgia, in 1919, never knew his father, who died in the flu epidemic of 1918. With no male head of household, the family was usually in difficult financial circumstances and lived largely among working-class people, although their tastes and inclinations set them apart as middle class. Lewis attended legally segregated white schools and the segregated University of Georgia. As a child, he learned the "etiquette of race relations" that defined life in the South since the end of Reconstruction.[4] But as a young man, he began to struggle against the prejudices that he found among his neighbors and within himself against black people. Although he worked in various places during his career, he mostly stayed in the South where he became an important sociologist of black-white relations and a prominent Southern liberal.

Lewis Killian and Dorothy Height became active civil rights workers during their lifetimes and both recognized the significance of the ruling that was handed down as a unanimous decision in *Brown v. Board of Education of Topeka, Kansas*. They understood that the decision reflected back on their own life experiences as black and white Americans and would change the future of American children: in the South where Jim Crow was written into law and built into custom, habits, and feelings; and in the North to which many blacks had fled to escape the rigors of Jim Crow legal codes. There too, daily life discriminated against blacks, as both blacks and whites carried their own inner worlds of racial understanding. Dorothy remembered no overt prejudice as a young child in Rankin, Pennsylvania, where she went to school with white friends. But when she was eight, her best friend told her that they could no longer play running down the hill together "because you're a nigger." She did not know exactly what the word meant but she "was crushed. I had heard the word before, and I knew it wasn't supposed to be used, at least not by anyone with manners."[5]

Killian and Height also knew that while the change heralded by the *Brown* decision was inevitable and the court had urged "all deliberate speed," it would likely take time for the effects of the ruling to be fully experienced by all American children. More than sixty years later, Americans still disagree about the effects of the *Brown* decision, but we celebrate it as a historic event that signaled a new emphasis on equality for all America's children as a national goal and offered a new vision of what our children need and should expect in their schools and in their lives.[6]

The Supreme Court's decision had been well prepared in a series of previous court rulings that questioned segregated schools—by the legal department of the National Association for the Advancement of Colored People (NAACP), whose head litigator Thurgood Marshall took desegregation of schools as his special province, and by the Chief Justice of the United States Supreme Court, Earl Warren. Warren understood that the decision was momentous and had to be unanimous.[7] The court had been prepared as well by a series of national emergencies that awakened American policy makers to the ways in which racial segregation was cruel and hypocritical in the world's most powerful democracy, and to how it hobbled America's ability to fully mobilize the talents of its population.

During World War II, America's segregated army had been an embarrassment when German prisoners of war traveling through the South were treated better than black GIs, or when white soldiers refused to salute black officers. The crippling costs of supporting two sets of schools had been revealed in the low scores of undereducated Southerners (white as well as black) on various measures of intelligence and literacy.[8] The modern army required its soldiers to read instructions as well as follow orders, and many Southerners failed on these measures. The modern army also required education at higher levels than was common in the South, and the army began providing such higher learning to some of its soldiers at colleges and universities across the nation. Once again, the South could not hold its own in instruction of this kind.

In theaters of war, black soldiers underperformed because their white officers were usually contemptuous of their abilities. Lewis Killian discovered this attitude during his own wartime service. Already a strong advocate of equal rights and commissioned through his membership in ROTC, he requested to "be assigned to serve with black troops. The army ignored my request, in spite of the fact that there were five battalions of black trainees at Ft McClennan," battalions commanded by white officers. The troops were viewed as a burden rather than as a resource. As Killian noted ruefully, "I learned later that there were many white officers in the black regiment who would gladly have changed places with me."[9] Having grown up where segregation and a deep sense of white superiority were pervasive and "any contact that might symbolize equal social status was so powerful as to produce physical reactions in whites," Killian himself experienced the revulsion that many whites felt in the presence of blacks. Young Killian recognized his conditioned responses even as his beliefs moved strongly toward questioning their basis and regretting their many consequences for whites as well as for blacks. "After I overcame my early indoctrination and began to shake hands with blacks, I found that it was easier to change my mind than my feelings."[10]

In the period after World War II, the problems of a segregated army were often on the minds of policy makers. The status quo seemed increasingly untenable as the South was incorporated more fully into the American economy and into national policies regarding manpower and military requirements. These were among the considerations that led President Harry S. Truman to desegregate the armed forces (against stiff resistance) during the Korean War, and it led many others to recognize that twentieth-century wars had transformed the United States. It was now a much more interconnected society, literally connected by a new interstate highway system completed in 1956 that was viewed as a means to strengthen national defense. The *Brown* decision made clear that these connections would have to be made between blacks and whites. Above all, American children, as they grew up, needed to be made aware of the complexities of the American population. In that way, the strong repugnancies and contempt by whites would gradually abate.

Height and Killian had very personal connections to the *Brown* case. Dorothy Height had been working to integrate the Young Women's Christian Association before the decision, and Killian was asked to prepare a report for the Florida Attorney General's Office in anticipation of the ruling. His task was to consider how the state should respond, by analyzing the views of Floridians. Where Height worked diligently in person to encourage an integrated vision for the YWCA, Killian learned from his surveys that desegregation would be greeted differently community by community and that it had many barriers to overcome. He found that there was "a great gap between the hopes of blacks and the expectations and attitudes of whites. . . . Blacks had far more faith in the good will and respect for the law on the part of whites than the white answers justified. Three-fourths of them believed that most white people agreed with the decision; 77 percent of whites believed the opposite."[11]

Height's response to news of the court's ruling embodied that high set of expectations. At the meeting of the YWCA she was attending, "We immediately adjourned. We felt like declaring a holiday!" It was an event that few ever forgot, Height insisted, and would begin "the push for comprehensive civil rights for Black Americans."[12] Killian and Height were both right. The *Brown* decision ushered in a new America, but it also precipitated an immediate fallout that sharply encoded the different perspectives of blacks and whites regarding their children.

In Jackson, Mississippi, where Edwin King was a white high school student when the *Brown* decision was announced, he and his friends were initially surprised by the front-page headline and article in the local newspaper "Blood on the Marble Steps," in which the editor predicted the violence that would greet the Supreme Court decision. At Carr Central High School, King recalled, they had "talked openly about the matter," in advance and were prepared for the decision. He himself had "come to hope the Court would rule against segregation," and so the newspaper coverage that day confused him. Edwin's membership in the Methodist Church helped lead him toward moderate views on race. His views were shared more generally, as "Teachers and students both assumed that the federal government would soon enforce the Court's decision—and that loyal citizens of Mississippi would, as Americans, of course, obey." But "it soon became clear that change would not come quickly." "The students who came back to that high school the next fall did not have open discussions about the Supreme Court or controversial issues. Those who still thought the Court was right *did not dare speak their minds*."[13] In Jackson, white society had closed its mind and its ranks. This was the reaction throughout much of the South.

In Pittsburgh, Pennsylvania, just five miles from Rankin, and also along the Monongahela River where Dorothy Height grew up, Annie Dillard's well-to-do and privileged family sent their children to private schools and spent summers in rustic cabins on Lake Erie. They attended the Presbyterian Church, and the children went to dancing school with others of their class (though not with Jews). Her mother and father had two black servants, who were treated warmly, almost as part of the family. Annie remembered that the chauffeur's drinking glass was always on the kitchen counter, as if among friends. When Annie's friend's brother, Tommy Sheehy, told her "go tell your maid she's a nigger," Annie complied, only to be strongly rebuked for this behavior by her mother. "She explained, and made sure I understood. She was steely. . . . She told me a passel of other words that some people use for other people. I was never to use such words, and never to associate with people who did so as long as I lived; I was to apologize to Margaret Butler [their maid] first thing in the morning and I was to have no further dealing with the Sheehys." This episode took place in the early 1950s. The Dillards were ready for the court decision.

Not long after this, Annie was taken by her mother to the closest public library. This library was in Homewood, an almost entirely African American part of town. "In the evenings, neighborhood people—the men and women of Homewood—browsed in the library, and brought their children." Allowed to take out books from the adult section of the library, Annie began to think about the many African Americans who had taken out the books of which she was especially fond, like the *Field Book of Ponds and Streams*. This shared reading made her aware of their common humanity. "With us, and sharing our enthusiasm for dragonfly larvae and single-celled plants, were, apparently, many Negro adults."[14] In the North and South,

American children brought many different experiences and expectations to the decision on desegregation whose aim was to affect them all.

It was children—broadly defined by the mid-twentieth century to also include teenagers—who were immediately on the front lines; young children who were asked to integrate previously all-white elementary schools in cities such as New Orleans; adolescents going to high schools in Little Rock, Arkansas, and Clinton, Tennessee; as well as those older teenagers and youth, who by the later 1950s participated in marches and in demonstrations and tried to integrate bus stations, restaurants, and soda fountains.[15] These children and youth were often surrounded by crowds of onlookers, many of them angry and vocally hostile, by local police, sometimes by federal troops, and by newspaper reporters and television crews. As historian Rebecca de Schweinitz argues about young people in the civil rights movement, "Before the 1950s, African American leaders asked young people ambitiously to pursue higher education and good jobs . . . to benefit the race. . . . In contrast, young people . . . after *Brown* very often chose to sacrifice, at least for a time, educational aims, professional success, parental support and material as well as physical well-being"[16] to become activists in the cause of civil rights. The events of the 1950s and 1960s would provide black and white children with very public experiences.

Ten years after the decision in *Brown*, child psychiatrist Robert Coles published a classic study of some of the young people who endured the battle to integrate the South. Trained as a doctor who was often asked to deal with delinquency, Coles faced very different issues as he turned his attention to the children who set out to end segregation in schools. Rather than observing ill health and maladjustment, Coles observed children coping with difficult historical circumstances; rather than delinquents, he dealt with young people who were often despised and outcast because they took on an honorable cause.

Psychological values surrounded the *Brown* case. In the most important brief submitted on behalf of the plaintiffs supporting public school integration, Dr. Kenneth Clark described his studies of dolls to illustrate how the sense of self-worth among African American

First grade, showing extremes in ages of pupils in a segregated African American class in Gee's Bend, Alabama (1939). Photograph by Marion Post Wolcott. Farm Security Administration—Office of War Information Photograph Collection, Prints & Photographs Division, Library of Congress, Image # LC-DIG-ppmsca-31891. Note the mixture of ages of students in the photograph even at the end of the 1930s. This was not unusual in the underfunded and poorly staffed schools of the segregated South.

children was wounded in a racist and segregated society. As children systematically chose white dolls over brown, Clark urged the court to understand how insidious the American racial system had been for the development of young black children. Coles found similar preferences among the black children whose lives he followed, children who drew pictures of themselves as smaller than white children, avoided black and brown crayons, and expressed the desire to be white. "One five-year-old colored boy had been unusually explicit in both his talk and pictures: he wished he was white, and that was that. . . . When I asked him whether he thought he was so, he said no, he was colored, but there was little harm in wishing otherwise."[17] Both Dr. Clark and Dr. Coles thought otherwise.

The emphasis on the psychological consequences of racism was common during the decade following the *Brown* decision,[18] but the importance of psychology for Americans was hardly confined to the subject of race relations. During the Second World War, psychologists and psychiatrists had joined the armed forces to underwrite a new perspective on battle readiness and on how war affected soldiers' mental and emotional well-being.[19] Studies of nervousness and anxiety were soon followed by discussions of "brainwashing" during the Korean War, as prisoners of war were subjected to extreme forms of indoctrination and their psyches preyed upon and altered.

The psychological underpinnings of childrearing had become a staple of twentieth-century advice well before the 1950s. And Americans were now regularly seeking psychiatric assistance for nervous and emotional disorders. From 1940 to 1964 the number of psychiatrists increased 600 percent.[20] These several sources created a predisposition toward psychological forms of understanding that flowered as psychology and psychiatry become dominant cultural perspectives in the 1950s and 1960s, when they informed legal briefs, literature, and other cultural products. Thus Robert Coles was working in very rich soil when he wrote about the psychological consequences of desegregation in the South in 1964.

In fact, Coles's study was much more than a psychological inquiry by an extremely sensitive observer of race relations. Coles understood that psychological insight needed to be historically situated. In describing "John Washington," a pseudonym for one of the young black youths who integrated an Atlanta school, Coles noted that John had been "strictly toilet trained." But he understood that this was the result of specific circumstances. The Washington family had migrated from a sharecropper cabin in South Carolina to the city of Atlanta, where the rules were different (and required much stricter attention to cleanliness). John's father was from a family of very poor sharecroppers but had returned home from the armed services with new ideas about possibilities for himself and his children. After basic training in New Jersey and a stint cooking for troops fighting in France, he did not want to return to his crude life as a "cropper." The food he ate, the clothes he wore, and his experiences of a good bed had made him eager for a different life when he returned. This moved him to take his wife and three children, including their newborn son (the parents had married very young—he at sixteen, his wife Hattie at fourteen) to the city of Atlanta. "He wanted schooling for his children, particularly his new son. He wanted to go northward, to Philadelphia or New York," but his wife did not want to leave at all, so they compromised on Atlanta.[21]

John's father eventually became an alcoholic, and the mother suffered repeated episodes of mental exhaustion and instability while raising seven children. But John, their eldest son, weathered the turmoil of his pioneering role in desegregating Atlanta's schools emotionally intact. A fairly ordinary student at his segregated elementary, junior high, and high school, John decided "on impulse to request a transfer" to an integrated school in eleventh grade. "Walking home one day with his friends, he heard some say yes, they would, some say no, they wouldn't think of going through mobs or sitting through insults at a white schools. . . . 'We kept daring one another and teasing each other. My friend, Kenny said he was going to do it, regardless; and the girls let out a big cheer and hugged and kissed him. Then Larry called him a fool. He said we would be giving up the best two years of our lives for nothing but trouble . . . the dances and football games—everything you hope for when you're beginning high school.'"[22] High school life had by the 1950s become a sought-after and valuable experience for African American youth, as it was for others, even in segregated schools.

It took John a week to convince his reluctant parents to sign the consent form. "They said, maybe *my* children, and I said *me*, so that my children will be the first really free Negroes. They always told me that they would try to spare me what they went through; so I told them I wanted to spare my children going through any mobs."[23] The civil rights struggle now redefined generational experiences, with schooling often at the center, just as it had done for the relationship between first- and second-generation immigrants. In Coles's words, John's parents "Eventually . . . gave their reluctant, apprehensive endorsements. They apparently were proud as well as filled with foreboding as they signed their names, itself not an easy task for either of them," since they were only marginally literate.

After many interviews, John became just one of two students chosen to go to the white high school near his old school. With determination, and after weeks of telephoned threats to his life, he settled into a routine at a newly desegregated high school where he spent his final two years. He had both endured and flourished, though not without academic setbacks and endless slurs spoken to his face and written in his textbooks. Watching John grow, make decisions, and develop over several years, Coles admitted that he could not have predicted it or even quite understand it. "As I watched John grow from a youth to a young man, and reflected upon his capacity to endure the simple trials not only of growing but of growing in a home such as his, of growing while a student in a white school, while taking a leading part in an important social change, I found the limits of my own particular professional training rather severely defined."[24] John Washington's strengths had induced humility in Coles. In addition to being a psychologist, Coles had been a witness to the history of a place and a time in which some things became newly possible for children and youth. Psychology had provided some valuable insights, but it was hardly a sufficient explanation for John Washington or for his experience.

II

Attention to matters of psychology in the 1950s began in the nursery. And in the nursery no one spoke with as much authority as Dr. Benjamin Spock, whose childrearing advice manual became a guiding text to several generations of mothers. From 1946 to the present, *The Common Sense Book of Baby and Child Care* (its original title) has gone through seven editions and sold more than fifty million copies. Spock was the first widely consulted child-care expert to adopt a manifestly Freudian perspective on children. The book, while still overwhelmingly organized around advice about nutrition, illness, and physical growth, also included advice on psychological development. Of course, it was never only to Spock's views and his guidance that mothers responded after World War II. While his gentle approach to babies became the dominant one and came to define parenting of the baby-boom generation, mothers continued to raise their children according to behaviorist theories that emphasized early and consistent habit training, in response to ideas of developmental appropriateness learned from Arnold Gesell, and by the guidelines set by church authorities and grandparents (something which Spock himself came to accept as appropriate in later editions of his book). No single child-rearing authority ever completely defined the horizons of child care, although Benjamin Spock probably came closest. And while children raised under his aegis were unlikely to remember the experience, their mothers did.

Part of Spock's appeal was simply that his advice was so practical and low-key. Drawing on his training in psychoanalysis, the work of developmental psychologists, and his own awareness of how much of a burden "proper" mothering was beginning to be in a society of experts with mass media access, Spock set out to provide American mothers with a way to become both knowledgeable and natural at the same time. He knew that the protective and overly conscientious mother could be a problem for her children from his own experiences as the son of such a parent, and he put that understanding to use in behalf of others. As Spock told them, "All parents do their best job when they have a natural, easy confidence in themselves." He described his own book as "sensible," and one of his early readers wrote to tell him that "[y]ou make me feel as if you thought I was a sensible person," too. Ann Hulbert, who has written perceptively about Spock and his milieu observed, "The book was irresistible."[25]

The baby-boom generation did not start out that way. Initially, the increase in births seemed to be one of those cyclical upswings in the birthrate that often succeed depressions or wars (in this case one following on the heels of the other) as people become more confident about the future. But by the mid 1950s, the figures had become a serious trend as Americans settled into having larger families, indeed, far larger than any previous time in the twentieth century. And confidence didn't seem to explain it, since the Cold War environment was hardly confidence building. Starting shortly after World War II, the growing tension between the United States and the Soviet Union—allies during the fight against Hitler and fascism—became an alarming shadow over all political life as the two became outright rivals for control of the allegiances of European nations and then of what became known as the Third World in Asia, Latin America, and Africa. After the Soviets acquired their own atomic bomb in 1948, and Mao Tse-tung and the Communist Party took over in China in 1949, the outbreak of hostilities on the Korean peninsula in 1950 turned the war red hot for three years. And the whole period was filled with domestic anxiety as the future of humanity itself seesawed precariously in a world defined by atomic bombs and atomic rivalry, while the loyalties of many US citizens were scrutinized as unreliable.[26] These fears—that treasonous Americans had aided the Soviets in acquiring their nuclear technologies, and that spies had invaded the highest precincts of American public life in the universities, the State Department, and Hollywood—turned the early 1950s into a theater of paranoia.[27] Some politicians, especially Wisconsin senator Joseph McCarthy, capitalized on this, but it was not McCarthy alone who created either the tension or the accusations. Instead, for more than a decade after World War II, American public life was filled with suggestions about plots and the exposure of plots, fears and the inflaming of fears, which hardly made childbearing a sure thing.

But still, the child population grew. Many factors contributed to the inflation of the baby boom—the growth of suburbs, the greater prosperity of ordinary Americans as the economy expanded with new jobs, the extra support for schooling and home ownership provided by the GI Bill.[28] But none of these features of the time explains it entirely. Instead, it might be useful to think of the period as one in which children were valued as children, and when the perceived rewards of childrearing provided mothers with a form of personal satisfaction. Childhood itself seemed to have became a national resource. This created a growing desire for adoption as childless couples sought validation as families.[29] In other words, the valuing of children fed on itself as parenthood became a desired and deeply socially approved status. Almost certainly, not all women felt this way, and dissatisfaction grew within the crevices of the national trend toward homemaking and childrearing, but overall the two decades after World War II, which coincided with the Cold War and with the baby boom, were a period in which a carefree childhood was set apart as especially important to the nation and to individuals who were meant to remember it as the happiest time of their lives. It was one in which Americans hoped to release the creativity and independence of the young through the toys they played with, the school buildings they inhabited, and the books they read.[30]

Dr. Benjamin Spock was there to oversee it all. With a sense of genial approval and a genuine love of children, Spock helped to sponsor and validate the baby boom and to encourage women to enjoy what they did as mothers. The half-century before the appearance of *Baby and Child Care* had seen women tutored and hectored as psychologists displayed their expertise about how best to make well-behaved and well adjusted children. Since they could not do this by themselves, they had enlisted mothers in the quest for perfection. John Watson had dreamed of a motherless utopia, but most psychologists had come to terms with the necessary partnership. As a result, women had often become riddled with anxiety (about getting it right) and guilt (when things seemed to go wrong) about fulfilling their roles well enough. Some historians have noted how this had led inevitably to creating images of the "bad mother" who neglected her children, or abused them.[31]

By the 1940s, the image of the bad mother had also become alarming in another sense as psychoanalytic theories proposed that unhappy, sexually maladjusted women could use their children as proxies for their own misplaced sexual drives. By 1942, *Time* magazine was beginning to worry about "Too Much Mother," and citing psychiatrist David Mordecai Levy to the effect that "excessive mothering [makes] problem children." Such "overprotective mothers" were portrayed as domineering and aggressive.[32] Out of this came the terrifying figure of "Mom," who exploited her children's love for her own emotional needs. Wilhelm Stekel wrote two volumes about frigid women whose influence, on their sons especially, was dire; and the popular writer Philip Wylie's book, menacingly titled *Generation of Vipers*, published in 1946, spread the fearsome image and the message.[33]

That same year, an army psychiatrist, Edward A. Strecker, used his experience with emotionally weak soldiers and those who had failed induction criteria to make a similar claim about "Mom and Her Silver Cord": Mom keeps "her children paddling about in a kind of psychological amniotic fluid rather than letting them swim away with the bold and decisive strokes of maturity." Observing that "There is nothing stronger in this world than the child-mother cohesion," Strecker laid out a series of sketches of mothering behaviors based on his view that there was a continuum from the frightful "Mom" to the true "Mother," who "uses the emotional ingredients sparingly and wisely," although he did note that in every mother, even the best, "there are traces of the mom." Strecker also provided a useful catalogue of "Mom Types." These included "the common garden variety of mom, the 'self-sacrificing' mom, the 'ailing' mom, the 'pollyanna' mom; the 'protective' mom, the 'pretty-addlepate' mom, and the 'pseudo-intellectual' mom," which might have been used in Hollywood casting departments for the films of the time.[34] Narcissistic and sexually repressed mothers, like these, undermined their children's independence and turned them into infantilized (and latently homosexual) adult weaklings. Many moms meant well, but their strained perfectionism was only aggravated by the very expertise to which they looked for help in rearing their children.

Benjamin's Spock's emphasis on the natural and the sensible took place against the backdrop of this already heavily psychologized relationship. His childrearing manual was meant not just to counteract the strenuous mothering encouraged by childrearing advice but to return to a time when parenting encouraged independence in children who were raised to be self-sufficient and autonomous in a democratic society. Spock thus wanted to liberate both mothers and their children, the latter from excessive mothering and the former from the tyranny of excessive expertise. This was a neat trick for a childrearing expert who had himself been something of a mother's boy.[35]

Like his predecessors concerned with the well-being and welfare of children, Charles Loring Brace and Horace Bushnell (one of whose descendants Spock married), Benjamin Spock was born and raised in Connecticut and went to Yale.[36] And while this was coincidental, he shared with these two a belief in the potentials of children to influence the society and a commitment to having them grow up to become effective adults. That path was strewn with obstacles by the 1950s. Americans had spent a century creating a childhood separated from adult concerns, and built up social and political institutions to protect them as children. They had extended the period of childhood

through expanded schooling, and adolescence had been institutionalized as a later phase of childhood.

Spock built on the belief that children "want to do grown up
things" and that a mother's emotional state was an example to her
offspring as well as the basis for her childrearing techniques. In this
way, he attempted to make both mothers and children more independent and self-sufficient as adults. Spock is deeply bound to his Connecticut predecessors of the nineteenth century, not only because
they shared a birthplace and a college, but because Spock was trying to recapture an older American childhood—more natural, more
fully congruent with and connected to an independent adulthood.

There was a hitch, of course. The American landscape of the 1950s
was nothing like that of the early nineteenth century, when Bushnell had elevated motherhood to a semi-divine status and liberated
children from the tyranny of innate sin. Mothers were the opposite
of divine in the portrait of "Mom." Childhood may have been liberated from sin, but it was deeply hemmed in so that it no longer
led easily to maturity through work and responsibility as Brace assumed it should. Mothers were now much more firmly in charge of
their children—too firmly, according to some of the critics.

Work as a goal had not only disappeared as a natural part of childhood, but even household chores receded, as middle-class mothers
took over almost all household tasks so that their offspring could
freely enjoy a childhood defined by play and school. Children did not
take care of each other, as they once had, in part because even in large
families most children were now born close together. They could
play together, but the assumption of a parental role, so common in
the nineteenth century, was now no longer part of growing up. A
childhood of play and schooling had, after all, become the ideal in
the late nineteenth century as reformers chased work out of the circle
of childhood and hoped to separate the young from adult tasks.[37]
Now, by the middle of the twentieth century, it seemed finally within
the grasp of the majority of Americans to make this kind of childhood available to all their children. Mothers had followed not just
the advice of experts; American mothers were expressing the values
of the whole culture. And that culture was not only American but

increasingly Western. The commitment to the freeing of children from the demands of work and the emphasis on their separation from adult responsibilities infused Western beliefs for more than a century. After the war, American children and their mothers were thus fulfilling a long cultural aspiration.

The general circumstances of life in American society, too, had changed. Almost all children now went to school, and schooling had changed the transition to adulthood in profound and inalterable ways. This was quite visible in the importance of the *Brown* decision, which elevated the ideal of equal schooling into a creed that was meant to cover all America's children, even the most previously marginalized populations. The *Brown* decision was as much a declaration of the right to childhood by all children as it was a statement about desegregation. Schools had reduced parents' authority as they took over most of the day from the time a child was five or six and filled it until she was sixteen, seventeen, or even eighteen years of age. And in the context of the high school, both mother's and father's authority had actually shrunk. This was something that novelist Richard Ford remembered keenly. Throughout his childhood growing up in Mississippi in the 1950s, he was extremely close to his mother. In fact, his mother (no doubt tutored by the experts of her time) often apologized for "smothering" him emotionally when he was little. But once he was in high school "I didn't see my mother much" as his "new friends took me up."[38]

After school, children played with other children, as they had in the nineteenth century, but they now also had many commercial toys and new media to engage their attention, especially as television became a commonplace; by the end of the 1950s, 90 percent of American homes had television sets.[39] Motherhood in 1955 was hardly what it had been in 1835. Neither was childhood. So, Spock's concern to reconnect to a more "natural" and a more "confident" time before childrearing experts had muscled in and psychoanalysts had exposed women's nastier side was never likely to succeed completely.

Spock's effort to revitalize independence for children was not altogether misspent, however. After World War II, the American middle class expanded rapidly, and young people enjoyed opportunities for advancement beyond those of their parents.[40] And despite the paranoia, the United States had won the war and become the most powerful as well as the most prosperous country in the world, a prosperity much more broadly shared than in the past. As was the case in the early republic, America's future seemed once again limitless and its children would define that future. They were its natural resource. Fostering an independent and innovative generation that would think beyond their parents' lives and succeed in new ways was visionary but not foolhardy. In this new world where literacy was basic to success and schooling was expanding rapidly, the future might well offer the independent-minded a source of significant advantage. Many designers of children's furniture, playrooms, toys, museums, and especially schools revived this image of the creative American child as a basic resource for America's future.[41] The old vision of the United States as unique among the nations was also being widely discussed with a new term: "exceptionalism." Thus, Spock's belief that he might help mothers and children fulfill a special destiny did not seem altogether illusory.

Like Robert Coles, Benjamin Spock understood that childhood was historically embedded. Erik H. Erikson would articulate this view most emphatically and fully when he became a psychoanalytic historian and wrote about historical figures like Martin Luther and Mahatma Gandhi.[42] He also became the favored psychological spokesman of an entire historical era. From 1950 to 1970, Erikson was a dominant public intellectual, and although his subject was childhood, it was childhood of a very special kind. As a good Freudian, Erikson emphasized the importance of the early years of a child's life and the sexual drives that defined these years, and he gave due attention to the Oedipal complex and the inevitable conflict between a son and his father. But Erikson came to focus increasing attention on a later developmental stage, one with which he became prominently identified: adolescence, a period of life that only became a serious subject of "scientific" investigation as a part of childhood in the twentieth century, and especially so in the United States. Starting in 1950 with his seminal book, *Childhood and Society*, Erikson applied Freudian concepts to various stages of childhood, associating each with special attributes and unique challenges to be overcome in order for the child to advance successfully toward the goal of an integrated and fruitful adulthood. Like Gesell, Erikson appreciated the importance of progressive development. Like Spock, Erikson saw the fulfillment of childhood in an integrated sense of self and well-functioning autonomous adulthood.

In *Childhood and Society*, he laid out these stages of development in what he called "the Eight Ages of Man," thus linking up his psychological stages to a long Western tradition.[43] Where childhood had once occupied one, or at most two, stages in the schema of the life cycle, Erikson emphasized its importance by dividing it into four stages. At each one, he posited a conflict between success and failure that determined the strength of a child's ego and affected the quality of adult life. At two years of age, for example, toddlers struggled for autonomy but could be inhibited by shame and doubt as they mastered body processes and experienced new inner states. "From a sense of self-control without loss of self-esteem comes a lasting sense of good will and pride; from a sense of loss of self-control and of foreign over-control comes a lasting propensity for doubt and shame."[44] As a child successfully proved himself at each stage, he could ascend to the next in a progressive evolution toward maturity. Erikson had extended these stages to encompass the full life cycle, moving beyond infancy and early childhood, into adolescence and adulthood, thereby suggesting that psychological well-being was the product of a lifetime.

In that cycle of growth reaching toward maturity, adolescence had an especially important place. It was at that point, by connecting childhood with adulthood, that, if successful, the unique individual became visible, integrating earlier successes and finally overcoming earlier failures. The result would be the creation of an independent ego. "With the establishment of a good initial relationship to the world of skills and tools [during the preceding school age of industry], and with the advent of puberty, childhood proper comes to an end. Youth begins. . . . In their search for a new sense of continuity and sameness, adolescents have to refight many of the battles of earlier years. . . . and they are ever ready to install lasting idols and ideals as guardians of a final destiny."[45] In Erikson's schema, adolescence became a connecting bridge, which often required that earlier conflicts be re-engaged successfully so that this stage could be traversed and "a final identity" established. But it was fraught with hazards as the ego

°seeks out strong allies in order to achieve the confidence necessary for independence. In giving adolescence this essential part to play, Erikson wrote a whole new chapter in childrearing advice. He also put his finger on the pulse of a historical moment.

During the Depression of the 1930s, and especially after World War II, American childhood expanded as some high school education became an expected experience for American youth. Even beyond high school, the GI Bill began to send millions of Americans to colleges and universities that newly opened their doors to many kinds of youths who had never previously dreamed of the privilege. As this happened, advanced training of all kinds became an essential part of the preparation for mature work lives. The new emphasis on equal education enshrined by the *Brown* decision thus meant far more even than desegregation of schools; it highlighted the fundamental importance of schooling.

Schooling had become a form of national policy as Americans invested in their youth. One of those investments was in colleges and universities that after the war became the beneficiaries of federal funds directed to programs in science and technology, as well as languages and fields of study viewed as necessary to national defense. College enrollments increased by 49 percent during the 1950s and 120 percent in the 1960s. By 1969, 35 percent of all youths aged eighteen to twenty-four were in college—an astonishing proportion of the population. At that point, unlike any other society, the United States had more college students than farmers.[46]

Erikson's emphasis on the strains of adolescence thus came at just the moment when adolescence had become a more extended process and also far more visible because the numbers of American children had ballooned during the baby boom. In Erikson's model, it also became more tortured as adolescents had to make choices about where and around whom to direct their energies and allegiances. Instead of leading quickly and efficiently through a door, as it did in societies in which the transition to adulthood was ritualized through some set performance, adolescence was a holding period of preparation in a sheltered space. The future was delayed as young people found themselves expectant but searching for just the right path to maturity.

III

In the late 1950s, Todd Gitlin was a brilliant math student at the Bronx High School of Science, a highly selective New York City public school. His parents were high school teachers and, like many other New York City middle-class Jews, they were liberal Democrats. They had not participated in the more self-conscious left that became part of the American scene from the 1920s through the 1950s, when a wide array of Socialist and Communist factions flourished. Gitlin himself was wild for Adlai Stevenson in his election bid against Dwight Eisenhower in 1956, hardly a sign of radical sympathy.

In high school, Gitlin started seeking a more inspiring set of beliefs to which he could attach his enthusiasm for American ideals of justice, and he observed such commitment among some of his friends who were "red diaper babies"—children of seriously committed leftists. His interest increased after he left home to attend Harvard College in the fall of 1959. At that point, influenced by a girlfriend, but also by others he met at school, including college instructors, he sought out various organizations and occasions to rally on behalf of goals he believed expressed a purer form of American idealism, in civil rights and other arenas of participatory democracy.

Eventually, fears about nuclear conflict, reawakened by the rise of Fidel Castro in Cuba, brought Gitlin more fully into politics as he lined up with other students and faculty in favor of nuclear disarmament. In this fervor Gitlin began to help organize public demonstrations like the one in Washington on February 1962.[47] The atomic bomb and the new threats it posed had been as much a product of World War II as the prosperity and the baby boom that fed the new college population. At the time, when Gitlin organized one of the largest anti-nuclear demonstrations in the nation's capital, he was not yet twenty years old. At this point, his exposure to ideals on campus, both inside and outside the classroom, led him to identify strongly with a new kind of leftist politics, rooted in the peace movement and the struggle for equal justice, which was eventually called the New Left.

Todd Gitlin's quest would take him to the forefront and a leadership position in the Students for a Democratic Society (SDS), which began forming at major universities during the early 1960s. He was doing things his parents had not done, committing himself deeply to a set of ideals, assisted by peers and friends, and demonstrating the courage of his convictions. In many ways, Gitlin exemplified the kind of adolescent Erik Erikson was writing about—a young person who threw himself fervently into various causes in the process of separating from his parents. Young people like these were creating their own identities through a process of affiliation with other like-minded young people who were also testing their beliefs through action. For Erikson this experimentation and supercharged willingness to try new paths was what set the period of adolescence apart. As they dreamed of adulthood, they found ways to distinguish their own future from the lives of their parents.

Of course, not all students had the talents to arrive at Harvard in the first place, or the drive to prove their independence with such determination. But in the 1960s, many more students were arriving at college and began to engage in a whirl of new activities, some of it political. The ability to do so, away from parental controls, during this stage that Erikson was identifying as part of a critical step on the route to maturity, would turn many students, like Todd Gitlin, toward intense political engagement. In their introduction to the "Port Huron Statement," its founding document, the founders of the SDS showed that they were fully aware of these conditions: "We are people of this generation, bred in at least modest comfort, housed now in universities, looking uncomfortably to the world we inherit."[48] The new generation was proclaiming its distinctiveness from a platform for social change.

Erikson, along with most other observers of youth at the time, based most of his conclusions on men, and his theories about development were firmly, though not explicitly, male-centered. This was often true of psychoanalytic theory generally at midcentury. In educational innovations too, women had temporarily taken a back seat to men after the GIs returned from their victories in Europe and the Pacific. Men were the recipients of government largesse and the wellspring of America's notion of manpower. That would not last long. For most of the twentieth century, American girls and women had been going to high school and college in the same proportions as men.

Indeed, women's attendance at colleges and universities was larger than that of men during the war years as military service sharply reduced the proportion of men on campus. Only briefly did this pattern recede when veterans crowded women out of higher education for a few years after the end of World War II. Then by the 1960s, women returned in force, graduating from high school and proceeding to higher education with as much momentum as their male peers.[49]

By the early 1960s too, veterans were disappearing from college campuses, and with them the more heterogeneous mixture of ages and the more fully focused adult-centered goals that they represented. Many GIs were already married when they went to college, and some even had children; and this gave that generation of post–World War II college students a patina of maturity and inclinations toward responsibility that soon moved off campus. By the end of the 1950s, college life was becoming deeply adolescent centered and peer directed. With that change came an intensification of many of the issues that Erikson identified with adolescence. Not all these issues were political. In fact, many observers in the 1960s were surprised by students' turn to politics, since American youth were frequently described as apathetic and deeply conformist. Psychologist Kenneth Keniston had published a book documenting this pattern, called *The Uncommitted*, in 1965. Indeed, Gitlin recounts how opposition to John Kennedy's response to the Cuban missile crisis in 1962 by some faculty and students provoked hostility on campus, as students expressed their firm support for government policies. "At Indiana University, a handful of anti-administration picketers were heckled, chased by a mob of two thousand students. . . . At Cornell, two professors were forced off the platform by stones and clumps of dirt. At the University of Minnesota, professors were splattered by eggs and oranges."[50]

Before the mid-1960s, adolescent solidarity and self-assertion against adults usually took the form of minor infractions of parietal rules (the many regulations that governed student social behavior), such as staying out after hours, drinking in dorm rooms, or having a friend of the opposite sex in one's room with the door closed. Anti-authority feelings had been expressed on American campuses since the nineteenth century.[51] American college students had always been inclined toward various pranks that undermined adult authority, and athletics and fraternity life often ruled campus culture. It would take more than high spirits or a sense of rebellion against adult rules to ignite what eventually became a very large and vocal student movement in the 1960s.

As Erikson knew, and as G. Stanley Hall had known before him, the coincidence of adolescence with puberty meant that not just youthful fervor, but sexual drives were among the urgent sources propelling the preparation for maturity and adult roles. The fact that women were now rejoining men on campuses refueled the sexual revolution that had begun on campuses in the 1920s and 1930s, as part of the growth of coeducation and of college populations. Peers propelled and enforced each other's erotic experimentation long before the 1960s. By the mid-1960s, the expansion of the numbers of women on campuses and the intensification of adolescent issues created the basis for new forms of sexual experimentation as well as new kinds of political engagement.

By the 1960s, colleges offered the setting and conditions for a lively youth culture, heavily fueled by the growing numbers of students on campus and a recognition among the young that they had the power to change tastes and styles. More than anything else, that culture was probably defined by music that included both high school and college students as part of its audience.[52] Starting in the mid 1950s, especially around the iconic figure of Elvis Presley, rock-and-roll music had the virtue of offending parents because it was different and raw while also being romantic. It was music drawn from Southern blues sounds much more than from the big bands their parents had admired. By the early 1960s, the enthusiasm for new music grew tremendously in response to the very different sounds of the Beatles and Bob Dylan. While a few young people, especially those who came out of the left, had begun listening to Joan Baez, Woody Guthrie, and others based in the folk tradition, Dylan brought that sound into the mainstream. The raucous, boyish sound of the Beatles and their innovative look challenged earlier styles in music in a completely different way, emphasizing youth with no apologies and in full stride. Music helped to give the young a sense of their distinctiveness and a connection in common generational tastes.[53]

Police car surrounded by students just after Jack Weinberg's arrest, Berkeley, California, October 1, 1964. Photographer unknown. Michael Rossman Free Speech Movement Photographs Collection, The Bancroft Library, University of California at Berkeley, Image # BANC PIC 2000.67:34. This was one of the first student demonstrations of the 1960s. The Berkeley campus of the University of California was one of the earliest sites for mass demonstrations, in this case, in response to infringements on free speech.

At the same time, the growing visibility of the civil rights struggle (now being seen on television as well as in print) gave adolescents a new sense of the possibilities of activism. Among black youth, the example of other African American youth ready to strike out against segregation stimulated identification and imitation. This was true for Julian Bond, the son of a college president. As he recalled, he had been a "happy-go-lucky teenager. . . . My role models . . . were white teenagers, . . . who danced five afternoons a week on ABC's *American Bandstand*. . . . But suddenly the nine brave young people of Little Rock's Central High School—the Little Rock Nine—replaced my former idols."[54]

Black youths' willingness to put their bodies on the line inspired whites as well. Todd Gitlin remembered, "Youth culture might have remained just that—the transitional subculture of the young, a right of passage on the route to normal adulthood—had it not been for the revolt of black youth, disrupting the American celebration in ways no one had imagined possible. From expressing youthful *difference*, many of the alienated, though hardly all, leaped into a self-conscious sense of *opposition*."[55] In 1964, the possibility of following the lead of black youth into civil disobedience came right onto college campuses when civil rights leaders recruited white students to help register voters on-site during Freedom Summer. The kinds of things that young Americans were learning at school, from the mass media, and from each other, had created broad new possibilities for generational identification and for tension between generations. Childhood and adulthood were connected through adolescence, but so differently articulated and understood by the generations as to produce a wide generation gap.[56]

Politics hovered over, without necessarily affecting, many of the young people from the beginning of the 1960s. The election of the youthful John Kennedy inspired a sense of new purpose and possibility. And Kennedy's shocking assassination on November 22, 1963, came all too soon afterwards. This was followed by a menacing intrusion of the Vietnam War into young Americans' consciousness as President Lyndon Johnson expanded America's commitment to a distant conflict in Southeast Asia. For early radicals like Todd Gitlin, it had been America's arrogant and aggressive internationalism that had ignited critical antagonism. The military draft spread the anger even more widely, and the earlier unfocused political energy on campus began to find a genuine center. The politically engaged students who, like Gitlin, had demonstrated against nuclear arms and the small group of Northern college students who joined the voter reg-

Student civil rights sit-in protest, second floor of Strong Hall, University of Kansas. (1965). Photographer unknown. University Archives, Kenneth Spencer Research Library, University of Kansas. Like the better-known schools, the University of Kansas, in the heart of the country, was home to a strong activist voice in the 1960s.

istration drive in Mississippi leavened the larger mass of students for whom active engagement now became a legitimate part of campus experience. Truly radical students were never more than a minority on most American campuses, but the growing war in Vietnam brought politics home to all students on campus, as the draft affected young Americans everywhere—in the Ivy League, the Big Ten, and small colleges as well as the many who never stepped onto a college campus. Being an adolescent now meant much more than preparing for work and marriage, the two features of adulthood emphasized by most psychologists. It also meant that graduation would lead to military training, fighting, and possibly dying in a far-off conflict about which most Americans initially knew very little and whose goals were being loudly disputed and questioned. How a young man (and his girlfriend) felt about the draft, and what he was willing to do about it, now became very much a part of the transition to adulthood.

The war in Vietnam finally ignited a genuinely broad-based student political revolt from 1967 through 1972 that kept students, faculty, and parents occupied and bewildered for years about its causes and consequences. Students adopted techniques of direct action to express their views and to make their differences with parents and college administrators clear. As demonstrators spilled into classrooms, faculty offices, and administrative buildings, and as police were called in to control the disruptions, the confrontations became bloody as well as angry. Eventually, police tactics and the National Guard presence on campuses such as Kent State University in Ohio, where several students were killed, added fuel to the fire.[57] Instead of bastions of civilized inquiry, colleges and, to some degree, high schools became embattled camps as the generations faced off against each other.[58] The very institutions that had privileged American adolescents and had set them apart from others in the Western world now became the sites for their oppositional attitudes. The generational antagonisms between parents (many of whom had fought in World War II) and their children as well as between students and adults on campus during the late 1960s and 1970s were as intense as their fundamental causes could be bewildering.

Eventually, some blamed an aging Dr. Benjamin Spock, himself a vocal opponent of the Vietnam War, for presiding over the creation of a generation of indulged and spoiled children who had never been adequately controlled, never grew up, and lacked patriotism. And while Spock had indeed sought to create the conditions for independent thinking among the young, the idea that he had been responsible for the activities of an entire generation seems very wide of the mark. In fact, very few people could have foreseen that a sizable portion of the baby-boom generation would behave as it did, not psychologists, not social scientists, and certainly not childrearing experts.

IV

In 1959, the year that Todd Gitlin went off to Harvard during the waning years of the Eisenhower administration, the president called a new White House Conference on Children and Youth into being, in order to commemorate the fiftieth anniversary of the first conference called by Theodore Roosevelt in 1909. More than six thousand delegates attended sessions that Eli Ginsberg, who edited the conference volumes, described as "dull." When the three conference volumes were republished in 1987, Ginsberg noted that most presenters had entirely missed the factors that would very shortly make for an explosion, on campus and off, as America's children and youth began to question how their elders handled politics and American society underwent a massive transformation. A social scientist himself, Ginsberg observed (with almost a chuckle) that "[t]he social scientist relies heavily on trends. But since trends do not persist, here is one important source of error."[59] In 1959, the staid papers were meant to bring the most recent and best knowledge about children and youth to a larger public, but most of these gave no hint of the events soon to follow. Few of the trends they observed led in the right direction toward the political engagement that was about to change the meaning of being young in America, and then in the Western world more generally.

One of the conference papers stood out as unusually perceptive about America's children, and its author also identified a social trend deeply relevant, if not to immediate experiences of the 1960s, then certainly to the decades that followed. In his discussion, "Work, Women, and Children," Henry David, then dean of the Graduate Faculty of Political and Social Science at the New School and soon to become its president, noted that American children had always occupied an unusual place in American society and in its culture. "No other major society in the world . . . provides as many or as varied educational opportunities for its young," and "probably no other society is as responsive to the consumption desire of its young." An expert on educational matters and national manpower questions, David was eager to see the larger national picture. Since they were so child-centered, Americans searched for the best and latest in childrearing advice. This child-centeredness, according to David, "[i]n part . . . grows out of the fact that Americans have long seemed far less disposed than other Western people to define a 'place' for their children, or to act on the belief that children should have a place and be kept in it whatever 'it' might be." In so describing the distinctive American treatment of children, David connected his observations to those of Tocqueville and Gurowsky a full century earlier. David continued: "Europeans . . . frequently find it odd that American adults encourage their young to voice opinions on the most complex and difficult social, economic, and political issues and that they manifest respectful attention to the views that children express on these issues."[60]

David could not have known in 1959 that a tradition of allowing children a vocal role would, within less than half a decade, become a very public and often defining experience as American parents were forced to listen to the very different views of their young on a variety of subjects, including race, sexuality, and the Vietnam War. The startling events on college campuses and in high schools during the late 1960s and early 1970s can be best understood within this tradition. The best-educated generation of children that Americans had ever raised, and the largest, expected their opinions to matter. They had institutions in which they gathered in large numbers, and they proceeded to express those opinions, in very direct language, not because they were permissively raised but because they had been raised in a democratic tradition.[61]

These young people had been provided with special institutional settings that prolonged their dependence on adults while encouraging them to think for themselves. It is also helpful to note that they were children only in twentieth-century terms. Had they been raised at an earlier time, most would have been considered adults. Even someone like Gitlin, who was very young (by our standards) when he became a leader of the New Left, was no younger than many young men who were already supporting families immediately after World War II.[62] He was just about the same age as Alexander Hamilton when he became George Washington's assistant during the Revolutionary War. He was certainly no younger than most Americans in the nineteenth and early twentieth century who, after eight years of schooling, set out to begin business careers and other ventures, sometimes in distant places. As young adults, these Americans believed that they had a right to their views and to a voice in determining their futures. Just past adolescence, young people in the 1960s, like Gitlin, felt that this was just what they were doing.

It was a peculiarity of the second half of the twentieth century (of which the generation of the 1950s and 1960s was the vanguard) that so many young people did not venture off to create independent lives but were still confined in educational institutions and governed by adult-imposed rules. Treated as dependent children, they remained in training to be adults and strained under the confines. Young people in the second half of the twentieth century were confronting the changing facts of an increasingly complex economy that seemed to require more schooling than ever before. In that sense, their experience was a byproduct of American prosperity. But because they were still in school (rather than serving as apprentices in adult-defined environments), the "independence" of young people had a special and unexpected character. Instead of being strictly individual, it was governed by group fervor that spread quickly among peers and along lines that were intensified by youth identification and youth culture, in its various forms of music, body styles, and dress. In the mid 1960s, the politics of generational self-expression became one of those cultural forms as well. Some youth, at the extreme political fringes, took their actions into genuinely militant and often violent directions; most did not. Politics was part of how they defined their progress toward adulthood. Because this was a very large group, and the experience was life altering, young people in the 1960s brought many changes to the American scene.

These changes had profound consequences for the larger society. Some were related to politics and helped to create a new legal conversation about the rights of young people. Others affected questions of personal appearance like hair (for men and women) and clothing, language practice that brought formerly taboo words into public speech, attitudes toward authority, and values regarding work, family, and approved forms of sexuality. As they confronted authorities on campus, at home, on the street, and in the government and expressed themselves vocally about these matters, the behaviors, beliefs, and visual imagery of the students of the 1960s have come to define what we remember about the time.

Youth assertiveness had an effect on law and political status in the most direct way, when the United States changed the voting age from twenty-one to eighteen in 1971, through passage of an amendment to the Constitution. This provided young people with direct access to the normal channels of political expression. But there were a host of other changes, some of them coming through rulings of the Supreme Court, which like other American institutions was witness to the changing times, that helped to bring forward a new perspective on children's rights. Perhaps the most important of these rulings, *In re Gault* (1967) altered the assumptions that prevailed since the institution of juvenile courts early in the twentieth century—that children should be differently treated legally, without any of the usual procedural rights that Americans had come to regard as part of citizenship. Under the guise of protection, children had been denied rights to legal representation and jury trial. By changing this practice, the Supreme Court began to include children more directly into citizenship rights. Court actions also extended to young people the right to public political speech regarding the war and other matters (*Tinker v. Des Moines*, 1969) previously unacknowledged.

Earlier in the twentieth century, the courts and the states had acted to protect childhood rather than to endow children with rights. This new push for the rights of the young in the 1960s did not last very long, as the courts began to backpedal in a variety of ways in the following decades.[63] Before that happened, some Americans began to question the scope of parental controls over their children in new ways. And the push for children's participatory rights had also spread far beyond the United States to become the basis for a fundamental rethinking in the 1989 United Nations Convention on the Rights of the Child. All in all, the 1960s marked a serious moment of change in beliefs that children had voices and rights apart from their parents. How these were to be represented and effected among younger children has still not been clearly established.[64]

In the United States, probably the most long-lasting consequence of the bold questioning of the conventions of adult power that was basic to youth assertiveness affected the roles of young women and girls. In the political rethinking taking place, students sometimes described women's oppression with language drawn from Karl Marx and, especially, Frederick Engels, and condemned bourgeois marriage as the culprit. But that line of argument did not go very far as many young women began to raise questions about inequalities that extended well beyond family life and located its sources in deep attitudes regarding gender that transcended economic systems. The period also saw a new peer-sanctioned normalization of premarital sexual intercourse. This was made possible because better forms of birth control—among them the birth control pill, invented in 1960, and the IUD, introduced at about the same time—reduced the potential for unplanned childbirth. The questioning of women's roles and the assertion of new rights in sex as well as in politics was a broad development that was often vocally promoted by young women, but its sources were just as much derived from the experiences of older women and their unequal treatment in the workplace and in all spheres of public and private life.[65]

The work of young women and girls in the American economy long antedated the demands for equality. Even very young girls, as we have seen, worked in factories, many worked as domestics, others on farms and at in-home industries. And women had been teachers for over a hundred years. By the twentieth century, women's education in academies, high schools, and colleges had introduced middle-class women into higher occupations as secretaries, librarians, nurses, and social workers. While some women worked after they married, and poor women as well as widowed and divorced women had sought employment in any form available, women in the workforce were usually unmarried and did not yet have children. This changed dramatically during and after World War II. The war emergency called upon the energies, resources, and talents of married women and mothers in very large numbers and in new ways, and although immediately after the war, many lost their foothold in the economy, this changed by the mid-1950s as women were once again welcomed into the workforce.[66]

Henry David understood how important this change was and drew attention to it in the fiftieth-anniversary volume of the White House Conference on Children and Youth. According to David, in their preoccupation with children, most Americans had missed the most significant social trend of the second half of the twentieth century, one with singular importance "for the rearing and development of their children and youth. That transformation is the one which has taken place in the employment of women—more particularly in the employment of wives and mothers—outside the home." David then sketched "the scale of the change." In 1890, one-sixth of the nation's workforce were women. "In recent years . . . women have accounted for about 30 percent of the nation's total labor force, and about one-third of all women fourteen years and older have been employed outside the home." Just as significant as their rising proportion was the composition of the female workforce. "As late as 1940, women above forty-five accounted for only a little more than one-fifth of all women in the labor force." Most of the women who worked in the early twentieth century were young and unmarried. But by 1959, almost half of all fifty-year-old women were in the labor force. In fact, young women no longer represented the most conspicuous fraction of the labor force. Their places had been taken by mostly married middle-aged women. "Early in the century, the typical working woman was not only relatively young, but she was also single. Today, she is married. Over the last several years, married women have accounted for 6 of every 10 women in the labor force." During the supposedly domestic 1950s, more than 30 percent of all married women were in the labor force, or as David concluded, *"Since the eve of World War II, the rise in the employment of married women has been spectacular."*[67]

This radical shift in the employment of married women in the workforce paved the way for a revolutionary set of ideas about gender equality, at a time that equality was very much on people's minds in regard to racial matters. Betty Friedan's call in the *Feminine Mystique* (1964) that women be liberated from the illusion that family life provided the only and best realm for women's satisfaction helped to crystallize these ideas. They also came to light when American youth called for the rejection of conventional thinking about politics, about the family, and about sexuality. While we usually do not think of the 1950s as creating a revolution in female experience, as women were then settling down to having larger families in suburban enclaves, surrounded by a growing list of modern conveniences, in fact, it was the 1950s that prepared the ground for the gender revolution.

As the primary caretakers of children, endowed since the nineteenth century with an almost divine maternity and provided in the twentieth with the assistance of scientific authority, the transformation in women's roles was probably the most profound and fundamental of the changes incubated in the 1960s. It would have many consequences for children, as Henry David brilliantly foresaw. Although David entirely missed the revolution on campuses that was just around the corner, in 1959 he was already deeply concerned that married women's growing presence in the labor force could leave children at home with inadequate supervision. And he worried as well about those children being cared for by people other than their mothers. There were no adequate data about "the quality of the care these children actually receive." In the 1950s, "among the ten and eleven-year-old children, 1 out of 5 was expected to care for himself while the mother was at work."[68] Like many observers in the 1950s, David worried that this would feed juvenile delinquency. David did not predict all the particulars of the vast transformation that was about to take place as changing perspectives on marriage, new work opportunities for women, new views of gender roles, and more effective forms of birth control were about to create a profound change in family life. Nor did he ask questions about how women's employment on a vastly larger scale was about to alter normal childhood experience. In fact, these changes initiated by women's increasing workforce participation were about to reshape the conversation about children and childhood as they ushered in a period of great anxiety.[69]

V

The immediate sign of the change was the decline in child bearing. As the number of children born dwindled and their proportion of the population shrank, the baby boom collapsed.[70] This was possibly the most startling result of the social revolution of the late 1960s and early 1970s. The infatuation with children and engagement with childhood of previous decades faded away as quickly as they had appeared. In each of the years 1966, 1967, and 1968, there were 69.9 million children in the population. Eighteen years later, in 1984, there were 62.5 million. While the population had increased from just 200 million to 235 million during this period, the absolute number of children had declined. In fact, the number of children in the population did not return to the 1967 level until 1995, when the population had increased by 70 million people.[71] This decline reflected the sheer drop in the rate of births among American women, from over

25 per 1,000 women from 1952 through 1957 to under 15 births per 1,000 women between 1973 through 1976.[72]

The changes in marriage and divorce statistics were similarly striking. Where women had married very young after World War II, at a median age of 20.5 in 1950, by 1990 the age had increased to 25, and it continued to rise thereafter. Men's age at marriage also rose, though not quite as steeply. In 1950, the median age at marriage for American men was 24 and, by 1990, it had risen to 26.5.[73] The delay in marriage age for women likely accounted for some of the decline in child bearing, but other factors were also responsible. Most conspicuous among these was the extensive use of birth control both by married women and by unmarried women. The latter were thus able to delay marriage but be sexually active, while married women could more carefully determine their pregnancies. And some married couples chose to remain childless, a matter increasingly identified in the media as a lifestyle choice. The *San Francisco Chronicle* headline said it all, "Child-Free Forever: Couples Who Choose 'Lifestyle' and Independence over Babies and the PTA."[74]

Divorce also changed radically during this period. The divorce rate had begun to climb in the 1920s and continued to do so throughout the first half of the twentieth century. After the 1960s, however, it became steep and remained high. Between 1960 and 1980, the divorce rate more than doubled for women in the United States. For those married in 1950, nearly one in three could expect to be divorced, but by 1980 one-half would have their marriages dissolved. In fact, the divorce rate was rising while the marriage rate was declining. The result was a dramatic transformation of expectations about American family life for women, men, and children. Americans were marrying later, and more were remaining unmarried, having fewer children, and divorcing even when there were children at home. This was a new pattern. In the past, not only were divorces more rare, they took place early in marriage and far more often among those without children.[75]

The revolution in ideas about women's roles and a new willingness to express dissatisfaction accounted for some of the change, as women began vigorously to seek a place in all parts of the economy and to demand more equal treatment at home. They could now be found in areas where they had not previously participated—among firemen and policemen, in the boardroom as well as the lunchroom. Women who had started serious careers were often unwilling to marry early or to have children at all, especially since men did not expect to help with either children or housework. When they did have children, it was hard to find adequate child care, as Henry David had discovered in the 1950s—before the pressures to find someone else to care for one's children increased dramatically. The child-care situation was never effectively resolved, even when the need became urgent, as women relied on their own resourcefulness rather than on new, systematic provisions for child care.

These many changes seriously affected children and parenting. As divorce became a more imaginable outcome of marital unhappiness, more women with children ended their marriages. These women often had no choice but to work, even with young children at home. More families were headed by and supported by women, and this became more common with the increase in non-marital childbearing, which picked up by the 1980s. Despite the decline in their absolute numbers, the proportion of children born outside marriage grew rapidly during this same period. By 1980, just over 18 percent of all births were to unmarried women. Twenty years later, that figure had almost doubled to one-third.[76] In the 1970s, on the eve of the great family transformation, that figure had hovered around what today would be considered an extraordinarily low level of just 10 percent.[77]

Federal policies were also changing. In the 1970s through the 1990s, unmarried women who had children could rely on federal financial support, since women who stayed at home to raise their children, without husbands in the household, could expect assistance through the Aid to Families with Dependent Children program, generally known as "welfare." Initially established in the New Deal as part of the safety net created by Social Security, the program was expanded after the war and then again in the 1960s. But in 1992, Democratic candidate Bill Clinton vowed to "end welfare as we know it." In 1996, he did just that when, as president, he signed the Welfare Reform Act.[78] Under the new law, welfare payments would cease after two years and women with young children at home were expected to work.

Welfare reform was accompanied by a number of measures to help struggling families through assistance with child care and earned income tax credits, as well as much more vigorous attempts to collect child support from fathers (both divorced and never married). But as a result, after the turn of the twenty-first century, ever more women were in the labor force, working to support themselves and their dependent children. By then the revolution in family life was complete, as women with even very young children could be regularly found working outside the home. This was in some ways a gradual process from the 1950s through the 2000s, as women became accustomed to leaving their younger and younger children to go to work. By 2012, 57 percent of all mothers of infants could be found in the labor force.[79] But it was hardly gradual from a historical point of view. Over the course of just two generations, women were working almost everywhere in the economy, married women were working at almost the same rate as married men, and women with infants were no longer expected and could not expect to stay at home caring for their children.

Someone who grew up during the student revolts of the 1960s, as I did, even one who was just marginally involved, often finds it hard to believe that anything truly important might have happened elsewhere than on campus or as a result of the shocks imposed by the revolts there. Certainly, the campus youth of the 1960s, and especially those on very activist campuses (I was at Columbia)—deeply influenced by the antiwar movement and demonstrations against the draft, by calls for greater racial equality, and by the early glimmerings of the women's movement—were instrumental in effecting serious social changes with long-lasting consequences. It was one of those historical moments in which people who, in late-twentieth-century terms, were still thought of as children had a clear influence on politics and social trends. But the experiences of students on campus and their attempts to upend conventions were neither sufficient for explaining the new patterns in family and parenting, nor the only sites for these historically significant transformations.

Those changes resulted in part from technological advances that resulted in more effective forms of birth control, such as the pill and the IUD. Initially available to married women only, they were very quickly made available to the unmarried as well.[80] The Civil Rights Act of 1964 barred discrimination based on sex as well as race and became the legal basis for strides toward greater equality of treatment and a profound elevation in young women's expectations. The strong and unremitting momentum toward higher divorce rates was accelerated by "no fault" divorce laws that swept through the states after the first of these laws was passed in California in 1967 and signed by Governor Ronald Reagan—a strong opponent of activist campus culture. Within less than two decades, almost every state had followed suit. The outlier, New York, finally adopted a version of the law in 2010.

The economy, too, had changed. The high wages for American workers, one of the sources of pride in American economic opportunity, began to seriously lag the pace of inflation and the desire for consumer goods essential to middle-class standards of living by the 1970s. Shortly after that, a more interconnected global economy eroded the basis for those wages in the good, stable, unionized manufacturing jobs that had supported family life through the 1950s and 1960s. In fact, by 1990, the opening up of free trade and rapid investment in developing parts of the world like China, Southeast Asia, Mexico, Brazil, and eventually many other places meant that the single-wage, male-headed household that had been the foundation of the family structure since at least World War I could no longer be viewed as an American standard. Women and men, or women without men, now earned a good part of the household income. By the end of the century, it was clear that these changes were irreversible. The stay-at-home American mother as the stable font of childrearing and child care was becoming a historical memory.

Other forces were also altering American families. The most important of these was immigration. In 1968, the United States passed an immigration reform act that removed the quotas that had once confined legal immigration to a population modeled along certain European lines. The new law also encouraged family reunification.[81] No one in 1968 could have predicted the degree to which this would transform the complexion of the American population, and it would not be until well into the twenty-first century that its consequences became visible across the country. Very soon, however, discussions of America's children would have to include many from Asia and Latin

America, as the United States was on the threshold of the largest immigrant surge of its history, one that, for the first time, would be centered not on people who brought Western ideas and habits with them but on those who came from a world far beyond Europe. That migration now brought the world's people into American homes. At a time that family life, views about women, the emphasis on more years of education, and other practices regarding children in Europe were becoming more and more like those in the United States, the new global immigration reintroduced Americans to the strong differences that newcomers could bring into private life and public institutions like schools. After the *Brown* decision, most Americans may have imagined that the most striking difference—that between black and white children—was about to become less important. But soon, other differences were added to the cauldron of America's pluralistic population. In fact, the commitment to all our children that *Brown* enshrined was not yet fully tested by the 1990s, when Americans realized that many others were also becoming part of the American community.

Some of those people were already here in the 1950s, though they were often not visible. In the year that the Supreme Court ruled that segregation in schools was illegal, a young Mexican American girl was following the harvest with her family in Texas. "For thirteen years I lived in the back of a 1942 Army surplus truck, which served as a home, while we followed the annual harvest of cotton, sugar beets, strawberries, cantaloupes, lettuce, and grapes back and forth across America," was how Elizabeth Loza Newby introduced herself to readers of her memoir, *A Migrant with Hope*. The family was lucky to have the truck, which Elizabeth's father had cleaned thoroughly and outfitted with sleeping quarters, water, a stove, and various provisions. It was far better than the crowded, dirty, and disease-ridden quarters that were usually provided for Mexican migrants in the Southwest, quarters that lacked any provision for family privacy.

Elizabeth went to twenty-two different elementary schools when she could go at all, since she was responsible for doing most of the housework in the truck and for preparing meals for her father and brothers. Nevertheless, because her English was so much better than that of her parents, Elizabeth translated for them and also for other migrants: "I was able to translate from English to Spanish while I was still a child. Consequently I was often called to the local courthouse to help migrants understand why they were being arrested, then to interpret for them during the court hearings." Her family, like that of most migrants, had never received professional medical care of any kind, and whatever the breadth of American prosperity and the child-centeredness of the American family, many migrant mothers still died in childbirth and many of their children died in infancy.[82] These children were largely off the national radar, even as the *Brown* decision challenged Americans to distribute its promises to children more equally.

Elizabeth was a gifted and eager student as well as a talented linguist, and despite her constant movement, managed to do well in her academic pursuits. She also found help from a concerned teacher, Mrs. Freeman, who became an important figure in her life, someone who encouraged her and gave her useful advice. But, according to Elizabeth, "In all my migrant life, I never witnessed a truant officer visiting a migrant camp near which we lived." Most students did not go to school and certainly not for long if they did. "Many parents, afraid of school, which meant progress and change, not to mention the lack of money for their children's school needs and clothes, deliberately discouraged attendance. Those who did attend were often placed in classes where they were the oldest, so they felt awkward and out of place. . . . Most migrant children drop out of school and find menial jobs rather than trying to put up with the struggles of securing an education."[83] Elizabeth described a situation that was hardly new in the American experience, since immigrants had reacted similarly earlier in the twentieth century, and many of their children, too, had received minimal schooling. But this deprivation now came as education was seen as central to success and an expected part of childhood—even extended way beyond traditional notions of childhood—at a time when the highest American court had insisted that schooling be made equal and available to all.

In 1954, just after the *Brown* ruling, Elizabeth also had an experience with prejudice, and it came at about the same point in her life as it had for Dorothy Height. As a seven-year-old in second grade, she made friends with a "little blue-eyed blond named Kathy, who happened to be the daughter of the town mayor. . . . She was the first real friend I had ever had. . . . We ate lunches together in school and talked about our families." But the camaraderie ended when Kathy's father saw the two walking from school together one day, at which point he grabbed his daughter by the arm and directed her home. "The next morning, when I stopped by the tree where we usually met so we could walk to school together, Kathy was not there." Nor did they ever play together again. Kathy explained to Elizabeth: "My father told me that you are different, and I am not allowed to play with you anymore." Elizabeth "was stunned," but found consolation in the wisdom and kindness of Mrs. Freeman, who explained some of the realities of American social attitudes to her.[84]

Elizabeth's experience of difference, of being required to help her parents, of moving from school to school, of translating for adults, and of a life shut out from the advantages of middle-class America would become a more common experience as immigration picked up in the last two decades of the twentieth century. So, too, did the attitudes of parents like the Lozas, some of whom kept their children from school, expected them to help by working in the household and outside, and had still to learn what America might offer their children.

The changing world economy with its implications for household finances, the altered roles for married women, new immigration resulting in a still more complex population, and the ever more dominant role of schooling in the lives of children began to set out a whole new agenda for American parents as the millennium approached. Instead of the heady confidence of worldwide victory after the war and the belief that where the United States led, the rest of the world would follow, Americans began to worry about the future and how to prepare their children in ways that, while not entirely new, were still challenging in their scope and persistence.

CHAPTER 6

What's the Matter
with Kids Today?

Americans aspire from a thousand different backgrounds and
special, atypical experiences. . . . So it is not only not possible
to describe in consistent detail all the steps taken by all the
different sorts of Americans in the journey toward adulthood,
but it is also not possible for any one of us to feel that the steps
were perfectly taken.

—MARGARET MEAD (1949)[1]

Never a complacent people, and with a long history of worrying about
the future of their children, Americans today have become ever more
vocal about their discontents. Since the 1980s, the sense of crisis has
been invoked in the barrage of books, articles, and online sites that
emphasize the problems of children and the travails of parenting.
Appealing to the public's normal anxieties, these have upped the ante
by presenting worries about the future as especially urgent in the context of a manifestly globalized and ruthlessly competitive economy.
Today, many parents seem obsessed with the success of their children
and eager to assure their progeny at least the standard of living they
have enjoyed.

The growing sense of urgency about these matters has accumulated like lava from the volcanic changes first observed in the 1970s.
Together, these changes seem to have smothered most attempts at optimism: the massive movement of mothers into the workforce and its
disruptive consequences at home; the difficulties finding adequate and
safe childcare; deteriorating public school performance as measured
against international standards; the expenses associated with college

and university attendance, now viewed as a necessity for success; the onslaught of new media penetrating first into the home and then into the hands of children; the problems of immigrant children who are inadequately absorbed into national life; and the high performance of some immigrant children at school that has made previously complacent parents turn fearfully toward schooling alternatives, testing, and additional preparation for their own. Finally, the growing inequality among American children now appears to be eroding the once regnant confidence in the possibilities of the American dream of opportunity. This list is hardly comprehensive. It doesn't touch on the direct threats to children's safety regularly paraded in public—kidnapping, drugs, guns, faulty car seats and play toys, dangerous vaccines, and sexual predators, now seen to be a problem not only on unfamiliar streets but in the ivied halls of college. At various points over the past thirty years, these and other dangers have stoked the fears of large segments of the parent population, fears fed by intense media attention.

It is quite rare today to come across a book that shines an optimistic and hopeful light on contemporary family life, such as the one published early in the twenty-first century by Peter Likins, the former president of the University of Arizona, as a paean to a new multicultural America. *A New American Family* (2011) offers family life as an ideal and suggests something about its complexities. Likins grew up in California, in a household supported by a single mother of four (her husband had abandoned them) who lived for years in a two-room backwoods cabin without electricity or heat during the so-called idyllic apogee of family life and economic prosperity of the 1950s. Married young to his high school sweetheart, Likins went through school on scholarships, fellowships, and an array of jobs that helped with expenses. After graduating from Stanford, he went on to MIT for graduate work, eventually returning to Stanford for a doctoral degree. After a stint as a practicing engineer, he enjoyed a highly successful career as a college professor and academic administrator. But his successful ascent from adverse personal circumstances is not at the center of Likins's story. Rather it is the unusual family that he and his wife, Patricia, created along the way.

Pete and Pat Likins adopted six children of varying cultural and racial backgrounds (African American, Native American, and Chicano), creating a family that looked like America even before the United States became a manifestly minority-majority culture: black, brown, white. It contained children who were talented and academically challenged, fat and thin, tall and short, athletic and clumsy. His family, Likins believes, represents a new American ideal, though it is hardly perfect, a family whose members supported each other and put up with the faults of its various and very different members and their tribulations, while glorying in its small and large achievements. Both Pete and his wife adore and value each of their children, even the one who became a drug addict and eventually died of an overdose that was as much a willful act as an accident. He, too, is part of what Likins calls in his subtitle "A Love Story," an emotional valence that the reader is made to feel on every page.[2]

This paean to children and parenting is increasingly rare at a time when personal memoirs are often exposés of abusive parents and difficult childhoods, and childrearing advice comes more and more frequently in response to fear and anxiety. Judith Warner, a popular author and sometime *New York Times* opinion columnist, argues that parenting has become "poisoned" through "a cocktail of guilt and anxiety and resentment and regret."[3] In the last two decades of the twentieth century and in the years since the start of the new millennium, as the United States entered a new global age, American parents became both the subject and the audience for a literature of complaint and disappointment. To review only the titles of some of these (in history, sociology and commentary) gives a sense of the matter: *Parenting Out of Control, Anxious Parents, All Joy and No Fun, Perfect Madness, Cut Adrift*.[4] The audience for these laments is heavily drawn from the upper middle class in social standing and aspiration. As we shall see, the American population of parents and children is much larger and their concerns more complex than those who worry about whether the kids get into Duke or Dartmouth, but it is often the smaller groups that set the tone of the conversation. And the relationship between the generations is far more subtle than that described in even the most engaging and insightful of the many books that have become famous examples of this genre and most likely to appear on best-seller lists.[5] We want to look at this varied array of relationships before we conclude either that we have a genuinely new crisis or, as the title of this book suggests, whether we have come to the end of a recognizably American childhood. And for those not old enough to remember the song whose refrain serves as the title of this chapter, it comes from *Bye Bye Birdie*, a 1950s musical about rock-and-roll music and the crazy teens who idolize one of its singers. The focus on "our kids," their travails, and generational misunderstandings is not new—something to remember as we ask how much has changed and why.

I

A good example of the tone of the books about parenting that define the genre today is *All Joy and No Fun*, Jennifer Senior's appealing reflection on what she calls in her subtitle "The Paradox of Modern Parenting."[6] Senior documents the many annoyances that accompany childrearing, the frazzled pace of modern mothers' lives, their sense of inadequacy as they make large demands on themselves and their children for high performance. Senior has a sharp understanding of several important facts about contemporary parenting. She knows that her middle-class readers invest money and time in their children's success. She recognizes the fundamental, unspoken, reality of parenting in our time—that giving birth is now a choice for most middle-class women, a choice with great potential consequences.[7] It is an investment in time taken from other areas, and one that is expected to be worthwhile as women forgo other satisfactions. Today, middle-class women who raise children are better educated than ever and more valuable to the economy. Women making the choice to have children are, for the first time in history (the exceptions in the past were a small minority), deeply involved in professional careers or work lives with which they identify and their contributions have a high social worth.[8] Senior's book is addressed to these women.

Senior understands the many problems faced by such women in the daily grind of parenting. At the same time, because it lacks real historical depth, her perspective is limited and some of what she has to say is misleading. Senior believes that one of the critical changes in parenting relates to the fact that after World War II, children stopped contributing to the household economy to become exclusively emotional assets to family life. Like many others who are engaged in the conversation about parenting, Senior has a very truncated sense of the history of parents and children in the United States, a history which, as we have seen, has followed many twists and turns to provide us with a complex inheritance. Children in middle-class households stopped being economically useful to their families long before World War II (although not all children left the work world entirely even after the war, and some are there today). Viewing children as the emotional center of family life and the objects of unconditional love has dominated our values since the nineteenth century. What happened after World War II had little to do with the economic marginalization of children, although it does relate to the vast democratization of expectations about family life, childhood, and schooling. Americans had emphasized emotional connections between parents and their children for more than a century, an emphasis sufficiently in place by the 1920s to make psychologist and childrearing advisor John Watson exert all his influence to try to put a brake on mothers' affections. And as far back as 1874, Christian Ross, Charley Ross's distraught father, was spending most of his time and resources demonstrating how much he loved his young son and how unwilling he was to calculate that love in economic terms.[9] What differentiates today's middle-class parents from those in the past is neither the fact that their children are not expected to work nor the emotional load of family relationships.

Conversations today about parents and children exist within a hazy vision of just how exactly contemporary parenting differs from parenting even fifty years ago when, in the aftermath of World War II, American children inherited a sense of the great potentials of their future lives. And few contemporary commentators realize that Americans have had a long tradition of worrying about whether they are doing all they can for their children. Margaret Mead understood that an emphasis on ideal parenting was built into the bloodstream of a fast-moving society where the aspirations of many newcomers intermingled with older dreams of perfection to create painful dissatisfactions.

Today's privileged middle- and upper-middle-class families, to whom most of the contemporary books and articles are directed, seem to be unaware of the difficulties, discomforts, and dissatisfactions that parents have long endured. Making them aware of the inherent difficulties of parenting is certainly one of the aims of Jennifer Senior's book. But why our concerns have taken the particular form they do today requires a fuller, more historically informed understanding than even Senior's thoughtful observations allow.

Unlike any previous time in history, child bearing is no longer seen to be part of the natural order, and having children today is a choice that may also involve a variety of other decisions. Indeed, not having children at all has become a real choice for many women. Twenty percent of all women who reach ages forty to forty-four today have no children—twice the rate of thirty years ago.[10] After that initial decision, parents make many other choices, not only about timing, but about the nature of the child (or children) they will bear and rear, since *in vitro fertilization* has become part of the process of conception for some and genetic testing for many more. The choice to parent at all, and how best to do so, is thus viewed as both subject to manipulation and freighted with consequences. Once the child is born, parents are confronted with a difficult balancing act about work and home that makes them eager to be as much in control as possible. It is the striving for control, not a new emotionalism, that differentiates family life today from that fifty or one hundred years ago.[11]

In the 1920s, by contrast, when women used birth control to limit and time conceptions, very few continued to work after their children arrived; and in the 1950s, mothers who went back to work did so when the children were already well along in school.[12] Spending their time at home with their young children was viewed as natural, and Dr. Spock tried to encourage that sense of ease. Today, many professional women go back to work very soon after childbirth, or if they feel overwhelmed by the multiple demands this places on their energy and the time they have with their young children, they fall

back into full-time parenting, although this is often not a fully satis-
factory alternative. Trained to succeed and to be rewarded, educated
women put as much "work" and effort into raising their children as
they do in demanding jobs and also expect to reap the rewards.[13] Once
having children is defined as an individual choice, American parents
often imagine that when they do not succeed or are less than completely successful, or their children are disappointing, it is somehow
their fault. Having made the choice, they are obligated to do it right.[14]
Rather than it being natural, it is seen as a strenuous battle.

Today's lamentations about family life and childrearing have such
a limited historical perspective that contemporary parents seem to be
the first ever to be overwhelmed or feel inadequately prepared for the
tasks they face and the sacrifices they are required to make. The reading
public is left blissfully unaware of the difficulties mothers like Harriet
Beecher Stowe faced as she tried to raise her seven children in straight-
ened circumstances (her husband, Calvin Stowe, was never a success),
while striving to write important novels and books about domestic life
in the middle of the nineteenth century. Even then, when mothering
was assumed to be an expression of divine grace, women were harried and needed advice (and consolation) for which they often turned
to each other or to women's magazines. Stowe too lived amidst challenging social changes that were deeply disquieting to many mothers.
And women complained then, too, about the lack of personal time,
the unending hard work, and their required self-denial even when sacrifice was believed to be in a mother's bloodstream. I use this example,
out of many, to suggest that even thoughtful writers eager to inform
readers about the necessary demands and difficulties of parenting have
no effective way to explain how we differ from earlier Americans in
regard to parenting because they are handicapped by a lack of historical depth. Current discussions about both children and their parents
are marked by a striking absence of substantial historical knowledge.
Even when a bit of history is introduced, it is usually far too short in
duration to provide an effective basis either for understanding where
our views come from or for making useful comparisons. As a result,
these discussions are not nearly as useful as they could be.

A deeper historical sense would allow us to realize that American views today rest on an unprecedented vision of the succession of

generations—that a parent's death will precede that of children. In fact, this view has come to seem "natural" only within the past century. It allows us to imagine that a child's death is the worst experience that can happen or has ever before befallen parents. Our memories are short indeed: only since the beginning of the twentieth century have killer childhood diseases like diphtheria and smallpox and many waterborne ailments deadly to infants come under our control; only in the middle of the twentieth century did very common diseases like measles and rubella, and scourges like polio, become fading memories as a result of vaccines; wounding diseases and life-threatening ailments like ear infections, meningitis, and pneumonia have been treatable only since the late 1930s because of sulfa drugs and antibiotics. The ability of mothers to exercise some "control" in such life and death matters began, as we have seen, in the second and third decades of the twentieth century and introduced a major alteration in parenting possibilities.

The historical blindness from which privileged Americans suffer is not the only source of discontent. Many Americans are becoming insulated from the real-life experiences of the less privileged as class lines have become more impermeable and neighborhoods more class stratified. As the distinguished political scientist Robert Putnam shows in *Our Kids*, the growing class divide that materialized over the past thirty years is affecting children's lives and their future prospects and severs the lives of the more privileged and the less advantaged from each other. This coincides almost exactly with the growing sense of crisis as expressed by middle-class parents. Putnam also shows how little those who are privileged know (or care) about the children of those who are not. This divide may well be a source of the fear that seems to haunt middle-class American parents as they imagine what an unsuccessful child might face in the future. But it also means that parents who hope to control their children's future fail to appreciate that their children, too, will need to respond to the unpredictable circumstances of change that are affecting the children of the less fortunate.

Children's lives today tend to break along different lines that involve not just class and ethnicity but household composition, and these social categories often overlap. If privileged parents suffer from the pains of high expectations, others suffer from the penalties that accompany bad choices in terrible circumstances or an absence of real choice. That unpredictability involves more than just economics. In the United States today, far fewer children than ever live with two parents, a problem less common among upper- and middle-class children than the children of the poor. Two-parent households, whether composed of heterosexual or same-sex couples, provide children with many important advantages. But, as Isabel Sawhill of the Brookings Institution has observed, for many Americans "[m]arriage is disappearing," and with it many of the benefits that a two-parent household provides. As the taboos on premarital sex have declined since the 1980s, the shame once attached to conception outside of marriage has subsided. Today, 40 percent of all children are born to unmarried women, some of whom are in temporarily stable relationships likely to dissolve within five years.[15] These children are often conceived thoughtlessly, either in the absence of contraception or by its ineffective use, by women who realize that they are unlikely to marry partners with solid jobs and prospects. The jobs their partners might once have held are now either transferred to other parts of the globe or made obsolete by technology.

While the problems of fragile families are often the target of conservative social critics, the struggles of these families are a subject that both liberals and conservatives agree on. Children in one-parent families are twice as likely to live below the poverty line and are much more likely to grow up in homes with rocky economic foundations even if they are not technically poor. The concerns of single mothers usually do not revolve around ideals of perfection.[16] Instead, these mothers are eager to maintain some minimal level of control over their children as their own lives are repeatedly disrupted by unemployment, underemployment, ill health, the need to maintain several jobs, inadequate child care, new and unstable boyfriends, unsupportive schools, and the general hazards of life lived in insecurity. Depending on the neighborhood they can afford to live in, they may also be deeply worried about crime, gangs, guns, and drive-by shootings.[17]

Even access to the technologies that make choice and the illusion of control available for some parents today is unevenly distributed. This is true for contraception and abortions, as well as for the techniques that can detect Down syndrome, since access to genetic testing is easily available only to those with money. Children with Down syndrome, according to Andrew Solomon, "are not evenly distributed across the population. Eighty percent of Down syndrome births are to women under thirty-five who have not had testing, and many of these are poor; wealthier people are more likely to seek prenatal testing even if they are not in a risk category," usually associated with women over thirty-five years old.[18]

Unlike most contemporary writing on parenting which deals with mundane discomforts and dissatisfactions of daily life, Solomon addresses the uncommon sorrows of parenting. By exploring the responses of parents whose lives have become a nightmare, parents whose children have disabilities such as autism or dwarfism, or suffer from severe mental illness or commit horrible crimes, he forces readers to confront the deep, inexorable riskiness of bearing children. Many of these conditions cannot yet be identified through even the most refined prenatal testing. Solomon thus inverts the perfectionism of contemporary middle-class family expectations and tries to connect parents from all socioeconomic and ethnic groups who share these extreme difficulties. A really troubled child, or one who is very far beyond our normal expectations, profoundly transforms the life of parents—and does so forever. Such a child forces parents to confront what it means to love one's child, presses up against the limits of one's devotion to caretaking, and destroys the dream of success. As one of the mothers of an autistic child (a woman who became "depressed, overwhelmed, even suicidal") tells Solomon, "I can't give up on my child. She didn't ask to be born; she didn't ask to have this problem. . . . If I don't take care of her, who's going to do it?"[19] Solomon and the reader are, in fact, impressed by the parents' endurance and love for their children, parents whose shattered lives make the minor complaints of most parents privileged to have ordinary children seem petty. As one mother, Angelica Roman-Jiminez, relates about her child with Down syndrome, "When your child is born with a disability, all your high hopes and dreams are shattered." She describes her joy when her daughter is able to pick up a Cheerio and her reaction to a doctor who would put tubes in her ears so she could be more adept at language. "So the doctor said, 'Well, she's not going to be perfect.' I felt, how dare he say that? He's never going to be perfect either."[20]

Some of Solomon's parents rise to very trying challenges; all of them have no choice but to cope. Many turn to others with similar problems for support and information. Laura and Harry Slatkin, wealthy New Yorkers, became deeply committed to helping other parents in similar circumstances, and endowed a special public school for autistic children, a school their own son could not take advantage of because of the severity of his disability. They have also worked with a program to train teachers who deal with such children. The Slatkins had tried everything they could for their own son, and paid for elaborate tutoring and skills training, but found that nothing worked. "Your son," they were told by their doctor, "is probably the most severely affected child I've ever seen."[21] The grief felt by parents like these transcends class, religion, ethnicity, and time and goes to the bone of what it means to be a parent.

In exploring how parents respond to children like these, and how they sustain their obligations, Solomon opens to view aspects of parenting ignored by most of the contemporary literature and to which most parents almost never attend. But his inquiry into extremes should be understood within the context of that broader literature. By the last decades of the twentieth century, after the rapid advance of the birth control revolution, within the context of legalized abortions and the advent and development of DNA science, and at a time that almost all children survive birth and early life, many privileged parents have been absorbed in illusions of control and ideals of perfection. These illusions affect the middle and upper middle classes especially, because they have the resources and access to professionals that allow careful supervision of nutrition during pregnancy, monitoring by genetic tests, and knowledge provided by the latest and best childrearing advice, now available for free and at a moment's notice online. In all this, the sense of control becomes the defining illusion of our time.

One of the more ironic results of the widespread availability of advice online is that the term "Mom," weighted with venom and spoken in tones of severe opprobrium after World War II when it was associated with emotionally destructive mothers, now dominates thousands of websites and blogs that offer advice and the opportunity for parents to respond and express their views.[22] These online communities exist to help mothers like those interviewed by Solomon by providing them with important networks and information. The online world also addresses those with more ordinary concerns—soccer moms, working moms, moms against vaccination, moms with children adopted from Asia or South America, vegan moms, and moms who seek perfection. The online world likes short words, so "Mom" has been rescued from its ignominy.[23] This virtual world gives expression to many contemporary parental concerns and can intensify the feeling that parents have control, since so much information is readily accessible and connections can be made at the push of a button or the tap of a screen.

Because this world is interactive, mothers (and fathers) can support and/or blame each other for their failures and reflect on them publicly. It also increases the barrage of both advice and complaints. As childrearing advisor Dr. Alanna Levine observes, "The blogosphere buzzes around the clock, chewing over new child-care fads that seem to crop up every month. The debates surrounding these fads are downright fierce, and the mommy boards are quick to scold parents who venture to stray from the latest accepted wisdom."[24] Judith Warner describes "the climate in which we now mother," as "in many ways, just plain crazy."[25] And the disappointment and craziness is overwhelmingly about experiences with normal children, not distress about children who take parents beyond the usual realm of family problems and into a world of extreme despair.

In *Battle Hymn of the Tiger Mother*, Amy Chua plays into the current middle-class obsession with control by castigating mothers for not doing their work well enough. As a result, in her view, most American children do not measure up. Shrewdly aware of the desire for perfection, she displays the academic and musical achievements of her two daughters, Sophia and Lulu, raised in traditional Chinese fashion to fear their mother and honor their ancestors. These girls are kneaded and baked according to old-world formulas where parental dictates take over the child's will to determine its current desires and future goals. Raised to fear and obey their mother, the girls are not allowed to have sleepovers (a modern middle-class ritual often resisted by im-migrant parents), must practice their musical instruments for hours (as Kate Simon also was required to do by her strict immigrant fa-ther in the 1920s), and are denied their toys and stuffed animals if they are recalcitrant. This "memoir" by a successful career woman and perfectionist mother appears to profoundly question the long-standing American commitment to the right of children to make their own decisions. Chua sees this belief as an American indulgence that encourages mothers to coddle their children and worry about their delicate psyches while permitting them to be easily pleased by mediocre performance.[26]

More explicitly, Chua is responding to the trend in the late twen-tieth century to elevate self-esteem among children as a basic goal of parenting (and schooling).[27] And indeed, the emphasis on self-esteem, while hardly exclusively American (many European parents have read the same literature), was commonly invoked as American parents became concerned about repression and its consequences for their children's sense of self-worth and confidence. Books like *Your Child's Self-Esteem* by Dorothy Corkille Briggs (translated into many European languages) and others like it were widely available and exaggerated the importance and ease of providing children with a guilt-free childhood. In this vision, an individual child's right to feel good about herself becomes the almost exclusive principle of good parenting. "Nos" are carefully hoarded for extreme situations. Early self-esteem in children was meant to lead to independence and cre-ativity in emotionally secure adults. "Some childish innovations, of course, cannot be accepted because they endanger health, safety, or are grossly out of place. But whenever possible, accept each sign of initiative," was one of Briggs's guidelines. For many, few issues seemed as burdened with developing self-esteem as potty training, especially among two-year-olds. "You go a long way toward preserving your sanity and your child's self-esteem by either forgetting toilet training during this period, or clearly indicating that he rules in this depart-ment."[28] Not surprisingly, potty training is an important point of con-tention in contemporary disputes over how best to raise children and often serves as the basis for accusations of coddling.[29] The failure of

American parents to train their children early in this area has often been seen as synonymous with their tendency toward permissiveness and toward letting their children have their way.

Since we sometimes blame psychiatrists and childrearing experts for the perceived American tendency to coddle egos and to indulge children, some childrearing experts have responded with a sharp eye to protecting their turf and their values. One very well respected child-rearing expert, Dr. Marilyn Heins, has posted on her website a some-what defensive response to Chua's book under the title "Tiger Mom vs Wimp Mom." "As I have said many times before, self-esteem is not only overrated in importance but it is not something a parent can bestow. It develops from the blending of UNCONDITIONAL LOVE given to the child and COMPETENCY developed by the child. It does not come about through incessant parental praise, parental indul-gence, or parental reluctance to discipline the child. . . . Learning, acquiring the skills needed to be a competitive part of the new global economy, and reaching your full potential is not optional. It is not a game. It is HARD WORK . . . . I believe there are too many US parents out there who never tell their kids that they expect them to do that hard work. . . . If you are a mom who is all cuddles and apt to wimp out when the time calls for demands, think about your parenting. Do you really want to give your child the message that mediocrity is OK?"[30] No doubt, this is sound advice, but it suggests how deeply Chua's book seems to question basic psychological values.

In fact, Chua's book became a sensation not because most Ameri-can parents today coddle children (although some do), but rather be-cause they are worried that whatever they are doing may not lead to their children's success. The book was the subject of extended cover-age in newspapers and magazines across the country, part of parents' conversations, and read in mothers' groups. It was also a stimulus to website advice like that of Dr. Heins because American parents fear that they may not know what the solution is and they are buffeted by so many demands and so many kinds of advice, all leading to ele-vated anxiety about their children's successful development and their adequacy to ensure it. The continuing commitment to an ideal of perfection in the midst of such anxiety is very troubling indeed. The publication of *Battle Hymn of the Tiger Mom* hit a sensitive nerve, and it is worth reflecting about the particular synapses that came into play when her book became a best seller in 2012.

II

Are Americans spoiling their children, undermining their character, and wrecking their chances for success? How much should children be directed to goals set by their parents? And is this a national crisis? These questions are at the heart of the response to Amy Chua's book, and it underlies much of the discussion about harried, worried, overwrought parenting in the last several decades. One recent study found that "Seventy-three percent of parents report that they worry occasionally or frequently about their ability to provide appropriate discipline."[31] These worries partly reflect new fears about worldwide competition for global economic success, as Dr. Heims' website makes clear. These fears are often expressed in educational terms, such as the relatively low ranking of American school children in PISA (Programme for International Student Assessment) testing, as well as lackluster performance in the growing number of tests now in place to evaluate how American schools are doing since passage of the No Child Left Behind legislation in 2001. Some of the fears result from a perceived "problem" that Amy Chua was also playing off—that the children of newer immigrants are displacing the children of Americans of longer residence at the head of the line academically and professionally.

In most cases, the American child is being implicitly or explicitly compared with standards derived from outside the United States, or with children from non-American backgrounds. As we have become aware of global competition, America's economic supremacy seems to have become wobbly. So, too, its educational edge, long a consequence of the extended democratic schooling offered to almost all American children, has been blunted. Of course, immigrants and the children of immigrants are also American, as Chua and her daughters are, and they are contributing not only to America's already diverse childrearing alternatives but to American success. But the matter is rarely seen in this way.

In thinking about Chua's book, we bring the question of childrearing back into an international context from which it first arose in the late eighteenth century after the Revolution, when Americans began to focus on their children's future and to ask how their childrearing practices should differ from others' in the circumstances of the New World and the new republic. Chua is not alone in doing this. During the past several years, what differentiates American children and their parents from children and parents elsewhere has been much on people's minds. Elsewhere today means not just Europe, from which Americans often differentiated themselves in the past, but also Asia and Latin America, from which the majority of all immigrants now arrive. In fact, European childrearing practices have grown closer to those of the United States since World War II. In the last half-century, especially, middle-class Europeans have embraced a much more democratic model of family relations with a much reduced emphasis on family hierarchy and paternal authority, while the European states have promoted higher levels of education for all children as part of their turn toward democratic values. Indeed, some European countries today are further along in their emphasis on children's rights than the United States; some like the Scandinavian countries have adopted the United Nations Convention on the Rights of the Child (1989), with its emphasis on children's active participation in decision making as a yardstick for their own policies.[32] At the same time, the robust growth of Asian and Latin American economies and steady immigration from these places to the United States are raising troubling questions about whether the habits of character and work that long made the United States enviously successful in the world will continue.

In their blockbuster books about the crisis in childrearing, both Amy Chua and Judith Warner argue for notable distinctions between how American mothers treat their children and how mothers elsewhere discipline and raise their young. Although they are interested in two different dimensions of the problem, their conclusions are remarkably similar: Warner believes American mothers would be far better off and far less overwhelmed if they were less self-sacrificing and brought more discipline to their interactions with their children; Chua argues that children would be better prepared for the world they will be facing if their mothers were far stricter in their discipline and more demanding regarding their children's performance. Both emphasize the need for adult demands and greater discipline, and both assume that Americans are weak in this regard. While Americans are often blamed today for being in thrall to childrearing experts, most commentators seem unaware of the fact that such looser styles and more lenient forms of discipline have a long history and were once viewed as the source of American competitive strength and the basis of American identity. And they seem ignorant of the degree to which childrearing experts have themselves been immersed in this tradition, conforming their ideas to values that long antedated their advice.

American childrearing practices are currently both under the microscope and under attack, and it is a good time to think about them in historical terms. By emphasizing the future over the past, resourceful innovation over convention and tradition, Americans have historically looked favorably to the independent spirit of children rather than to an imposed discipline that would reproduce the past.[33] This should not be confused with imposing no boundaries on children's behavior; in fact, parents from many backgrounds used discipline to rein in unacceptable behavior. Rather, as Count Gurowsky observed in the middle of the nineteenth century, and economist Henry David understood in 1959, in the United States children's "place" was less clearly delimited and defined. Is this still a good guide to how to raise children in the twenty-first century? This question is at the root of contemporary conversations about "wimp" mothers.

Despite a long tradition of allowing children a great deal of freedom to define their own paths, there is very little evidence that the majority of American parents past or present have been inattentive to the task of effectively overseeing their children's development and preparing them for the future. Today, however, an obsession with perfection by upper- and middle-class mothers in the context of a changing world, fears about future success, and continuing self-criticism and criticism by others are redefining the terms of the problem. Increasingly fearful that the slightest deviation in oversight will ruin their children's carefully prepared path into the future, parents yield to their most directive instincts and attempt to manage all parts of their children's lives, whether those children are two months or two years, twelve or twenty: better strict supervision than failure. And this perspective has begun to organize how we view and evaluate the parenting of others. We expect all parents to oversee their children in minute detail, and when they do not, many parents are tempted to call the police. As *New York Times* columnist Ross Douthat has noted about this trend, it begins with "upper class, competition-driven vision of childhood as a rigorously supervised period in which unattended play is abnormal, risky, weird. This perspective . . . has encouraged bystanders and public servants to regard a deviation from constant supervision as a sign of parental neglect."[34]

Historically, negative comments about the lack of discipline of American children were attached to contemptuous views about the habits of Americans generally, while concerns about negligent supervision were applied to the ruder classes. One nineteenth-century observer noted, "Baby citizens are allowed to run wild as the Snake Indians and do whatever they please." The comment suggests the equivalence drawn between Americans' lack of restraint on their children and their "less civilized" circumstances. Americans were accused, and sometimes accused themselves, of a wayward disregard for authority that was transferred to their children. Children were less often instructed in the niceties of polite deportment, which offended those who believed in a more refined and proper upbringing. Thus the *Presbyterian Magazine* in the 1850s observed, "The signs of the want of family discipline appear in the waywardness of the children while yet they are young" who are "allowed to treat their parents with disrespect—indulged in all their whims and caprices." These children would naturally become rude and overly familiar with strangers.[35] This view neatly corresponds to Warner's observations about "the breakdown of boundaries between children and adults and the erosion, for many families, of any notion of adult time and space" in the twenty-first century. "Nowhere," a nineteenth-century French commentator concluded, "are children so free, so bold, such *enfants terrible*, as in America."[36] Back from France, where they were impressed by mothers' easier time in the early twenty-first century, two recent commentators on American children, Judith Warner and Pamela Druckerman, echo this sentiment.[37] Certainly much has changed in two hundred years, but the tendency to evaluate Americans as insufficiently cultured and their children as undisciplined seems to have endured.

Scholars agree that cultural patterns and values influence child-rearing and that childrearing reinforces these patterns.[38] And, certainly the American imagination has produced plenty of examples of children who are rude and saucy but also cute, natural spirits, from Huckleberry Finn to Dennis the Menace and Bart Simpson. This cultural preference does not mean that American parents encourage their children to be disrespectful or helplessly abdicate parental controls over children. Of course, some normally caring American parents do lose control. This happened in the 1950s to even the most attentive readers of Dr. Spock, who mistook relaxed engagement for permissiveness, and it happened earlier in the century, sufficiently often to make the first serious historian of the family, Arthur Calhoun, condemn modern parents for inattention to their children as they pursued their materialist goals in a capitalist economy.[39]

Similarly, accusations that some parents show disregard for children's welfare and neglect their needs was deeply part of the middle-class reform impulse since the mid-nineteenth century, when the Children's Aid Society, and later the Societies for the Prevention of Cruelty to Children, set out to rescue the abused. These commitments led to the creation of social work in the early twentieth century and to campaigns against child labor. And they underwrote the origin of the Children's Bureau, the first federal agency devoted to children's health and welfare. Fears regarding the results of neglect and disregard for children's needs were at the root of the welfare state. Americans have worried about children whose parents seem unable or unwilling to care adequately for them since early in the history of the republic. But neither attempts to assist those who are perceived as negligent nor attacks on Americans' lack of discipline in themselves and in their children should be confused with a general cultural disregard for the proper rearing of children. These were, instead, signs of the importance of childrearing as a national commitment.

Margaret Mead understood why American childrearing patterns could be so confusing to observers. American aspirations were such an amalgam of immigrant sources attached to a native belief in an ever-improving future and a desire for individual perfection that they were difficult to define and pin down. "Are there not unbridgeable gaps between the immigrant mother who sets her baby gently in a cradle that she brought from the Old World and the young American mother imbued with ideas of schedules and hygiene who sternly lets her baby in its thumb-sucking-proof blanket cry its heart out because it is not time for the next feeding, and the ultra-modern mother who has abandoned schedules and feeds her baby on self-demand? . . . [H]ow indeed can one say anything at all about American babies, and about how American babies become men and women, able—or unable—to love and beget children?"[40] Mead nevertheless concluded that Americans did have recognizable forms for producing the next generation.

Certainly, the accusation that American mothers coddle their children is not new. One American observer of family life in the early twentieth century noted that "the average American baby is cared for in abject worship by its mother and the household is turned topsy-turvy for the benefit of this smallest member"—a sentiment the mothers interviewed by Jennifer Senior and Judith Warner would no doubt fully understand.[41] Children have been the focus of middle-class households for at least a hundred years. As mothers' chores became easier in the late nineteenth century and the number of children in the family declined significantly, it was possible to turn childrearing into the focus of domestic attention. These same changes also released older daughters from many family obligations to the household, so they could turn instead to school and to work outside the house, and toward participation in public reform efforts.[42] This dual reality—one in which children became the central concern of mothers, while women were liberated into a larger world, is today the source of the complaints about women's frazzled and overburdened lives and the difficult choices they need to make. The changes in women's experience have not taken place suddenly. They are a product of a long history.

What foreigners and Americans have in mind when they challenge Americans' effective supervision of their children while accusing them of excessive coddling are usually confusions about the proper balance between caring guidance and the traditional commitment to encouraging "independence" in children. Both John Dewey in promoting "progressive" education and Benjamin Spock in emphasizing children's "autonomy" in the nursery understood just how delicate this balance could be. Both were also accused of permissiveness. The conscious commitment to independence continues to distinguish American parents from what may seem to be quite similar child-centered patterns among Europeans, as ethnographers Sara Harkness and Charles Super discovered when they compared American and Dutch parents. American parents much more frequently emphasize individual attention, active interaction, and the developmental needs of the child, matters they view as effective means for developing independence in their children. Dutch parents put their faith in regularity of habits (rest, quiet, and cleanliness) and family time together, especially around meals, thus emphasizing the unified goals of the family group. One result of these different goals in households equally devoted to children's welfare was that American parents were often tired and appeared frazzled. They tended to complain about their children's sleeping habits and gave in to their demands because they were too exhausted to fight in the middle of the night. Dutch parents rarely had a problem with their children regarding sleep because they simply adhered to a strict schedule. The devotion to viewing the child as an individual seems to be much more deeply part of how American mothers and fathers approach childrearing than is the case for the Dutch, with the side effect that American parents seem to be more confused and are often sleep deprived.[43]

In fact, despite their overt dedication to independence, the specifics among American families have varied quite a lot. American childrearing advice today and in the past has been all over the map on issues such as weaning, toilet training, or sleeping patterns, with some experts encouraging a more laissez-faire attitude and others a more rigid enforcement of rules. None of these matters in themselves define American childrearing.[44] A study of the views of the five currently most popular childrearing experts has shown that a broad set of possibilities are offered to parents today. This includes the intensive demands of attachment parenting promoted by Penelope Leach, the more discipline-heavy views of John Rosemont, and the sin-soaked evangelical strictures offered by the Reverend James Dobson. This complex picture of alternatives suggests that advice has not just seesawed over time, as Ann Hulbert argues in her detailed discussion of changing fads in twentieth-century childrearing advice, but that there has been an array of choices at most times. Even Benjamin Spock, the most uniformly admired authority of the 1950s and 1960s, changed his views over time on various particulars. As historian Philip Greven has shown in regard to colonial Americans, child-rearing strategies have never been uniformly adhered to; they reflect the experiences of parents as children as well as their commitments in politics, religion, and aesthetics. They still do.

This does not mean that there have not been changing trends over time. Most Americans today are more child-centered and inclined to be more lenient than their ancestors were in the early republic. They also appear far more reluctantly committed to the exercise by their children of real independence than they were fifty years ago. But their choices have never been simply handed over to experts. They bring their own views and needs as parents with them to the exchange with experts, along with their varied traditions, questions, and concerns. Given the almost continuous infusion of immigrants to the United States, and the tenacious tradition of evangelical Protestantism, it would have been strange had it been otherwise. Immigrants from different places brought varied techniques in their treatment of children and integrated these with the advice they received from many sources—from doctors, midwives, ministers, neighbors, and their own parents as well as pamphlets, books, and articles on proper child-rearing. To read only the latter would give us a very selective idea of what was current in the past or in the present.[45] Besides, as Lenore Skenazy, one of the saner observers of contemporary parenting (and one of the wittiest) has commented about the situation that faces parents today, childrearing advice is confusing; it "keeps coming at us: an endless avalanche of breakthroughs proving that whatever you sort of thought made sense . . . is actually fraught with peril."[46] Today's parents, like those in the past, are not just overwhelmed by the avalanche but find their own ways of burrowing through to the light. That has not stopped the books and articles of advice, of complaint, and of despair from coming.

Despite these variations, American childrearing practices have developed a historical tendency that has generally encouraged individualism and independence (sometimes called self-reliance)[47] rather than a simple deference to parental authority. This has been a tradition since the early nineteenth century, and we struggle with it still. It has been deeply imprinted in many aspects of the culture, such as educational theories and in childrearing advice. That advice has emphasized child development, placed high value on a child's ability to find in the family a forum in which to express and articulate its needs (even as infants), and subordinated household routines to those needs. This can be mistaken for (and can also sometimes lead to) catering to children.

III

If Americans have often in the past been described in ways that would be familiar today and if today's parents continue to value independence, what, if anything, has changed? Today's middle-class parents are much more often seen as hovering than hands-off, and their faults lie in excessive supervision, not the reverse. This new condemnation of "helicopter" parents and worries about coddling and indulgence suggest that the real concern may be about how the commitment to independence can be maintained in a highly competitive world without sacrificing the success that parents want for their children. Parents have not only become fearful of allowing children to become too independent lest they make bad choices; they have a selective vision of how success and genuine independence are related. In a study of how parents deal with insecurity, sociologist Marianne Cooper has found that some well-educated and wealthy mothers choose to leave their professions in order to steer their children more effectively toward success. Of the sixteen upper-class families she studied, only two mothers had continued to work full time; the others had either quit working entirely or cut back to much shorter hours and less-demanding professions.[48] A recent survey of working women by David Leonhardt of the *New York Times* also discovered a new trend, unevenly distributed throughout the country, toward staying at home with children. As a result, in 2014 more women were not

"*Thank Goodness I Didn't*
'Train' the Fun
Out of My Babies"

**"I simply gave them lots of love...
the right kind of food . . . and My
Book House," says this commonsense mother**

"I DON'T believe in over-training children," says this wise and successful
mother. "Time and again I've seen how too
much fussing and worrying can rob children
of their fun and *naturalness* . . . and even
give them the dangerous idea that they are
some sort of special 'cases'. I know that my
babies are just normal, healthy, average
American children with the right to have a
lot of fun while they are growing up into
worth-while men and women. MY BOOK
HOUSE fits in perfectly with that conception, and I am perfectly willing to give it
third place in the list of important influences in my children's lives."

MY BOOK HOUSE can do as much for your
child. It can for *any* child. It contains the
finest of childhood literature from 47 nations. It is completely absorbing and fasci-
nating for the child himself. Yet it is a
carefully and definitely graded plan for the

natural de-
velopment...
through sug-
gestion and
example . . .
of the best
traits of dis-
position, per-
sonality and character. MY BOOK HOUSE
is not for the "problem" child . . . it is for
every child . . . for his own pleasure and
enjoyment . . . and to help him in a natural
way to grow up the way you want him to!
It's impossible, of course, to give you anything like a complete picture of MY BOOK
HOUSE here. We hope you will mail the
coupon so we may send you full information. You will find it interesting.

The BOOK HOUSE *for* CHILDREN
360 N. Michigan Ave., Room E-50, Chicago, Ill.

MY BOOK HOUSE

DAD.. *If Your Wife Hasn't
Already Sent This Coupon..*
YOU DO IT!

"Thank Goodness I Didn't 'Train' the Fun Out of My Babies." "I don't believe in over-
training children," says the wise and successful mother." Advertisement for the Book
House for Children in *Parents' Magazine* 11 (May 1936), 85. This ad from the 1930s illustrates the emphatic belief that children should be allowed to play and act on their own
without too much parental interference.

"Sometimes I think we want this more than he does."

"Sometimes I think we want this more than he does." Cartoon by Kim Warp. *New Yorker*, May 12, 2014, 47. *The New Yorker* Collection, The Cartoon Bank, Condé Nast Collection.

employed (30 percent) than in 1999 (26 percent). At least part of this is the result of mothers who decide that their children need them at home.[49]

Judith Warner and others describe a constant round of chauffeuring and party planning, obsessive attention to school performance, and enlistment in sports and artistic activities, all of which go way beyond infancy and early childhood. One of Warner's interview subjects noted that "[t]he children are the center of the household and everything goes around them,"[50] and while the remark could have been made a hundred years ago, there are aspects that reflect contemporary rather than historical circumstances. They suggest not that children are being indulged but that they are supervised in great detail. And there seems to be no end in sight as children age. In the 1950s and 1960s, many women went to work once their children were in junior high school or high school, so that they could afford to send them to college. Today, many stay home so they can help them to apply to college.

Contemporary plaints about children reflect growing uneasiness with demands on parents' time and attention that last much longer than ever before, combined with a sense of helplessness about results. This comes at a point when working mothers seem to have less time than they once had to give their children the attention parents think they need. Allowing children to play a significant role in the household continues a long and identifiable American tradition. But perhaps contemporary parents are able to provide children with only half of the traditional formula for success. They are giving children, even older children, what they believe is autonomy without a real sense of responsibility. And they do this not because they are bad parents, but because the circumstances have made their hovering and supervision seem necessary. This translates into children who are over-controlled and over-indulged at the same time, while mothers are run ragged.

In the past, by the time they were adolescents, young people had been provided with the tools to lead them on a road toward adulthood. For middle-class youth today, that is less and less likely as school life lasts beyond adolescence and into the twenties, and it is *success in school* that seems uppermost in parents' minds. But as one of my children once told me, school seems to lead only to more school rather than to "real life." Has the middle class thus failed its children by too much attentive involvement at a time when the outcome seems very far off?

Not according to family sociologist Annette Lareau. In her stimulating contrast between how lower-class and middle-class parents raise their children and its consequences for how successfully children negotiate their lives, Lareau found serious differences with very significant effects on children of the privileged middle class and their lower-class peers. And Lareau believes the differences are much more a matter of class than of race or ethnicity.[51]

Middle-class parents, Lareau argues, encourage their children to act with confidence in their dealings with their doctors, teachers, and others. These children boldly articulate their views and demands, characteristics that allow them to achieve their goals, by making them proactive and autonomous actors. This does not release them from parents' oversight, however, since middle-class parents spend large amounts of time engaging in what Lareau calls "concerted cultivation," supervising sports and leisure activities. They are also deeply involved in overseeing their children's academic work and schooling. Unlike working-class households, which are more adult-centered and where children are subordinated to adult routines and needs, middle-class children are the central drivers in their households. This leads to their success in a wide variety of institutional settings that protect their class standing as they grow up, and the school success that provides them with a place in the privileged middle-class in the future. In a more recent study of class differences, Robert Putnam comes to similar conclusions.[52]

Lareau has identified one of the basic concerns of parents today, since the consequences of class privileges are much on their minds as they observe the growing inequality in the society and conclude that privilege seems to be increasingly inherited. Thus, in a 2014 article, *New York Times* columnist Nicholas Kristof reflected on the failings of many of his working-class childhood friends in a small town in Washington State and concluded that for middle-class kids, "Their big break came when they were conceived in middle-class American families who loved them, read them stories, and nurtured them with Little League sports, library cards and music lessons. They were programmed for success by the time they were zygotes."[53]

Lareau thus provides a basis for understanding how this privilege is bound up with differences in child outcomes. The patterns that Lareau ascribes to the middle-class are distinctly connected with those qualities (boldness, autonomy, self-assurance) that are historically connected to America's commitment to independence and were believed to set American children apart from children elsewhere.

Lareau suggests that American middle-class kids, at least, are still being given the tools to be successful. By contrast, Lareau argues that working-class children are not. They are treated as subordinates in a family hierarchy in a home environment that emphasizes respect for parents and other elder family members to the detriment of the personal success of children. As we shall see, this pattern is also closely identified with various immigrant groups as they negotiate their transition to American life.

In Lareau's portrait, most middle-class parents are the opposite of permissive. They are caring and careful rather than indulgent as they herd their children into innumerable activities that effectively prepare them for future success and provide real world advantages. Parents are still overtly committed to strength and independence in their children, but also expect that their own hard work will be rewarded through their kids' successful school achievement and admission to excellent colleges and universities, followed by highly rewarded careers. These are the choices parents are making for their children. Whether these children are given genuine choice or leeway for self-direction or are tightly managed by parents intent to maintain their class position is an open question. At the same time, given the extensive efforts involved, one can also imagine the disappointment that failure can bring and the fears that loom in such a culture of expectation.

What is undoubtedly different from the past is that children of all classes, but especially those from the middle and upper groups, are expected to remain "children" for much longer periods of time, regardless of whether they address their parents as equals or not. The condition of childhood dependency and the absence of the real perks of adulthood even after adolescence have been vastly extended by schooling, now understood to be necessary for the maintenance of middle-class status. This takes a toll on the ability of young people to act on their own as they move toward maturity, as previous generations had done by, among other things, setting up their own households.[54]

Whatever the continuing affinity of American parents for aspects of past traditions in the self-conscious treatment of their children, the alteration in circumstances creates an immense divide between them and their ancestors. Paradoxically, early maturity, like early responsibility, is much more likely to be part of childhood in less-affluent, often immigrant households, than in those of the native middle class. This delay in social maturity should not be confused with the rapid advance of physical development that has taken place in the United States over the course of the last century, as both boys and girls arrive at sexual maturity earlier. The delay in one and advance of the other compounds the problem, as children look like adults but can't aspire to an equivalent cultural position.

Part of this delayed maturity results simply from the extensive requirements of certification in a society that values higher levels of literacy and other skills increasingly located in school. This certification merely begins with a high school diploma (once a mark of serious achievement) and can continue into various post-college degrees. In this process, the signposts of maturity—regular work, marriage, and childrearing—are delayed way beyond the experience of earlier generations.[55] In the nineteenth century, aspiring young men also took a long time to settle into their final occupation, but this usually followed several work experiences in the adult world. Similarly, while the early age at which Americans married after World War II was unusual, one would have to go back more than 150 years to find the kind of delays in marriage experienced by the current generation.[56]

Today, middle-class and even many working-class American children go to school longer than ever before; therefore, the schooling requirements for all kinds of jobs have become more demanding, forcing everyone to run faster in order to catch up. This creates real disadvantages for those who either put less emphasis on schooled knowledge or are less adept at academic learning, or those who cannot afford the cost of advanced schooling. This is why the United States and Western societies generally (but the US more than any other) have developed a passionate interest in attention deficit disorder as an explanation for the failure of children who are not willing or able to put up with the extended periods of quiet and concentration required by life in school and why Americans have invested heavily in diagnosing and controlling the disorder.[57] The medications to treat it have become a common study aid for high school and college students. The dependence on schooling also disadvantages children from the working class if, as Lareau suggests, their failure to articulate their needs and to demand attention leaves them at a disadvantage with teachers and other school officials.

While the traits encouraged by the "concerted cultivation" of middle-class parents seem to foster qualities like self-confidence and outspokenness that Americans have valued historically, they are also potentially newly problematic. Does the kind of "success" that results from such cultivation by adults lead children toward deep personal ambitions, an appreciation of innovations, a willingness to endure failure and difficulties, and a strong drive for creativity? Or does it encourage competent performance that will satisfy parents and teachers? Lareau argues that children who approach their tasks with confidence and the ability to work well with others are likely to succeed in the American school and the American workplace, or at least that they do better and are more successful than their working-class peers. But the evidence is not so clear.

Middle-class children feel and express their privilege through what Lareau describes as a sense of entitlement, and she views this as a positive quality. But does a sense of entitlement, so often commented upon by observers of today's privileged youth, provide an effective attitude when young adults are faced by new circumstances and their competence is not automatically acknowledged but must be earned through hard work or real independence of mind? Some critics of higher education, such as William Deresiewicz, have singled out the herd-like mentality of entitled undergraduates that leads them to the "best" schools and into what seems the most lucrative and currently popular subjects,[58] as a troubling trend for both true individual success and national effectiveness.

Some observers have been especially acerbic about parents who continue to define and control their children even as they move through college and university, a time when one should expect young people to exercise their independent judgment. Academic life is full of stories of parents continuing to micromanage children's selection of courses and activities and to supervise their performance. Margaret Nelson discovered that her college students leaned on their parents often. "When they have questions, meet difficulties, or simply want to report on their days, they reach out for their 'mom' and, somewhat less often, their 'dads.'" She also cites polls that show that

"13 percent of first-year and 8 percent of senior students reported . . . that a parent or guardian 'frequently intervened on their behalf to help them solve problems they were having at the college.' "[59] If this is the result of "concerted cultivation," one might seriously question its benefits for youth who will need to face new challenges in their future careers and lives. Some parents, at least, may confuse cultivation that will develop their children's skills and competences with a zealous oversight most likely to lead to immediate success, much as some parents substitute coddling for real attention to children and their needs. This is the conclusion of Nelson, among others. If this is permissive childrearing, it certainly has a very limited view of what is allowed.

These tense and contradictory indicators help to underwrite the anxiety of parenting today, an anxiety usually expressed by the vocal and articulate middle class, though also experienced by those whose children grow up without a sense of entitlement. What characteristics, after all, are required for success in a world that seems to change almost by the moment and moves so fast that no one can predict its future direction? In many ways, that was the basis for the promise of the United States—that parents' past and the limits of their experience would not determine their children's future. Americans always hoped and usually expected that their children would do better—an essential component of the American dream. Polls show that today's parents often believe the opposite, that their children are unlikely even to achieve their own level of success.[60] As a result, they are less uncomfortable directing their children's future, hoping in this way to maintain the next generation's hold on a perch in the middle class.

There have been other points in the past when parents were faced with major economic transformations that led to anxiety about class and concerns about the future of children. One of those took place in the middle of the nineteenth century, when major changes in the organization of the economy, during the industrial transformation of the Northeast, created downward pressures on class mobility and fears about the future of children among mothers. In response, many sought to encourage self-control and prudence in their children and a sense of inner purpose as they prepared for vast changes in the future. They, too, hoped to guide them and did so by charting a path that frequently led through church attendance and carefully cultivated habits of respectability.[61]

In the context of today's shift in the worldwide economy, as industrial labor is supplied outside the United States, while high levels of literacy have become a standard job requirement and acquiring new skills is necessary for success, American parents worry endlessly about their children's preparation for the future. This perspective is often expressed by concerns about the right schools and colleges. Even parents' frantic efforts on their behalf are no guarantee that their children will succeed.[62] Changes in the economy and the fundamental importance of higher education today may be giving an advantage to children from societies with very different parenting styles, such as India, China, or Korea. And some American parents are asking why these children are better prepared, or what their parents have done to prepare them more effectively? At such times, Americans question whether their emphasis on independence and on allowing children flexibility to chose their own future is the right course. Who will be a success, what qualities are required to achieve it, whether extended schooling is the best preparation for the innovative intelligence required at a critical juncture of change --these questions fill the modern media and have penetrated the American childrearing conversation as parents try to provide their children and themselves with assurances that are simply not possible to achieve.

Amy Chua, a successful Yale Law professor, a woman of Chinese descent, a ferocious mother intent on assuring her daughters' stellar future as a tribute to her own family's glorious traditions and history of success, had indeed hit a very sensitive nerve.

IV

The daughter of migratory agricultural workers, Elizabeth Loza, whom we met in the preceding chapter, was born poor. She had no sense of privilege or entitlement. Neither did her brothers, who interrupted their studies to help their father in the fields. Elizabeth took care of their Texas truck house and went to school when she could. Exploited and often cheated, all members of the family contributed their labor for the benefit of the group as a whole. This had been the common experience of many European immigrant families earlier in the century as well, as the family economy became the basis for survival. And it is this perspective on children that Annette Lareau describes as basic to working-class family life and habits. It is one in which children are subordinated to adults and take their orders from parents. Children are taught the importance of the wider kin network, and most of their social activities are restricted to the family group. Children like these, according to Lareau, tend to be timid and undemanding in their interactions with outsiders, quiet and well behaved when they are not acting out and being rebellious. This more subservient model for children is likely what visitors to the United States saw as the alternative when they criticized American children as wild, undisciplined, and unmannerly.

In the case of the Loza family in the 1950s, the children—apart from Elizabeth, who was academically talented and very lucky to find a mentor—hardly had a path to success in America. In their efforts to help their families and their obedience to their elders, these children went to work rather than to school. The children simply could not take schooling seriously, and their parents were not thinking ahead but concentrating on their immediate needs. This had been the case for poor Italian, Polish, Irish, and many other European immigrants before them. Earlier in the century, neither the legal requirements for education nor economic necessity had made extended schooling an imperative. This changed over the course of the twentieth century.[63] But even in the early twentieth century, some immigrants took schooling and its contribution to success in America very seriously and invested it with their aspirations for the future. As philosopher Sydney Hook, who grew up at the beginning of the twentieth century in Williamsburg, Brooklyn, noted about Jews, for example, even in their most impoverished and difficult days, "hope was sustained by a faith that the door of opportunity would be opened by education."[64]

Difficult circumstances today often inhibit full participation in schooling by many impoverished immigrants, but almost all immigrants now are much more likely to grasp the importance of education for the future success of their children. This was why some Hispanic immigrants in the Bushwick section of Brooklyn gathered to decry bilingual programs that were designed to assist their children because they feared that these would be an impediment to success in school. As *New York Times* education columnist Samuel Freedman explained, "they condemned a system that consigned their children to a linguistic ghetto cut off from the America of integration and upward mobility." Freedman describes the parents as "Spanish-speaking immigrants who struggled to reach America and struggle still at low-wage jobs to stay in America so that their children can acquire and rise with an American education."[65] Today's immigrant parents may well still need the help of their children, at home and at work, but the emphasis on schooling in the society is so pervasive that they can no longer ignore its imperatives.

Still, some immigrants are more keenly aware of the importance of schooling and more deeply committed to their children's education as one of the goals of migration. In 2013, of almost one million people who received lawful residence status in the United States, almost 400,000 (two-fifths) were from Asia, led by the People's Republic of China, with India a very close second (68,000 and 65,000, respectively). The Philippines provided a third significant Asian source (53,000). Mexico remains the country of origin of the largest group of American *legal* immigrants (28 percent of the almost 41 million total immigrants in the United States in 2013, they were the single largest number of documented immigrants that year: 134,000).[66] But of all those who immigrated *legally*, the total of the three Asian groups surpassed that of Mexico. While much of the most vocal discussion about immigration focuses on immigrants from Latin America, Asian immigration has clearly become a major influence on American society and culture, and the children of Asian immigrants and their achievement now help to define certain issues in the public mind. These figures, based as they are on the number of immigrants with legal papers, do not fully represent the situation in the United States, where many people from Mexico and Central America are undocumented, but it does give a sense of the complex picture of American immigration. Many Asian immigrants are also without appropriate documents, having overstayed their visas.

Immigration from China and India, most of it since the changes in the immigration law of 1965, represents a new experience for the United States.[67] Long excluded by law and treaty, marginalized, harassed, and confined to narrow niches of the economy, Asian immigration has transformed American identity over the past two generations. Of those who immigrated from China and India in 2013, more than one-quarter of the former and a full half of the latter came on employment-based visas, reflecting the skilled and educated quality of many (though hardly all) of the immigrants in these groups. Asian immigrants and their children have become a conspicuous success in many parts of American economic life, not only in the high-tech fields with which they are frequently identified, but also in commerce and entrepreneurship, in education, and in entertainment-related industries. How these immigrants raise their children—their success in academics and their future prospects—is now a significant part of the American conversation about parents and children. It is also a profoundly American story.

Whether the parents came here legally or were undocumented, from Asia or Latin America, whether they are skilled or not, working or middle class, in most immigrant families, one of the children will operate as a liaison to and as a cultural broker for American institutions and language. These "kids in the middle" in Vikki Katz's felicitous phrase, are a necessary part of the functioning of immigrant families, where lack of facility with the English language, and unfamiliarity with the culture and with how American institutions operate provide one child with the opportunity to become mature, dependable, and knowledgeable long before similarly aged or placed American children are. As Katz demonstrates in her study of poor Hispanic immigrants in Los Angeles, their role is not entirely advantageous, as these kids struggle with accelerated maturity and with adult matters for which they are not always well prepared. They can also feel overworked.[68] Nevertheless, their role encourages resourcefulness, while their parents' dependency on their children subtly alters the usual hierarchical assumptions of immigrant families in which children are expected to obey their elders. The phenomenon has been most intensely studied in Latin American families where even children whose families are without legal documents are required to attend school and therefore learn English much faster than their parents, especially their mothers.[69] They often provide translation services in community institutions such as hospitals and clinics, with employers, and, as Elizabeth

Loza learned, in judicial proceedings. These children know early on about their parents' finances and other adult matters. Even in families where the demand for children to honor their ancestors is intense and can lead to sharp generational conflicts over the children's goals—often the case within Chinese immigrant families—children provide essential services for their parents and others, which alters the generational equilibrium.[70] Like children in the early nineteenth century, these young people are better able to adapt to the new world than their parents.

Kids in the middle can feel resentful, since they are required to provide their time to parents and other relatives and to subordinate their peer relations and even schoolwork to their duties. But their sense of responsibility and competence also develop through these activities. And these children have an enhanced status in the household, at the same time as their own strengths as individuals develop, because they operate on behalf of their families. Annette Lareau's depiction of working-class families, because she pays so little attention to ethnic factors, ignores this important aspect of the mechanism by which success can be achieved in non-middle-class contexts. The experience of these children reminds us of the unusual maturity and responsibility achieved in the early republic by Ulysses Grant on the family farm, or by Anna Howard Shaw and her siblings when they found themselves setting up a homestead on the Michigan frontier. In such new circumstances, young people like these can have a distinct advantage over their more obviously privileged American peers. Their motivation and maturity can also have important educational benefits.

Immigrant families almost universally fear loss of authority over their children, and parents are frequently repelled by their perception of the looser control Americans exercise over their children. Some judge American discipline to be extremely lax and view American children as disrespectful. While their own families are changing as parents become dependent on the knowledge and skills of their children, the expressed opinions of immigrants often remain very traditional. West Indian immigrants, for example, insist on maintaining discipline through physical punishment that is often condemned by school authorities and social services. As Mary Waters and Jennifer

Sykes observed about the West Indians they interviewed in New York, they "believed that parents had a moral obligation to discipline their children, and that, if parents did not beat them, children would turn out badly. In fact, the absence of physical punishment was often cited by respondents as the cause of America's juvenile delinquency problem."[71] East Indian parents had similar concerns, as they feared losing their authority over children, including their children's marriage choices. Immigrants' sense of achievement and self-worth is often bound up with the degree to which their children adhere to Indian values.[72] Adjusting to the United States can be a conflicted and confusing process.

Chinese immigrants, who now occupy many upper- and middle-class positions often act as parents in ways that counter expectations of their class in Lareau's schema. Almost all aim to maintain inherited values and expect their children quietly to defer to parental desires and traditional strictures that emphasize reverence for elders and ancestors. Rather than giving their children a voice in household affairs, they expect obedience. Thus the daughter of one Chinese immigrant, "Tricia Sung," described her mother as "very open-minded" but, at the same time, noted that the mother always assumed the children were wrong, "So I don't challenge her." Asked about her mother's approach to childrearing, "Tricia Sung" said, "She does reason with us, but she just thinks that we're wrong and she's right." Another interviewee, "Sandy Wang," whose father was born in China and has a degree from MIT and whose mother was born in Boston and has a degree from Boston University, described her parents (clearly middle class) as "VERY LIBERAL" but noted that "I never let them down: I never did anything bad." Her other siblings were not similarly obedient and were treated much more harshly.[73] Middle class in their expectations about their children, such Chinese parents are engaged in a quite different kind of "concerted cultivation," subordinating their children's desires to ideals of family respect and honor. Children in Chinese families are held to high standards as a measure of family success as well as a means to their own.

Part of the effort to maintain control over their children is the normal response of immigrants eager to cement a lasting identification between their progeny and their own communities, culture, and past. But part is also a response to perceptions about different childrearing strategies among American middle-class families where overt obedience is usually not high on the agenda of goals or means. This has historically been the case for each successive wave of immigrants to the United States, who found American childrearing lax and children spoiled and unresponsive to their parents' desires. In many cases in the past, children were ashamed of their parents' lack of American knowledge, old-fashioned views, and lack of experience with commercial culture and then as now it has led to conflict within families. Today, such conflict is often most intensely experienced in Chinese immigrant households. In the past, generational conflict often had an economic dimension, since poor immigrant parents maintained control in order to secure their children's contribution to the household economy. Although still a concern of poor immigrants today, economic considerations have retreated while other objectives have taken their place. The distance between contemporary immigrants and their American environment can be especially acute because so many come from non-Western societies in Asia, the Middle East, and South America, where views about the roles of women and children remain deeply traditional and patriarchal ideals stand in sharp contrast to the direction of family life among Europeans and Americans since World War II.[74]

There is evidence that even immigrants with a strong orientation to tradition have begun to adjust their childrearing patterns as they adapt to the United States. Korean second-generation mothers now emphasize autonomy and self-determination because they see this as a key to effective functioning and success in American society. Many see the old-fashioned emphasis on rules and authoritarian control as retrograde and ineffective.[75] Most also maintain many of the ideals with which they were raised, and, like their parents, emphasize schooling success. As in most periods of very substantial migration, the delicate balance between older patterns and the adoption of American ways proceeds along many routes. These routes can be perplexing as second-generation daughters rely on their own (immigrant) mothers and mothers-in-law for child care.

These adjustments can be even more complicated in the families of the very large number of undocumented migrants. Those from Latin America, especially, maintain ties across borders, and undocumented migrant parents can be separated from their children for years and even decades.[76] In the context of global economic changes, the very process of assimilating has taken on complex forms, with transnational identities becoming a new option for recent Americans and peer groups operating to maintain continuity by emphasizing deep friendships among children within homogeneous groups while also enforcing a range of adaptations to American life.[77]

The experience of second-generation children in American schools today is similarly intricate, and it is difficult to describe all the patterns of success and failure that prevail. The literature in this area is growing, and no simple summary here can do justice to the many facets of what can be a bewildering story.[78] Some immigrant groups such as the Chinese, South Asians, and Koreans have achieved notable levels of academic success, while some Latino groups, especially those from Central America, have had a much harder time. But this pattern is hardly uniform. The success of working-class Chinese American children can be very much like that of middle-class Chinese families, and contrary to the pattern described by Lareau, results not from the development of self-confidence and independence within the family but from the intense investment of Chinese mothers in the success of their children and in family honor. At the same time, not all Chinese families have the time to exercise rigorous oversight, and class can have its consequences even among what is sometimes designated as the "model minority." At a time that college has become a necessary route into the middle class, large numbers of Asian immigrants from all classes are admitted to the most desirable colleges and universities. But there are many Chinese students who do not succeed despite their parents' aspirations. As one study of parents and children in Chinese American households demonstrates, even middle-class Chinese families sometimes have to cope with children who did not succeed in college despite the fact that "the parents expect good academic performance and college education for all the children." In the case of one family interviewed by Victoria Chen, two of three daughters dropped out of college.[79]

Nevertheless, the statistics on admission to prestigious public and private universities is telling. In 2014, 18.1 percent of those admitted to Princeton were Asian American. At Columbia and the University of Pennsylvania, Asian Americans were 25 percent and 24.4 percent, while the proportion at Yale was similar to Princeton's, with 17.4 percent Asian Americans admitted to the 2014 class. At the public University of California at Berkeley, in the fall of 2013, almost 19 percent of all freshman were of Chinese descent, 7.4 percent were South Asian, and 5.3 percent were Korean. In the entering class of 2012 at the University of Michigan, 13.4 percent were Asian.[80]

By way of contrast, there is a much greater tendency for children from Mexican and Central American families to leave school early, often without graduating from high school.[81] In 1990, the completion rate of Hispanic students from high school was under 60 percent. But this has been changing. In 2009, that proportion reached almost 77 percent. Not only have completion rates been rising, but many students of Hispanic background are beginning to participate in higher education and moving toward professional careers. According to the Pew Research Center statistics, "a record seven-in-ten (69%) Hispanic high school graduates in the class of 2012 enrolled in college . . . two percentage points higher than the rate (67%) among their white counterparts."[82] Still, this last statistic tells us very little about the type of college that Hispanic students attend, with many from Latin American backgrounds staying close to home by going to inexpensive community colleges, while their Asian peers attend prestigious universities. In general, despite their larger proportion of the American population, Hispanic students attend prestigious institutions at only half the rate of Asian Americans. Berkeley's 2013 freshman class included 8.4 percent Mexican Americans with 3 percent other Latinos; at Princeton, 7.9 percent of students admitted to the 2014 class were Hispanics; at Columbia, 16 percent; and at Yale, 8.6 percent.[83]

Sociologist Alejandro Portes argues that a challenging pattern of "segmented assimilation" exists today among poor second-generation children who live in inner-city neighborhoods. For these immigrants, older patterns of mobility and success through assimilation are no longer relevant. Assimilation for youth often means adapting to local peer groups who do not support school success and are contemptuous of middle-class values. In contrast, often the most successful second-generation students are those who remain close to their parents and their ethnic identities (many "kids in the middle" fall in this category). These latter continue the aspirations of their parents to make a success in the United States, which almost all immigrants today understand is most likely to be achieved through schooling. Of the students studied by Portes, the most successful were Cubans in Florida, who remain close to peers of their own backgrounds and whose commitment to schooling is very strongly reinforced by their attendance at Catholic schools.[84]

There remain powerful differences in motivation and achievement among second-generation children, and many factors—including length of residence and socioeconomic class—affect school success. At the same time, there is considerable evidence that students who are themselves immigrants often set very high goals for themselves and perform well despite language handicaps. Comparing their opportunities in the United States with their previous deprivations, many try to take advantage of what the United States can offer them.[85] As one team of prominent researchers in this area has noted, "Most children recognize the sacrifices their parents have made for them. . . . These parental sacrifices propel many immigrant students to launch themselves wholeheartedly into their educational journey." Immigrant students also view their schooling in the United States as an opportunity they would not have had in their home countries, and teachers find that these students are good to work with because they are both more motivated and more respectful.[86] So many factors operate here that it is difficult to locate the one best reason for these success stories. Nevertheless, one factor may well be the most consequential. First-generation immigrant students have not yet been fully adapted into the mainstream of their local peer group and American youth culture. In addition, over the course of the past half-century, various forms of affirmative action have been devised by institutions of higher education to meet the needs of students whose initial deprivation and continuing schooling circumstances would otherwise make their route to college difficult.

This view of the advantages of being a first-generation immigrant has not gone unquestioned. In what she describes as "subtractive schooling," Angela Valenzuela has suggested that the difficulties and obstacles that many Latino students face in American schools actually undermine their ability to learn. In devaluing their past cultural experiences and being largely oblivious to the handicaps of many who are barely literate when they arrive in the United States, adolescents from Mexico in American high schools especially can be made to feel stupid as teachers sideline them. One student, for example, testified that he felt "*avergonzado*" (embarrassed); his inability to read and write even in Spanish was treated by people at school "like if we had a disease."[87]

While the jury is out on the advantages and disadvantages of immigration for many students, the forced attendance at high school probably differentiates many contemporary experiences from those of equally ignorant immigrant populations in the early twentieth century. Then, many if not most adolescent immigrant students were ignored (after a stint in a "steamer class," intended to quickly teach them English) once they reached thirteen or fourteen. When they reached the age at which attendance was no longer required, or just short of it (many also lied about their age), they avoided high school altogether as they went to work instead. Only the most motivated went to school. Today, everyone has to attend, whether or not they are prepared, literate, or motivated. As the law and expectations regarding school attendance changed over the course of the twentieth century, the problems that confront immigrant adolescents have also changed. Any comparison between children (especially older students) in school today and those in the past needs to take this changed context into account.

There are few easy conclusions to draw about the schooling success of the immigrant children who accompany their parents to this country and their second-generation siblings. What is clear is that their presence in the schools—both as successful competitors and as evidence of schooling failure—has deeply affected the perceptions of Americans regarding the problems of the current generation. So, too, affirmative action has turned some parents and students into cynics regarding the possibilities of successful competition. Both the successful new immigrants and the experiences of and policies regarding the less successful have influenced the context of the parenting literature of complaint. These help to define anxieties about success and provide a source for the fears regarding the future of American children in the twenty-first century.

V

Parents today also experience a serious sense of disorientation because of dramatic changes in the sequencing of childhood. Older categories once used to understand children's behavior no longer fit, as age has changed its meaning and the contours of childhood are redefined. New concepts, like "tweens" (eight to twelve years of age), are upending earlier views about how children develop and when they could be expected to become preoccupied with sexual matters and consumer goods. A voracious media-influenced culture of consumption targets younger and younger children and sexualizes children well before adolescence. All this affects how parents believe they should supervise their children's activities. As the age of menarche has dropped and the clothing industry dresses girls like teenagers by the time they are seven or eight, the world of preteenagers looks different than it once did. Toys also add to the anxiety; physically explicit dolls like Brats became the rage in the early twenty-first century, and new games that could be accessed online made earlier limits on the viewing of violence, once understandable by age categories in movies, obsolete. Pornography, too, is now available on the computer at any time of day or night to children of all ages, affecting boys especially. As a result, American parents no longer understand how their children move from childhood into adulthood, once the domain of adolescence and the province of the high school.

Adolescence has always been troublesome, both as a concept and as an experience. In the twentieth century, it came to define an essential stage in the life course once G. Stanley Hall took an amorphous nineteenth-century idea about the jittery period surrounding puberty and gave it flesh, blood, and spirit. In the huge tome he published in 1904, Hall described the difficult physical and emotional changes that accompanied the sexual maturation of boys and (to a lesser degree) girls.[88] Dreamy and unfocused, adolescents were physically awkward and socially inept. Striving toward self-realization, they stumbled over their limbs, which often grew at different rates, as well as their inchoate desires.

Over the course of the twentieth century, the adolescent problem grew beyond the physical and spiritual into a social issue. In the 1920s, it was still a new enough idea for Margaret Mead to suggest that adolescence existed in the United States because of conditions created by modern life and modern family dynamics.[89] Mead understood that it was not only a transitional stage but a historically situated concept. As conditions changed at the end of the twentieth century, redefining schooling, work, and sexuality—the three areas most significant to its successful fulfillment—adolescence itself changed as an experience and then became less and less useful as a concept. Today, traversing adolescence successfully can no longer be read as a signal of social maturity and the period from age thirteen to age eighteen is no longer a central pivot of the life course as it was in the twentieth century. Erik Erikson and his idea of the crucial role of the adolescent identity crisis have disappeared from public conversation. Adolescents are still difficult to handle and can still be troublesome to themselves and to their parents, but as a stage of development and as a way of understanding one's progress through life adolescence is no longer an efficient social concept.

The first adolescents to catch the public's attention in the twentieth century were "juvenile delinquents," young men and women who failed to abide by the rules and laws set for them by adults. During the twentieth century, those restrictions actually increased as reformers focused on protecting young people by keeping them away from hazardous work and sexual experience, hoping thereby to extend to older children the sheltering umbrella of childhood innocence and dependency. It was adolescents they had in mind when they invented the juvenile court and set it apart from ordinary judicial procedures. Delinquents dropped out of school or were truant; they smoked, drank, swore, stole or sold goods on the streets, gambled, or had inappropriate sexual relations.[90] Over time, the list of matters that could contribute to delinquency among adolescents grew, from an initial attention to adverse home conditions, inherited criminal tendencies, the dangers of work, and adult male seduction of young girls to cultural products like movies, comic books, drugs, music, video games, and the Internet. Adolescent girls always had a special niche in the literature on delinquency, since their maturing bodies were ripe for exploitation and could also create problems of illegitimacy and prostitution. Turning adolescent girls into responsible adults thus involved additional social provisions. At the turn of the twentieth century, reformers eager to protect girls directed their energies toward raising the age of sexual consent as well as toward shutting down brothels. By the middle of the century, homes for wayward girls where unmarried mothers could give birth and then give up their infants for adoption became another part of the social map of adolescent supervision, together with juvenile courts and reformatories.[91] And in the last several decades, Americans have been riveted by studies of how the still-immature brain of teens works.[92] This view has been enshrined in a Supreme Court ruling that now excludes young people under the age of eighteen from the death penalty.[93] In so doing, the highest court in the land has not only incorporated the new science of the brain into law but effectively made the period of adolescence very much a part of childhood—a period of continuing physical development rather than of emergent maturity.

For the non-delinquent, adolescence was viewed for most of the twentieth century as a distinctive and important period during which youth learned to adjust to requirements that would bring them toward successful work and mating. This was how Erik Erikson understood the matter at midcentury. Like Hall, he saw the process as fraught with dangers, but normal adolescents would struggle to gain a sense of confidence and define their life's commitments while moving toward responsible citizenship, work, and marriage. Erikson believed that modern adolescence provided individuals with the time to experiment as they integrated their personalities in ways that would lead to adult success through well-chosen work and in satisfying sexual relations. Some misbehavior could be expected as a result of this experimentation, but it was a byproduct of the normal process rather than a deviant path. Erikson was able to take this moratorium on adulthood for granted because high schools had become the chief institutional setting for these several things to happen. Young people prepared for the future while putting off decisions about family and work. Civics classes, as well as training in advanced literacy and even sex education classes and parenting classes made the high school the ideal venue for maturing adolescents.[94] They were supervised by adults but also were allowed freedom for social development and the arena in which to test their talents and exuberance in the extracurricular realm as well as in academics. High school students did not all learn exactly the same things, but most, more or less, could be assumed to have learned about these essential matters, and even the many students who, until midcentury, never graduated from high school were exposed to them to some substantial degree. The high school was thus effectively a fundamental expression of adolescence in the United States.[95]

Then in the 1970s, just when over 60 percent of American youth were graduating from high school, social conditions changed so that neither adolescence nor a high school education could any longer provide an effective way to understand the challenges facing American youth. First, fundamental changes in the economy meant that the credentials defined by high school graduation rapidly became insufficient for successful advancement into the middle class. Second, changes in sexual mores and in gender roles upended earlier expectations about sexuality and marriage. Finally, the vast expansion of higher education made high schools into anything but "high" schools as they had once been understood, rendering their services not only inadequate to most middle-class aspirations but also irrelevant as places where students could be vocationally prepared, as many had been earlier in the century in an assortment of nonacademic tracks. These vocational tracks were now transferred to community colleges, and later to private for profit "colleges," as high schools identified themselves as democratic institutions aiming to educate all to levels of comparable achievement. Tracking was viewed as an impediment to educational access rather than as an effective means to prepare some students for future vocations.

For most students by the end of the century, high schools lost their relevance to careers and work. Going to high school became a stopover during the teen years, with very little to offer beyond academic selection for those who would go on to college and university, while creating academic obstacles for those who would drop out and settle for low-paying jobs. They were also a place of torture for those who could not keep up with the youth culture that became the price of admission to popularity among peers.

For the first two-thirds of the twentieth century, high schools had also been an important force for assimilation in immigrant communities because children remained in school during their adolescent years and were exposed to the English language and American ideals as well as to peers from whom they could learn to adapt to mainstream culture. Their immediate friends were often, like themselves, from immigrant homes, but they managed the rocky process of acculturation together, and high schools were generally composed of more than one ethnic group. This, too, changed in the last third of the twentieth century. As Gary Orfield and the Harvard Project on School Desegregation have demonstrated, schools became more segregated in the last decades of the century, so that immigrant children often had little exposure to high-achieving students from other groups.[96] In the context of the beehive that was the social life of high school, many of these students actually turned away from the educational aspirations of their parents and their non-American-born siblings to engage with peers who disdained academic achievement while embracing the popular culture of the inner city. Immigrant parents often struggled against the influence of the high school peer world as they tried to keep their children focused on achievement.

Alejandro Portes suggests that this has led to a reverse relationship between assimilation and success in the United States, as it was once understood. Those students who moved most strongly away from their parents' culture moved toward peer cultures and values that were not middle class and devalued schooling. This impeded their mobility. Even second-generation Asian American children engaged in one form of this assimilation as they distinguished between the "whitewashed" who assimilated and the FOBs (or fresh off the boat); and by the third generation, some Asian American children had lost the drive for academic success.[97] The steaming social cauldron of the high school now produces different results than once imagined. Of course, in wealthy suburbs and in selected urban environments, it remained a place in which middle-class kids, adept at manipulating schools toward their own ends and under their parents' careful supervision, learned to succeed by playing the game. But those ends now had little to do with learning meaningful work in high school or effective socialization to adult standards. Instead, they were concerned overwhelmingly with admission to future colleges. For those lower-class children, not so adept, it provided not even an effective credential or a salubrious environment for advancement into the middle class.

By the end of the century, the high school had also become a very different place in regard to preparation for marriage. Until the 1960s, adolescent girls who became pregnant or married, and even those known to be sexually active, could be dropped from school. High schools upheld and enforced the dominant sexual standards. High schools were places where girls learned to maintain their virtue and delay marriage as they picked up the behaviors associated with their academic achievements. It also meant that many girls never finished school because of their sexual delinquency. Thus the high school was able to maintain normal cultural expectations. That changed dramatically when the implications of Title IX of the Civil Rights Act became clear. In outlawing discrimination based on gender, girls could no longer be punished for behavior that boys were not punished for, and schools could not drop pregnant or sexually active girls. Instead, various provisions were made to accommodate them.[98]

The postponement of sexuality for adolescent girls (at least) until marriage, thus upholding middle-class assumptions, became moot as the high school no longer reinforced these standards. At the same time, the sexual revolution removed older restraints on sexuality among peers.[99] This much more open sexual regime even made it into childrearing and parenting advice. In 1967, Haim Ginott published *Between Parent and Teenager*, opening up the dialogue about sex as a basic concern of parenting. Other experts similarly began to include frank conversations with adolescents in their advice manuals. As this happened the adolescent period could no longer serve as the bridge to marriage, since marriage was no longer the necessary goal of sexual desire or of sexual experimentation, as it had been when young people dated earlier in the century.

By the end of the century, adolescence and its primary institution—the high school—led nowhere. Its value as an extended moratorium on adulthood had been eclipsed for both middle-class and lower-class kids as the adult objectives toward which adolescence was supposed eventually to lead had been redefined. The decline in marriage and the rapid increase in births to single mothers in the last twenty years confirms the disconnect that has taken place. As an article in the *New York Times* put it, "It used to be called illegitimacy. Now it is the new normal. . . . [M]ore than half of births to women under 30 occur outside marriage. Once largely limited to poor women and minorities, motherhood without marriage has settled deeply into middle America."[100] The rapidity of the transformation testifies to the ways in which institutions no longer function as they once had. In 1980, only 20 percent of all births were to women outside of marriage. This figure more than doubled by the end of the first decade of the twenty-first century. The changes in society had moved the goalpost so that adolescence became nothing more than one additional step in development.

These changes in the meaningfulness of adolescence and the relevance of high schools are deeply implicated in the confusions of parenting today. Parents with aspirations for their children worry about how to raise their infants so that when they become teenagers, they will be set on the right path, away from risky choices and toward the right colleges and universities. Today, the high school is not a bridge but a resource to be manipulated for immigrant children eager to advance up the ladder through school achievement as well as the means toward college admission for middle-class children in the know. Finding the "right" high school for ambitious immigrants and prosperous middle-class Americans has become the holy grail as parents seek out places to live for the schooling advantages they would provide their children, while becoming distrustful of public schooling.[101] One young woman of South Asian background told sociologist Marianne Cooper that as a high school freshman, she immediately signed up for the classes she would need to get into the right college: "If you want to get into a highly distinguished school [college], these are the classes you need to take each year. . . . I have ten or eleven copies of the same sheet, of what classes I need to take." When asked why she had so many, she replied that there were numerous meetings held for parents concerning "different colleges' and university requirements," and "My mom, being my mom, went to every single one. . . . She just likes to be really informed and know everything."[102] The burden on moms to "know everything," and therefore remain very much in control, has become great.

The high school is paradoxically less relevant but more consequential. This is not because of what the schooling itself offers adolescents as part of their transit to adulthood, nor for the guidance it provides during this period of life. Whatever it is that comes after adolescence is now much more likely to be viewed as the bridge to adulthood, and even then, adulthood is in no way just around the corner.

While juvenile delinquency has declined as a dominant concern, the public is often directed toward the pathologies of adolescence. As Karen Sternheimer points out, our image of youth is totally distorted as we concentrate on the extreme, on guns and shootings in high schools and colleges and, given the new emphasis on the "unfinished" quality of the adolescent brain and its lack of responsibility, the extremes of body decoration, cutting, or obesity.[103] Without the guidance of seeing this change as a byproduct of adolescent experimentation, as Erikson did, parents are inundated with visions of irresponsible behavior and fear the worst. In response, parents seek to remain firmly in control. Americans seem to be at war with youth, a reversal of the generational configuration sixty years earlier, when coming out of World War II, the peace seemed all for the children. We don't trust our young people to be normal since the former categories of normal no longer fit.

During the major economic recession that began in 2009, parental confusion and angst grew when even those progeny who had been successfully guided through graduation from college came home because they had not been effectively prepared for advantageous careers and needed to lean on parental resources.[104] It is unsurprising that colleges and universities have now come under the same pressure for demonstrable results that has affected the lower schools. These post-adolescents are usually sexually active at school and delay marriage and childbearing for longer and longer periods of time, especially as grown daughters inherit their rights to successful careers.

With preparation for work and for marriage no longer part of normal adolescence, the concept of adolescence itself has lost its cogency. Parents view it as just one more leg in a process of child development, rather than a separate and unique part of the life course. American parenting has become more complicated, not because the issues that adolescence had once addressed disappeared, but because parents no longer seem to have the tools to deal with them. "Adolescence" had once provided parents with a means to understand children who were growing up and growing away.[105] That understanding provides very little guidance today.

Many middle-class parents gave up trying to supervise the sexual behavior that had defined one of the key issues of adolescence, settling for protection against pregnancy and STDs as good enough as their sons and daughters matured. And even pregnancy without marriage was now, for many, an acceptable alternative as rules about sexual behavior changed. But the other matter of how their children would become financially independent became a much more pressing subject with no obvious answers. In this new context of potentially ongoing dependency, parents need ways to understand how exactly they could guide their children to independence. This phenomenon has now created a new category, "boomerang kids," and a literature of advice to accompany it, including titles like *How To Keep Your Kid From Moving Back Home* (2012) and *The Accordion Family: Boomerang Kids, Anxious Parents, and the Toll of the Global Economy* (2012). A recent book, *When Will My Child Grow Up?* (2013), in which family advice writer Elizabeth Fishel teamed up with Jeffrey Arnett, who invented a new stage of the life course that he calls emergent adulthood (from the end of teenage through the twenties),[106] suggests that kids coming back may be quite acceptable, even normal. The book gives advice about how to maintain the privacy of parents and children in the circumstances. But this literature neither quells the anxiety nor offers much comfort to parents who are being forced to adjust to a new kind of "childhood."

With independence put off much longer than in the last century and far longer than in the nineteenth century, Americans have begun to question the idea of independence, or at least to reevaluate its meaning for their children. Today, finding a path toward success has stressed parenting in ways that were rarely seen in the twentieth century, and the decline of adolescence as a useful social category reveals just how much has changed as parents struggle to find other ways to understand what has happened to them and to their offspring. Without effective tools to understand it, the life course has become much murkier and riskier. In response, parents have tried to shield their children from risk whenever they can, as young children in playgrounds, as teenagers engaged in sexual activities, and even as supposed grown-ups unable fully to engage in the job market.

Adolescents, who became known as teenagers by the fourth decade of the twentieth century, were never easy for their parents to understand. But at least at midcentury, parents could expect certain things from them as they became rock-and-roll fanatics or experimented with various kinds of premarital sexuality such as petting and going steady. They were repeating earlier patterns familiar to their parents, now with different music and different margins for sexual controls.[107] The musical *Bye Bye Birdie* tried to explain teenagers to their parents by showing that they were basically good kids gone mad with the music of their idol, Conrad Birdie. The majority could be expected to settle down soon and mellow out. Adolescence was a transitory phase which parents had learned to manage. And the high school had been a known institution that operated to protect their children and advance their interests.

By the early twenty-first century, the so-called millennials—the generation born between the 1980s and the end of the twentieth century—were something else entirely: a generation with unclear goals, embedded in a new world of Internet rules and Facebook friendships.[108] They had sexual hookups rather than dates, and had created a new relationship, "friends with benefits," where sex was sex without window dressing, a phenomenon without obvious earlier precedents for respectable middle-class kids. Without a means to understand them, parents felt helpless to figure out where they were going and tried mightily to bring them toward a safe harbor. Much like immigrant parents, who seek to control their children because they fear losing them to gangs if they get absorbed by popular culture, or forget where they came from if they succeed in school, Americans generally are looking to control their kids as a solution to their difficulties in understanding the many changes that have taken place. Control, above all, became the guiding principle of "successful" parenting during the past thirty years. In this way, parents could protect their kids from predators, from unsafe sex, from failure at school. Protection became more important to parents than independence, more important than giving children the freedom to choose their own futures. In that sense, American childhood as it had evolved over two hundred years of changes had come to an end, in no small part because the end of childhood was not clearly defined.

Parents love their children, but they also love themselves. In fact, they often love and cherish their memories of their own childhood when they worry about their children. Jean-Jacques Rousseau, in his mid-eighteenth-century thoughts about the natural wonderfulness of childhood—thoughts that continue to influence us today—understood very well how large a dose of memory clings to our beliefs about childhood. This is one of the dilemmas of parenting in the modern age, when love and self-love are both deeply part of generational relations.

For many Americans today, their own memories help to define what is most normal and desirable about childhood, and they often judge their children's lives in the light of their own experiences. In so doing, they disregard a fundamental dimension of all situated historical experiences. Children's lives are always enmeshed in the changing cultural and political landscape of their time, and each generation will have a somewhat (and sometimes drastically) different set of social conditions influencing its life. This does not mean that there are no continuities in either nurture or children's culture, in a commitment to caretaking by parents, and in games and reading materials; nor does it mean that parents cannot influence their children's experience. Parents not only have this power, but they often exercise it without giving much thought to its appropriateness. But American parents have, from the beginning of our national life, also been aware that children can make claims on their own experiences and should be given the space to do so.

In the United States, this recognition was fundamental to our earliest visions of childhood and children's rights—that these be aligned with the future and able to change in order to succeed on their terms.

But generational memories are difficult to dismiss or to forget. This is especially the case when many things change in a short time—schooling and technology, mass media and norms of behavior—as has been our experience over the past thirty to forty years, the span of less than two generations.

In fact, American conditions have never remained stable and, as I hope this book has demonstrated, changes have often been rapid and disturbing. In the United States, enormous changes over the past two centuries—the result of wars, economic transformations, massive immigration, and governmental policies—re-created the context within which Americans lived their most intimate lives. Over time, these changes created great variety in a nation whose people are different both in their pasts and in their aims. Still, it is important to be aware of the common factors that have come to bind the many different forms of this relationship together. In the early republic, certain shared conditions of the new country were basic to how childhood was experienced. Americans valued their children's work and resourcefulness, while ideas of republican independence, a discounting of paternal power, and an elevation of women's roles in the family all contributed to a special view of how children were to be treated as they became the source for the nation's future. This lived past became the basis for an American version of the relationship between parents and children, one that continued to inform American behavior and ideals.

Later in the nineteenth century, in the context of war, industrialization, and immigration, philanthropic and state agencies as well as new cultural models of parental authority modified the American vision. In creating social limits on how children could be raised, institutions such as schools, the activities of voluntary (often religiously inspired) agencies, and popular culture emphasized that children needed to be loved and deserved protections beyond what the family could sometimes provide. These also put a spotlight on what society expected from parents—love as well as caretaking, the right to play rather than labor. This remodeled childhood became the dominant ideal by the end of the century as various reformers began to emphasize the mother's vital role in child survival and development. Eventually, it was not reformers but doctors and psychologists who became most deeply engaged in questions of how children could be best brought up in the home.

The exploding possibilities in the relations between parents and children in the twentieth century, as immigrant populations became larger and more varied, not only strengthened the demands made on schools and social agencies, they also powerfully augmented the role of scientific ideas and medical guidelines. These have both aided parents and reduced their autonomy during the twentieth century. And over time, more and more popular media have provided instructions that judge and regulate as they propose normative evaluations. Though not a new phenomenon—women's magazines did these things in the nineteenth century—the media today take many more forms and their seeming intimacy can be more intrusive and importunate.

In this book, I have tried to outline certain fundamental historical features of generational relationships and to suggest why Americans often see themselves as culturally unique in this matter. Together, these several features of how Americans have addressed matters of child-hood and generational obligations over the past two hundred years have created a history that provides its own strong force for common-ality. Without understanding this history, Americans are hard-pressed to understand why they respond as they do today. In fact, many of our discussions float on anxieties that flourish without the understanding that would allow participants to make sense of how and why we treat our children as we do. We are self-conscious about childrearing with-out being truly aware of how our childrearing ideas developed and what makes them compelling to us. In fact, our conversations about what the generations owe each other are the result of values we have inherited as well as contemporary conditions that require a shrewd adaptation as circumstances and knowledge change.

That Americans are connected to this common history does not mean that all children are equally well protected and enabled toward a successful transit through this crucial period of life—far from it. Today, as in the past, vastly different and materially unequal child-hoods define the territory. Those inequalities do not track completely with commonly invoked social categories, like race, class, gender, or locale. Parenting is such a fine art, and parents and children interact in such diverse ways, that many of the most privileged may be poorly served (the subject of *Rebel Without A Cause*, a canonical film about children and youth), while others among the poorest and most recently arrived can be embedded in rich networks of caring parents, kin, and neighbors. In the past, even slave children—badly used, almost entirely unprotected—could be deeply loved and cherished, something brilliantly portrayed by Harriet Beecher Stowe in *Uncle Tom's Cabin*. Still, inequalities in social condition have had serious consequences for children and their parents, as any social welfare worker, teacher, or parent of a foster child can attest. Today's conversations about inequality among children of different backgrounds, and in their different opportunities—in schooling or in health care, for example— are necessary conversations, but they will not provide us with all the answers.[1]

As a historian, my task has been to chart the development of both the commonalities and the differences, to suggest how we function as Americans but remain different as parents and children, different in our outlooks and goals, and in our racial, class, and ethnic identities. But as a parent, I, too, have experienced the fears and dilemmas faced by other parents. And so, it is difficult not to draw a personal conclusion. American parents today (I do not exclude myself) worry too much and provide their children with too little space to grow. That space was essential to the relationships that Americans carved out in the early republic, as they saw that their children's lives would necessarily be different than their own. It was, it should be noted, based on confidence in the possibilities that the future offered. Trust in their children's ability to make their own way was tested throughout the nation's history as Americans became ever more self-conscious about parenting and about what their children required in order to grow up. Benjamin Spock understood how much that trust could be eroded by the growing advice industry that first gave welcomed guidance to American parents and then overwhelmed them. Today this confidence and the trust that accompanied it seem no longer at the vital center of our generational relations, and the change has affected the tone and content of our discussions about children and what they need. Still, it is well to remember that it was no easier being a parent (or a child) in the middle of the nineteenth or twentieth century than it is today, and we may want to bear this in mind as we let our children move toward their own adulthood in their own ways.

At a time when the United Nations Convention on the Rights of the Child (1989) emphasizes children's competence and active engagement, not just their dependence as helpless recipients of adult care and provision, it may be useful for Americans to reconnect to their own past in which this was such a strong component of how we viewed and treated children. I have tried to provide ample examples of children's capacity to act in ways that allowed them to create strong futures. Rather than looking to the resourcefulness of children and how this can sustain the nation, many American parents are overseeing their children in great detail, fearful that a lack of vigilance will imperil their children's success. Of course, children need guidance and protection, but today's middle-class parents may be overdoing both. In fact, Americans today may need a vision that is both larger, so that it embraces all the nation's children, and full of a sturdier confidence in our own progeny. Otherwise, we may provide a narrow success that stymies our children's growth while ignoring the degree to which our children's future depends on the common good of all.

In fact, the relations between parents and children are even more tangled than my already complicated picture would suggest. In this book, I have looked only at one part of the generational equation— what parents owe their children. But historically, it has often been the reverse that was on the minds of ordinary people who wanted some security for their own care in old age when they could no longer provide for their needs. Many Americans used the lure of inheritance to secure their old age.[2] In the nineteenth and early twentieth century, widows and widowers often lived with grown children and grandchildren, one form in which this mutuality of obligation was expressed. Many children benefited from that relationship, as Margaret Mead did and some still do.

By the twentieth-first century, this palpable expression of generational interdependence had mostly (though never entirely) disappeared as Social Security, other pensions, and Medicare, as well as residential facilities, gave the elderly greater resources. Social policies, changing medical interventions, and demographic patterns have tended to obscure the obligations of children to their parents. That we less often see this part of the generational equation does not mean, however, that it does not exist or is any less important. As the parents of their own growing and home-leaving (and now sometimes home-returning) children are discovering, their obligations to the previous generation do not go away even after they have left the parental nest or when the oldsters have moved into a nursing facility. This part of the American generational equation needs to be left to another discussion, one that has already begun among historians, but it is important to recognize its relevance to everything I have been describing in this book.

American assertions of independence for children grew out of commitments to the independence of adults. It was an innovative and generally positive perspective. However much modified over time and augmented with a sense of children's manifold needs, that image of the independent child has never been entirely lost in the culture. But the complex and delicate nature of the relationship between parents and children means that independence is only part of the story. The needs of each generation must be seen to if the generations are to become part of a historical chain, a chain that weaves its way into the larger history of the United States, binding it together.

INTRODUCTION

1. I have drawn the title "Young in America" from Sheila Cole's beautiful picture history book of American children, *To Be Young in America: Growing Up with the Country, 1776–1940* (New York: Little, Brown, 2005).

2. For an excellent historical analysis of just such cases in fin-de-siècle Vienna, see Larry Wolff, *Child Abuse in Freud's Vienna: Postcards from the End of the World* (New York: New York University Press, 1995); see also Paula S. Fass, *Kidnapped: Child Abduction in America* (New York: Oxford University Press, 1997).

3. See, e.g., Edmund Phelps, "What Is Wrong with the West's Economies?" *New York Review of Books* 62 (August 13, 2015), 54–56.

CHAPTER 1

1. Gordon Wood has been especially sensitive to these many social and cultural changes as part of the American revolutionary outlook. See especially Gordon S. Wood, *The Radicalism of the American Revolution* (New York: Vintage, 1993).

2. For how these changes were anticipated before the revolution, see Jay Fliegelman, *Prodigals and Pilgrims: The American Revolution against Patriarchal Authority, 1750–1800* (Cambridge, UK: Cambridge University Press, 1982). For the consequences of the revolution, see James E. Block, *The Crucible of American Consent: American Child Rearing and the Forging of Liberal Society* (Cambridge, MA: Harvard University Press, 2012).

3. From the inaugural edition of Willis's publication *The Youth's Companion* (1827), quoted in Mary Lynn Steven Heininger, "Children, Childhood and Change in America, 1820–1920," in *A Century of Childhood 1820–1920* (Rochester, NY: The Margaret Woodley Strong Museum, 1984), 1.

4. Quoted in Bogna W. Lorence, "Parents and Children in Eighteenth Century Europe," *History of Childhood Quarterly* 2 (1974), 16.

5. See Lynn Hunt, *The Family Romance of the French Revolution* (Berkeley: University of California Press, 1993).

6. Block, *Crucible of American Consent*. Gordon Wood has also registered the vast changes that took place after the Revolution; see especially *Radicalism of*

the American Revolution. For the explicit radicalism regarding patriarchy, see Winthrop R. Jordan, "Familial Politics: Thomas Paine and the Killing of the King, 1776," *Journal of American History* 60 (September 1973), 294–308.

7. For the postrevolutionary changes, Hunt, *The Family Romance of the French Revolution,* 154–203, and Pavla Miller, *Transformations of Patriarchy in the West, 1500–1900* (Bloomington, IN: University of Indiana Press, 1998).

8. Alexis de Tocqueville, *Democracy in America,* vol. 2, trans. Phillips Bradley (New York: Vintage, 1990), 192.

9. This included Latin American countries as Nara B. Milanich has shown; see *Children of Fate: Childhood, Class, and the State in Chile, 1850–1930* (Durham, NC: Duke University Press, 2009).

10. Tocqueville, *Democracy in America,* 2:192–193 (my emphasis).

11. Tocqueville, *Democracy in America,* 2:194, 195.

12. Count Adam de Gurowski, *America and Europe* (New York: D. Appleton, 1857), 380–381.

13. Mother of Mary Lundie Duncan, *America as I Found It* (New York: Robert Carter & Bros, 1852), 25–26.

14. Ulysses S. Grant, *Personal Memoirs of U. S. Grant,* 2 vols. in 1 (New York: Charles L. Webster, 1894), 20.

15. Gurowski, *America and Europe,* 7.

16. Grant, *Personal Memoirs,* 21, 22.

17. Howard P. Chudacoff describes the ample outdoor and unsupervised play available to children of this time in *Children at Play: An American History* (New York: New York University Press, 2007), chap. 2.

18. Daniel Drake, *Pioneer Life in Kentucky, 1785–1800,* ed. Emmet Field Horine (New York: Henry Schuman, 1948), xiii, 7, 15, 38, 74.

19. See the introduction by Louis C. Jones in *Growing Up in Cooper Country: Boyhood Recollections of the New York Frontier,* ed. Louis C. Jones (Syracuse, NY: Syracuse University Press, 1965), and the excerpts from Henry Clarke Wright's *Human Life* in that volume. It is the editor who notes the range of Wright's tasks in his introduction to the volume (17).

20. Mother of Mary Lundie Duncan, *America as I Found It,* 30.

21. Alison Gopnik, Andrew N. Meltzoff, and Patricia K. Kuhl, *The Scientist in the Crib: What Early Learning Tells Us about the Mind* (New York: William Morrow, 2000).

22. Caroline A. Stickney Creevey, *A Daughter of the Puritans: An Autobiography* (New York: G. P. Putnam's Sons, 1916), 74–75, 98, 101.

23. Anna Howard Shaw, *The Story of a Pioneer,* with Elizabeth Jordan (New York: Harper & Brothers, 1915), 30.

24. Rachel Q. Buttz, *A Hoosier Girlhood* (Boston: Richard G. Badger, 1924), 11–13.

25. Enos Hitchcock, *Memoirs of the Bloomsgrove Family,* vol. 1 (Boston: Thomas and Andrews, 1790), 16 (my emphasis).

26. Catherine Beecher, *A Treatise on Domestic Economy* (New York: Schocken Books, 1977; first published in 1841 as *Treatise on Domestic Economy for the Use of Young Ladies at Home and at School*), 16–17.

27. Beecher, *Treatise on Domestic Economy*, 17.

28. Stanley Katz, "Republicanism and the Law of Inheritance in the American Revolutionary Era," *Michigan Law Review* 76 (November 1977), 18. See also Carole Shammas, Marylyn Salmon, and Michael Dahlin, *Inheritance in America: From Colonial Times to the Present* (New Brunswick, NJ: Rutgers University Press, 1987), 65–67. While eldest sons continued to be preferred in a few states, most laws differentiating between children in inheritance had disappeared by the 1790s, and "by 1800 in most states, sons and daughters received equal shares in real and personal property," according to Shammas, Salmon, and Dahlin (67).

29. Katz, "Republicanism and the Law of Inheritance," 17 (emphasis in original).

30. See Donna C. Schuele, "Love, Honor, and the Power of the Law: Probating the Avila Estate in Frontier California," in *On the Borders of Love and Power: Families and Kinship in the Intercultural American Southwest*, ed. David Wallace Adams and Crista DeLuzio (Berkeley: University of California Press, 2012), 141–162.

31. In her examination of the family and childhood in Chile from the mid-nineteenth century, Nara Milanich, *Children of Fate*, provides an excellent contrast with American conditions. Chile had a republican and liberal government, but children's status was rigidly defined throughout the society. According to Milanich, "the Chilean Civil Code carefully delineated the rights and obligations that existed among family members. The complex legal architecture surrounding filiation reflects how the bonds of right and responsibility between parents and children were of particular concern" (175–176). Similar kinds of restrictions were imposed through most of continental Europe.

32. Both quoted in Michael Grossberg, *Governing the Hearth: Law and the Family in Nineteenth Century America* (Chapel Hill: University of North Carolina Press, 1985), 203–204.

33. Timothy Walker, *Introduction to American Law* (Philadelphia: P. H. Nicklin. & T. Johnson, 1837), 188–189, 273.

34. Peter W. Bardaglio, *Reconstructing the Household: Families, Sex, and the Law in the Nineteenth Century South* (Chapel Hill: University of North Carolina Press, 1995).

35. Buttz, *Hoosier Girlhood*, 23.

36. Sabrina Loomis Hills's letters describing her life were published privately as *Memories*, by Mrs. Nathan Cushman Hills (Cleveland, 1899); quote on p. 12.

37. See, e.g., Philip J. Greven, Jr., *Four Generations: Population, Land, and the Family in Colonial Andover, Massachusetts* (Ithaca, NY: Cornell University Press, 1970); Edward Morgan, *American Slavery/American Freedom* (New York: W. W. Norton, 2003).

38. Grossberg, *Governing the Hearth*, 19.

39. Susan E. Klepp, "Revolutionary Bodies: Women and the Fertility Transition in the Mid-Atlantic Region, 1760–1820," *Journal of American History* 85 (December 1998), 910–945.

40. Anne L. Kuhn, *The Mother's Role in Childhood Education: New England Concepts 1830–1860*, Yale Studies in Religious Education (New Haven: Yale University Press, 1947), 34, 38.

41. Quoted in Kuhn, *Mother's Role in Childhood Education*, 4.

42. John C. Burnham, *Bad Habits: Drinking, Smoking, Taking Drugs, Gambling, Sexual Misbehavior, and Swearing in American History* (New York: New York University Press, 1993).

43. See especially Carroll Smith-Rosenberg, *Disorderly Conduct: Visions of Gender in Victorian America* (New York: Oxford University Press, 1986).

44. Horace Bushnell, *Christian Nurture* (New York: Charles Scribner, 1867), reprinted in Philip J. Greven, Jr., *Child Rearing Concepts: 1628–1861* (Itasca, IL: F. E. Peacock Publishers, 1973), 164.

45. Bushnell, *Child Rearing Concepts*, 165.

46. Sarah Pugh, "Diary of Sarah Pugh, October 1851," in *Memorial of Sarah Pugh: A Tribute of Respect from Her Cousins* (Philadelphia: J. B. Lippincott, 1881), 40; accessed online in North American Women's Letters and Diaries, Document 23, http://search .ebscohost.com/login.aspx?direct=true&db=edsasp&AN=edsasp.ASPS744-D088 .CWLD&site=eds-live.

47. Mrs. Child (Lydia Maria) *The Mother's Book*, online at http://digital.library .upenn.edu/women/child/book/book.html (accessed July 18, 2013); Kuhn, *Mother's Role in Childhood Education*, 154; John S. C. Abbott, *The Mother at Home: Or the Principles of Maternal Duty Familiarly Illustrated* (New York, 1833), online at http://digital .lib.msu.edu/projects/ssb/display.cfm?TitleID=556 (accessed July 18, 2013).

48. Reprinted in Donald M. Scott and Bernard Wishy, eds., *America's Families: A Documentary History* (New York: Harper, 1982), 289.

49. Creevey, *Daughter of the Puritans*, 52–53.

50. Quoted in Mary Ann Mason, *From Father's Property to Children's Rights: The History of Child Custody in the United States* (New York: Columbia University Press, 1994), 60.

51. Hendrik Hartog, *Man and Wife in America: A History* (Cambridge, MA: Harvard University Press, 2000), 209. For the circuitous path taken by the case, 93–135.

52. Cornelia Gray Lunt, *Sketches of Childhood and Girlhood: Chicago, 1847–1864* (Evanston, IL: Evanston Historical Society, 1925), 44, 35, 11, 14.

53. S. G. Goodrich, *Recollections of a Life: Men and Things I Have Seen* (New York: Miller, Orton, 1856), 1:53.

54. Erik H. Erikson, *Childhood and Society* (New York: W. W. Norton, 1950), 309.

55. Florence Kelley, *The Autobiography of Florence Kelley: Notes of Sixty Years* (Chicago: Charles H. Kerr, 1986), reprinted from four articles originally published between 1926 and 1927, 30–31, 30.

56. Creevey, *Daughter of the Puritans*, 13, 128.

57. Hills, *Memories*, 3.

58. Fanny Newell, *Memoirs of Fanny Newell; Written by Herself* (Springfield, MA: O. Scott & E. F. Newell [Merriam, Little], 1832), 102.

59. I do not agree with those who see a constantly changing reconfigured patriarchy as the basic Western pattern, especially as it affected children. Instead, I think that there were significant changes in the structure of the household in the United States that makes the term not particularly relevant after the American Revolution. In this, the American experience could have been different from that of other countries. For a contrary view, see Miller, *Transformations of Patriarchy*.

CHAPTER 2

1. Drew Gilpin Faust, *The Republic of Suffering: Death and the American Civil War* (New York: Alfred A. Knopf, 2008), xviii. For the most recent casualty figures, see http://www.nytimes.com/2012/04/03/science/civil-war-toll-up-by-20-percent-in-new -estimate.html?pagewanted=all&_r=0 (accessed October 7, 2014).

2. For young men in the Civil War, see James Marten, *The Children's Civil War* (Chapel Hill: University of North Carolina Press, 1998).

3. *The Brothers' War: Civil War Letters to Their Loved Ones from the Blue and Gray*, ed. Annette Tapert (New York: Times Books, 1988), 151–152, quote on p. 151.

4. Ulysses S. Grant, *Personal Memoirs of U. S. Grant*, 2 vols. in 1 (New York: Charles L. Webster, 1894), 659.

5. Peter W. Bardaglio, *Reconstructing the Household: Families, Sex, and the Law in the Nineteenth Century South* (Chapel Hill: University of North Carolina Press, 1995).

6. Jacob Stroyer, *My Life in the South* (Salem, MA, 1898) in *African American Voices: The Life Cycle of Slavery*, ed. Steven Mintz (St. James, NY: Brandywine Press, 1993), 87.

7. Ira Berlin, *Many Thousands Gone: The First Two Centuries of Slavery in North America* (Cambridge, MA: Harvard University Press, 1998), 130.

8. Steven Mintz, *Huck's Raft: A History of American Childhood* (Cambridge, MA: Harvard University Press, 2004), 98.

9. Marie Jenkins Schwartz, *Born in Bondage: Growing Up Enslaved in the Antebellum South* (Cambridge, MA: Harvard University Press, 2000), 132; George Jackson is quoted on 110.

10. Ira Berlin and Leslie S. Rowland, eds., *Familes and Freedom: A Documentary History of African-American Kinship in the Civil War Era* (New York: New Press, 1997), 5–7.

11. Peter Lesley, as quoted in Sydney Nathans, *To Free a Family: The Journey of Mary Walker* (Cambridge, MA: Harvard University Press, 2012), 159.

12. John T. Greene, ed., *The Ewing Family Civil War Letters* (East Lansing: Michigan State University Press, 1994), 81. The letter by George Ewing is dated June 16, 1863.

13. Priscilla Ferguson Clements, *Growing Pains: Children in the Industrial Age, 1850–1890* (New York: Twayne, 1997), 24–25. See also Berlin and Rowland, eds., *Families and Freedom*, 21–78.

14. Tapert, ed., *Brothers' War*, 36. The letter is from Oliver Wilcox Norton and written on January 28, 1862.

15. From a report by James Bryan, July 27, 1863, in Berlin and Rowland, eds., *Families and Freedom*, 62.

16. This was the figure for the number of slaves up to age fourteen in the population in 1860. Jack E. Eblen, "Growth of the Black Population in Antebellum America, 1820–1860," *Population Studies* 26 (1972), 276.

17. Wilma King, *African American Childhoods: Historical Perspectives from Slavery to Civil Rights* (New York: Palgrave Macmillan, 2005), 80. For the situation facing young African Americans in the South during the period after Reconstruction, see Leon Litwack, *Trouble in Mind: Black Southerners in the Age of Jim Crow* (New York: Alfred A. Knopf, 1998).

18. Charles S. Johnson, *Shadow of the Plantation* (Chicago: University of Chicago Press, 1934; reprinted in 1969) 65.

19. See Milanich, *Children of Fate*, for a similar kind of circulation of children in Chile, especially among the very poor.

20. According to the latest figures on war casualties, the higher number of deaths (the current estimate is from 575,000 to 750,000) would mean 90,000 more orphans than was previously believed. http://www.nytimes.com/2012/04/03/science/civil-war-toll-up-by-20-percent-in-new-estimate.html?pagewanted=all&_r=0 (accessed October 7, 2014).

21. For an excellent discussion of these children, see Timothy Gilfoyle, "Children as Vagrants, Vagabonds, and Thieves in Nineteenth-Century America," in *The Routledge History of Childhood in the Western World*, ed. Paula S. Fass (London: Routledge, Taylor & Francis Group, 2013), 400–418. The problem and its treatment are discussed in Robert Mennel, *Thorns and Thistles: Juvenile Delinquents in the United States, 1825–1940* (Hanover, NH: University Press of New England, 1973).

22. Hugh Cunningham, *Children and Childhood in Western Society since 1500*, 2nd ed. (Harlow, UK: Pearson, Longman, 2005), 148–149.

23. See David J. Kertzer, *Sacrificed for Honor: Italian Infant Abandonment and the Politics of Reproductive Control* (Boston: Beacon Press, 1993).

24. Julie Miller, *Abandoned: Foundlings in Nineteenth-Century New York City* (New York: New York University Press, 2008), 5. For the importance of the problem of foundlings throughout the West in the nineteenth century, see Ivan Jablonka, "Social Welfare in the Western World and the Rights of Children," in Fass, ed., *Routledge History of Childhood*, 380–399.

25. Gilfoyle, "Children as Vagrants," 402.

26. Quoted in Stephen O'Connor, *Orphan Trains: The Story of Charles Loring Brace* (Chicago: University of Chicago Press, 2004), 81.

27. Boston Children's Aid Society, *First Report of the Executive Committee* (Boston, 1865) in Robert H. Bremner et al., eds., *Children and Youth in America: A Documentary History* (Cambridge, MA: Harvard University Press, 1970), 1:734.

28. Boston Children's Aid Society, *First Report of the Executive Committee*.

29. Gilfoyle, "Children as Vagrants," 401.

30. O'Connor, *Orphan Trains*, 88.

31. Quoted in O'Connor, *Orphan Trains*, 78–79.

32. In fact, many of the "orphans" sent to work were not expelled from the house but rather urged to use the agency as a kind of temporary employment bureau, as hard-pressed families used the Children's Aid Society for their own purposes. For this, see Bruce Bellingham, "Waifs and Strays: Child Abandonment, Foster Care, and Families in Mid-Nineteenth Century New York," in *The Uses of Charity: The Poor on Relief in the Nineteenth Century Metropolis*, ed. Peter Mandler (Philadelphia: University of Pennsylvania Press, 1990). A useful summary of the ways in which historians have understood child labor is provided by Brian Gratton and Jon Moen, "Immigration, Culture, and Child Labor in the United States, 1880–1920," *Journal of Interdisciplinary History* 34 (Winter 2004), 355–391.

33. For the strong cross-national influences, see Ivan Jablonka, "Social Welfare in the Western World and the Rights of Children," in Fass, ed., *Routledge History of Childhood*, 380–399, especially 387–388.

34. Linda Gordon, *The Great Arizona Orphan Abduction* (Cambridge, MA: Harvard University Press, 1999).

35. Michael Katz, *In the Shadow of the Poorhouse: A Social History of Welfare in America*, rev. ed. (New York: Basic Books, 1996), 111–112, 109; Brace quote on p. 111.

36. For the continuing difficulties of agencies and courts faced by these decisions, see, e.g., Michael Shapiro, *Solomon's Sword: Two Families and the Children the State Took Away* (New York: Basic Books, 2002); and Nina Bernstein, *The Lost Children of Wilder: The Epic Struggle to Change Foster Care* (New York: Pantheon Books, 2001).

37. See Nell Irvin Painter, *The Exodusters: Black Migration to Kansas after Reconstruction* (New York: W. W. Norton, 1992).

38. For an excellent discussion of the rudeness, profanity, and other ills that afflicted children in the new West, and especially on the mining frontier, see Elliott West, "Heathens and Angels: Childhood in the Rocky Mountain Mining Towns," in *Growing Up in America: Children in Historical Perspective*, ed. N. Ray Hiner and Joseph M. Hawes (Urbana: University of Illinois Press, 1985), 369–384.

39. James Kent, *Commentaries on American Law*, 11th ed. (Boston, 1867), quoted in Bremner et al., eds., *Children and Youth in America*, 1:364.

40. On the attachment of American law to the family as the basic institution of nurture, see Martin Guggenheim, *What's Wrong with Children's Rights?* (Cambridge, MA: Harvard University Press, 2007); Paula S. Fass, "The Past Is Not a Foreign

Country: The Historical Education of Policy," in *Raising Children: Emerging Needs, Modern Risks, and Social Responses*, ed. Jill Duerr Berrick and Neil Gilbert (New York: Oxford University Press, 2008), 9–26.

41. The *New York Times* account (April 10, 1874) that I have used for the details is reprinted in Bremner et al., eds., *Children and Youth in America*, 1:185–186.

42. One recent example can be found on the front page of the *New York Times*, May 9, 2011, A1.

43. See Linda Gordon, *Heroes of Their Own Lives: The Politics and History of Family Violence, Boston 1880–1960* (New York: Penguin Books, 1988), 27–58, on what the affected families often called "the cruelty."

44. For a similar case twenty years later in Chile, see Nara B. Milanich, *Children of Fate: Childhood, Class, and the State in Chile, 1850–1930* (Durham, NC: Duke University Press, 2009), especially 1–3; for Vienna at the end of the nineteenth century, see Larry Wolff, *Child Abuse in Freud's Vienna: Postcards for the End of the World* (New York: New York University Press, 1995).

45. Viviana A. Zelizer, *Pricing the Priceless Child: The Changing Social Value of Children* (New York: Basic Books, 1985). For Victorian illustrations, see Anne Higonnet, *Pictures of Innocence: The History and Crisis of Ideal Childhood* (New York: Thames & Hudson, 1998), 31–71.

46. Gordon, *Heroes of Their Own Lives*.

47. Jacob A. Riis, *The Making of an American* (New York: Macmillan, 1903).

48. Timothy J. Gilfoyle, "Street-Rats and Gutter-Snipes: Child Pickpockets and Street Culture in New York City, 1850–1900," *Journal of Social History* 37 (Summer 2004); Jacob A. Riis, *The Children of the Poor* (New York: Charles Scribner's Sons, 1892; repr., New York: Arno Press and New York Times, 1971).

49. Rose Cohen, *Out of the Shadow* (George H. Doran, 1918; repr., Ithaca, NY: Cornell University Press, 1995), 81, 89–90.

50. Cohen, *Out of the Shadow*, 90.

51. Paula S. Fass, "A Historical Context for the United Nations Convention on the Rights of the Child," *Annals of the American Academy of Political and Social Science*, no. 633 (January 2011), 17–29.

52. For child labor as a subject for reform efforts in the United States and Europe, see Hugh Cunningham, *Children and Childhood in Western Society Since 1500*, 2nd edition (Harlow, UK: Pearson, Longman, 2005), 140–146; Colin Heywood, "Children's Work in Countryside and City," in Fass, ed., *Routledge History of Childhood*, 125–141. For the traditional incorporation of children into work regimes and the attitudes of immigrant parents, see Stephen Lassonde, *Learning to Forget: Schooling and Family Life in New Haven's Working Class, 1870–1940* (New Haven: Yale University Press, 2007.

53. This marks a change from earlier in the century, when the work of adolescent girls was initially taken as a good thing. See Thomas Dublin, *Women at Work: The Transformation of Work and Community in Lowell, Massachusetts* (New York: Columbia University Press, 1981).

54. On schooling in this period, see William J. Reese, *America's Public Schools: From the Common School to "No Child Left Behind"* (Baltimore: Johns Hopkins University Press), 45–78. For similar experience in Sweden, see Bengt Sandin, " 'In the Large Factory Town': Child Labour Legislation, Child Labour and School Compulsion," in *Industrious Children: Work and Childhood in the Nordic Countries, 1850–1990*, ed. Ning deConinck-Smith, Bengt Sandin, and Ellen Schrumpf (Odense, Denmark: Odense University Press, 1997), 17–46.

55. The archtypical story was told by Theodore Dreiser in his novel, *Sister Carrie*, first published in 1899.

56. For age of consent changes, see Mary E. Odem, *Delinquent Daughters: Protecting and Policing Adolescent Female Sexuality in the United States, 1885–1920* (Chapel Hill: University of North Carolina Press, 1995). For amusements and the temptations of commerce, see Kathy Peiss, *Cheap Amusements: Working Women and Leisure in Turn of the Century New York* (Philadelphia: Temple University Press, 1986).

57. Riis, *Children of the Poor*, 43–44.

58. Gordon, *Heroes of Their Own Lives*.

59. For the story of the "lost boy" and its broad influence, see Paula S. Fass, *Kidnapped: Child Abduction in America* (New York: Oxford University Press, 1997), chap. 1.

60. Quoted in Norman Zierold, *Little Charley Ross: America's First Kidnapping for Ransom* (Boston: Little, Brown, 1967), 36.

61. On the importance of fathers for women reformers, see Ellen Condliffe Lagemann, *Education in the Lives of Progressive Reformers* (Cambridge, MA: Harvard University Press, 1979).

62. For this matter as it applied especially to Britain and the United States, see John Gillis, *A World of Their Own Making: Myth, Ritual, and the Quest for Family Values* (New York: Basic Books, 1996). For the American Victorian family, see also Steven Mintz and Susan Kellogg, *Domestic Revolutions: A Social History of American Family Life* (New York: Free Press, 1988). I think that most historians have placed this transformation too early in the American context, assigning it to the nineteenth century generally, when it really applies only to the period after the Civil War.

63. Henry Seidel Canby, "Life in the Nineties: Home and Parents," *Harper's* 169 (1934), 271, 271. Stephen M. Frank provides a revealing discussion of the relationship between fathers and sons in his reading of Civil War letters. In evaluating the father's role, Frank concludes that these were affectionate relationships that were also characterized by a certain level of authority; " 'Rendering Aid and Comfort': Images of Fatherhood in the Letters of Civil War Soldiers from Massachusetts and Michigan," *Journal of Social History* 26 (Fall 1992), 5–31.

64. Clements, *Growing Pains*, 36–80.

65. Anne F. Hyde, "Mixed-Race Children in the American West," in Fass, ed., *Routledge History of Childhood*, 344–359. See also Hyde's *Empires, Nations, and Families: A New History of the North American West, 1800–1860* (Lincoln: University of Nebraska Press, 2011).

66. West, "Heathens and Angels," 375.

67. Lawrence R. Friedman, *American Law in the 20th Century* (New Haven: Yale University Press, 2002), 431–432.

68. For these class etiquettes, see Karen Haltunnen, *Confidence Men and Painted Women: A Study of Middle-Class Culture in America, 1830–1870* (New Haven: Yale University Press, 1982).

69. Kate Douglas Wiggin, *My Garden of Memory: An Autobiography* (Boston: Houghton Mifflin, 1923), 47–48.

70. For the role of schools in the late nineteenth century in Western societies generally, see Pavla Miller, *Transformations of Patriarchy in the West, 1500–1900* (Bloomington: University of Indiana Press, 1998). Miller also demonstrates how fatherhood was reconfigured and strengthened in various public ways in the late nineteenth century.

CHAPTER 3

1. Charles Darwin, *The Expression of the Emotions in Man and Animals* (London: John Murry, 1872).

2. Felix Adler, *The Moral Instruction of Children* (New York: D. Appleton, 1893).

3. An American Mother, "The Modern Son and Daughter," *Ladies' Home Journal* 17 (March 1900), 17.

4. Sophonisba P. Breckinridge and Edith Abbott, *The Delinquent Child and the Home: A Study of the Delinquent Wards of the Juvenile Court of Chicago* (New York: Survey Associates, 1912), 8.

5. Breckinridge and Abbott, *Delinquent Child and the Home*, 288 (my emphasis).

6. Breckinridge and Abbott, *Delinquent Child and the Home*, 292 (my emphasis).

7. For a discussion of these matters and how "parental schools" operated, see Julia Grant, *The Boy Problem: Educating Boys in Urban America, 1870–1970* (Baltimore: Johns Hopkins University Press, 2014), chap. 3.

8. For this matter, see Mary E. Odem, *Delinquent Daughters: Protecting and Policing Adolescent Female Sexuality in the United States, 1885–1920* (Chapel Hill: University of North Carolina, 1995), for cases related to Los Angeles; and Eric C. Schneider, *In the Web of Class: Delinquents and Reformers in Boston, 1810s–1930s* (New York: New York University Press, 1992).

9. Linda Gordon, *Heroes of Their Own Lives: The Politics and History of Family Violence, Boston 1880–1960* (New York: Penguin Books, 1988); see especially chaps. 1–4.

10. Eliza Cook, "How to Make a Home Intolerable," *Ladies' Repository* 15 (November 1855), 673.

11. For this change, see Gordon, *Heroes of Their Own Lives*.

12. Sheila Rothman, *Woman's Proper Place: A History of Changing Ideals and Practices, 1870 to the Present* (New York: Basic Books, 1978).

13. Suellen Hoy, *Chasing Dirt: The American Pursuit of Cleanliness* (New York: Oxford University Press, 1995), 85–149.

14. L. Emmett Holt, *The Care and Feeding of Children: A Catechism for the Use of Mothers and Children's Nurses* (1894; repr., New York: D. Appleton, 1923). William Cadogan, *An Essay upon Nursing and the Management of Children from Their Birth to Three Years of Age; by a Physician* . . . (London: J. Roberts, 1749). For William Cadogan, see Morwenna Rendle-Short and John Rendle-Short, *The Father of Child Care: Life of William Cadogan, 1711–1797* (Bristol, UK: John Wright & Sons, 1966).

15. For how reform varied over time regarding infant mortality from the mid-nineteenth century through the 1920s, see Richard A. Meckel, *Save the Babies: American Public Health Reform and the Prevention of Infant Mortality, 1850–1929* (Baltimore: Johns Hopkins University Press, 1990).

16. For the Children's Bureau, see Kriste Lindenmeyer, *"A Right to Childhood": The U.S. Children's Bureau and Child Welfare, 1912–46* (Urbana: University of Illinois Press, 1997). Nancy Tomes, *The Gospel of Germs: Men, Women, and the Microbe in American Life* (Cambridge, MA: Harvard University Press, 1998).

17. *Third Annual Report of the Chief, Children's Bureau, to the Secretary of Labor, Fiscal Year Ended June 30, 1915* (Washington, DC: US Government Printing Office, 1915), 8; accessed online from Google Books, August 4, 2013.

18. Hugh Cunningham, *Children and Childhood in Western Society Since 1500*, 2nd ed. (Harlow, UK: Pearson, Longman, 2005), 155.

19. Louis Starr, *Hygiene of the Nursery: Including the General Regimen and Feeding of Infants and Children, and the General Management of Ordinary Emergencies of Early Life*, 2nd ed. (Philadelphia: Blakiston & Son, 1889), ix; accessed online from Google Books, August 4, 2013.

20. Alice Birney, quoted in Alice Boardman Smuts, *Science in the Service of Children, 1893–1935* (New Haven: Yale University Press, 2006), 21.

21. Holt, *Care and Feeding of Children*, 42.

22. US Department of Labor, Children's Bureau, *Infant Mortality: Montclair, N.J.: A Study of Infant Mortality in a Suburban Community*, Infant Mortality Series 4, Bureau Publication 11 (Washington, DC: US Government Printing Office, 1915), 16.

23. Edwardo Porter, "Income Inequality Is Costing the Nation on Social Issues, *New York Times*, April 29, 2015, B1, 8.

24. For a discussion of this conflicting and sometimes contradictory advice, see Ann Hulbert, *Raising America: Experts, Parents, and a Century of Advice about Children* (New York: Knopf, 2003).

25. *Second Annual Report of the Chief, Children's Bureau, to the Secretary of Labor, Fiscal Year Ended June 30, 1914* (Washington, DC: US Government Printing Office, 1914), p. 8; accessed online from Google Books, August 4, 2013.

26. Children's Bureau, *Infant Mortality: Montclair*, 12.

27. Quoted in Hulbert, *Raising America*, 110.

28. See Lindenmeyer, *"A Right to Childhood,"* 103–107.

29. Lawrence K. Frank, "Forces Leading to the Child Development Viewpoint and Study" (1939), Lawrence K. Frank Papers, MS C 280b History of Medicine Division, National Library of Medicine (b.11, A2). I want to thank Dennis R. Bryson for providing me with this material.

30. For the importance of the Iowa Station, see Hamilton Cravens, *Before Head Start: The Iowa Station and America's Children* (Chapel Hill: University of North Carolina Press, 1993).

31. Quoted in Hulbert, *Raising America*, 103.

32. Howard P. Chudacoff, *How Old Are You? Age Consciousness in American Culture* (Princeton, NJ: Princeton University Press, 1989).

33. For this new role for doctors, see Judith Walzer Leavitt, *Brought to Bed: Childbearing in America, 1750–1950* (New York: Oxford University Press, 1988).

34. "The Misbehaviorist," chapter 5 of Hulbert, *Raising America*. For Watson, see also Paula S. Fass, *The Damned and the Beautiful: American Youth in the 1920s* (New York: Oxford University Press, 1977), 100–107.

35. US Department of Health, Education, and Welfare, Children's Bureau, "The Story of Infant Care," (Washington, DC: Children's Bureau, 1965), 5, 11–12.

36. Children's Bureau, "The Story of Infant Care," 21.

37. Peter N. Stearns, *Anxious Parents: A History of Modern Childrearing in America* (New York: New York University Press, 2003).

38. Lindenmeyer, *"A Right to Childhood,"* 76–107.

39. See Fass, *The Damned and the Beautiful*, 100–116; Caroline M. Hinkle, "Creating 'Dad': Finding a Place for Father in the Middle-Class Home, 1900–1929" (PhD diss., University of California at Berkeley, 2011).

40. For Watson's biography, see Hulbert, *Raising America*, chap. 5; and Watson's own discussion in *A History of Psychology in Autobiography*, ed. Carl Murchison (New York: Russell and Russell, 1961), 3:271–281.

41. Quoted in Hulbert, *Raising America*, 136.

42. For the German case, see Dirk Schurmann, "Childhood and Youth in Nazi Germany," in Fass, ed., *Routledge History of Childhood*.

43. See Nathan G. Hale, Jr., *The Rise and Crisis of Psychoanalysis in the United States: Freud and the Americans, 1917–1985* (New York: Oxford University Press, 1995).

44. For example, E. L. Coolidge, "Modern Substitutes for Spanking," 31 (September 1914); S. Merwin, "A Father's Relation to his Children," 40 (July 1923); and J. J. Walsh et al., "Should Children Be Punished?" 41 (March 1924)—all in *Ladies' Home Journal*.

45. For the use of psychiatry in public trials in the 1920s, see Paula S. Fass, *Kidnapped: Child Abduction in America* (New York: Oxford University Press, 1997), chap. 2.

46. William Alanson White, "Nervous and Mental Hygiene among Children in Present-Day Life," in *The Child: His Nature and His Needs*, ed. M. V. O'Shea (New York: Children's Foundation, 1924), 205.

47. Helen Faw Mull, "Love Them and Tell Them So," *Parents' Magazine* 13 (July 1938), 17, 65; Lawson G. Lowrey, "The Family Melting Pot," *Parents' Magazine* 8 (November 1933), 20–21; James Lee Ellenwood, "Are You a Dictator?" *Parents' Magazine* 13 (November 1938), 16–17, 48; Helen Van Pelt Wilson, "Education Is a Two-Way Street," *Parents' Magazine* 19 (April 1944), 24–25.

48. Ruth Heller Freund, "We Don't Keep Our Children in the Dark about Family Problems," *Parents' Magazine* 20 (December 1945), 72.

49. Marion LeBron, "Relax and Enjoy Your Children," *Parents' Magazine* 16 (January 1941), 29, 81.

50. Lorine Pruette, "Mother's Job," *Parents' Magazine* 7 (November 1932), 18–20, 40; Louise Cruice, "The Ballade of the Modern Mother," *Parents' Magazine* 8 (November 1933), 84 (emphasis in original).

51. Julia Grant, *Raising Baby by the Book: The Education of American Mothers* (New Haven: Yale University Press, 1998).

52. Margaret Mead, *Blackberry Winter: My Earlier Years* (New York: William Morrow, 1972), 19, 25–26, 28. This does not mean that household work for girls was not also declining. See Jane H. Hunter, *How Young Ladies Became Girls: The Victorian Origins of American Girlhood* (New Haven: Yale University Press, 2002).

53. Mead, *Blackberry Winter*, 46–47, 53–54.

54. Lucy Sprague Mitchell, *Two Lives: The Story of Wesley Clair Mitchell and Myself* (New York: Simon and Schuster, 1953), 49.

55. See Cravens, *Before Head Start*.

56. Smuts, *Science in the Service of Children*, chaps. 8–9. For the important role of foundation support in the 1920s and 1930s, see Dennis Raymond Bryson, *Socializing the Young: The Role of Foundations, 1923–1941* (Westport, CT: Bergin & Garvey, 2002). For the development of a scientific perspective on childrearing, see also Elizabeth M. R. Lomax, Jerome Kagan, and Barbara G. Rosenkranz, *Science and Patterns of Child Care* (San Francisco: W. H. Freeman, 1978).

57. Smuts, *Science in the Service of Children*, chap. 10, provides the best discussion of Gesell.

58. Gesell is quoted in Hulbert, *Raising America*, 164 (emphasis in original).

59. For Chicago as the site of the most important initial studies of juvenile delinquency, and a book that examines the work of Healy, Glueck, Thomas, and Shaw, see Harold Finestone, *Victims of Change: Juvenile Delinquents in American Society*, Contributions to Sociology 20 (Westport, CT: Greenwood Press, 1976).

60. Smuts, *Science in the Service of Children*, 140. See also Margo Horn, *Before It's Too Late: The Child Guidance Movement in the United States* (Philadelphia: Temple University Press, 1989).

61. For the general failure, see Schneider, *In the Web of Class*; Franklin Zimring, *American Juvenile Justice* (New York: Oxford University Press, 2005). James Gilbert provides a good summary of the work done over the course of half a century in this field in *A Cycle of Outrage: America's Reaction to the Juvenile Delinquent in the 1950s* (New York: Oxford University Press, 1986), chap. 8.

62. White House Conference on Child Health and Protection, *The Young Child in the Home: A Survey of 3000 Families*, ed. John E. Anderson (New York: D. Appleton Century, 1936).

63. William Allen White, *The Autobiography of William Allen White* (New York: Macmillan, 1946), 27, 28.

64. White, *Autobiography*, 44, 47.

65. White House Conference, *Young Child in the Home*, 23.

66. White House Conference, *Young Child in the Home*, 72, 84.

67. Quoted in *Time*, February 17, 1936, 55.

68. White House Conference, *Young Child in the Home*, 206, 208. Stearns, *Anxious Parents*, chap. 5.

69. Steven Ruggles, "The Transformation of American Family Structure," *American Historical Review* 99 (February 1994), 103–128.

70. The most elaborate expression of this was in the work of Talcott Parsons. See Talcott Parsons and Robert F. Bales, *Family: Socialization and Interaction Process* (Glencoe, IL: Free Press, 1960). For a critique of this literature, see Paula S. Fass, "Perspectives on Family Theory: Families in History and Beyond," in *Family, Self, and Society: Toward a New Agenda for Family Research*, edited by Philip A. Cowan, Dorothy Field, Donald A. Hansen, Arlene Skolnick, and Guy E. Swanson (Hillsdale, NJ: Erlbaum, 1993), 143–152.

71. See Grace Abbott, "A Sister's Memories," *Social Service Review* 13 (September 1939), 351–407.

72. For Elsie Clews Parsons, see Rosalind Rosenberg, *Beyond Separate Spheres: The Intellectual Roots of Modern Feminism* (New Haven: Yale University Press, 1982).

73. Sarah Blaffer Hrdy, *Mother Nature: A History of Mothers, Infants, and Natural Selection* (New York: Pantheon, 1999). While historically and in terms of evolution, it was probably women who most often filled these roles, they were by no means restricted to them. Elliott West shows how men from outside the family often filled in to help provide love and instruction to children who suffered neglect as a result of circumstances on the mining frontier. See "'Heathens and Angels': Childhood in the Rocky Mountain Mining Towns," in *Growing Up in America: Children in Historical Perspective*, ed. N. Ray Hiner and Joseph M. Hawes (Urbana: University of Illinois Press, 1985), 369–384.

74. See Fass, "Perspectives on Family Theory," 143–152. See also Stephanie Coontz, *The Way We Never Were: American Families and the Nostalgia Trip* (New York: Basic Books, 1992).

75. Frank, "Forces Leading to the Child Development Viewpoint," 1, 2.

76. Mitchell, *Two Lives*, 74, 55, 62.

77. Mitchell, *Two Lives*, 58–59, 60.

78. Mitchell, *Two Lives*, 72.

79. A comprehensive study of these early criminologists is provided by Jon Dundee Snodgrass, "The American Criminological Tradition: Portraits of the Men and Ideology in a Discipline" (PhD diss., Sociology, University of Pennsylvana, 1972); see also Finestone, *Victims of Change*.

80. See John Watson's short review of his life in Murchison, ed., *History of Psychology*, 3:271–281. For the university and the city, see Steven J. Diner, *A City and Its Universities: Public Policy in Chicago, 1892–1919* (Chapel Hill: University of North Car-

olina Press, 1980). For the development of the university as the center of social science research, see Everett Rogers, *History of Communications Study* (New York: Basic Books, 1994), chap. 5.

81. Michell, *Two Lives*, 87–88.

CHAPTER 4

1. As Michael B. Katz and Ian E. Davey have shown, in the case of Hamilton, Ontario, the increase in high school attendance is by no means historically predestined. In a midcentury Canadian city like Hamilton, young people between ages thirteen and sixteen at first went to the newly organized upper school in that city in much larger numbers than they would a decade later, once jobs became available through industrialization. The Depression in the United States in the mid-twentieth century radically reduced job opportunities for young people, but the vast majority of these did not subsequently return to the workforce once jobs became available except for the brief period when the United States was at war. Instead, going to high school became a regular and expected activity for all American youth. See John Demos and Sarane Spence Boocock, eds., "Youth and Early Industrialization in a Canadian City," in *Turning Points: Historical and Sociological Essays on the Family*, supplement, *American Journal of Sociology* 84 (1978), S81–S119.

2. Kriste Lindemeyer, *The Greatest Generation Grows Up: American Childhood in the 1930s* (Chicago: Ivan R. Dee, 2005).

3. Leonard Covello, with Guido D'Agostino, *The Heart Is the Teacher* (New York: McGraw-Hill, 1958). For a discussion of how this belief continues today into the college period as immigration has once again become a dominant American experience, see Paula S. Fass, *Children of a New World: Society, Culture, and Globalization* (New York: New York University Press, 2007), chap. 1.

4. James G. Carter, *Essays upon Popular Education* (Boston: Bowles and Dearborn, 1826; repr., New York: Arno Press and *New York Times*, 1969), 20.

5. Carter, *Essays upon Popular Education*, 20, 21 (emphases in original).

6. Thomas Jefferson, *Notes on the State of Virginia*, ed. William Peden (New York: W. W. Norton, 1972).

7. David B. Tyack, *The One Best System: A History of American Urban Education* (Cambridge, MA: Harvard University Press, 1974).

8. For the little red schoolhouse in the American imagination and in reality, see Jonathan Zimmerman, *Small Wonder: The Little Red Schoolhouse in History and Memory* (New Haven: Yale University Press, 2009).

9. Bernard Baruch, *My Own Story*, in *Childhood Revisited*, ed. Joel I. Milgram and Dorothy June Sciarra (New York: Macmillan, 1974), 35.

10. Chet Huntley, *The Generous Years: Remembrances of a Frontier Boyhood* (New York: Random House, 1968), 90, 91, 16, 68, 88.

11. For the importance of play as recorded in memoirs, see Howard P. Chudacoff, *Children at Play: An American History* (New York: New York University Press, 2007).

12. Kate Douglas Wiggin, *My Garden of Memory: An Autobiography* (Boston: Houghton Mifflin, 1923), 44 (quote), 53.

13. Edna Ferber, *A Peculiar Treasure* (Garden City, NY: Doubleday, 1960); Sidney Hook, *Out of Step: An Unquiet Life in the 20th Century* (New York: Harper & Row, 1987), 12; Gertrude Edelstein Berg, *Molly and Me*, reprinted in Milgram and Sciarra, ed., *Childhood Revisited*, 42.

14. White House Conference on Child Health and Protection, *The Adolescent in the Family: A Study of Personality Development in the Home Environment*, Report of the Subcommittee on the Function of Home Activities in the Education of the Child, E. W. Burgess, Chairman (New York: D. Appleton-Century, 1934), 26.

15. I have borrowed this term from the title of Kate Simon's second volume of memoirs, *A Wider World: Portraits in an Adolescence* (New York: Harper & Row, 1986).

16. William J. Reese, *America's Public Schools: From the Common School to "No Child Left Behind"* (Baltimore: Johns Hopkins University Press, 2005), 181, 182; *School Life* as quoted in Reese, *America's Public Schools*, 181.

17. Claudia Goldin, "America's Graduation from High School: The Evolution and Spread of Secondary Schooling in the Twentieth Century," *Journal of Economic History* 58:2 (June 1998), 347.

18. Goldin, "America's Graduation from High School," 358, 361.

19. Ferber, *Peculiar Treasure*, 93.

20. White House Conference, *Adolescent in the Family*, 3.

21. On the importance of schooling in the creation of the nation-state, see Pavla Miller, *Transformations of Patriarchy in the West, 1500–1900* (Bloomington: University of Indiana Press, 1998), chap. 6. A good example of the foreignness of schools in certain regions is captured in Miller's description of language usage in Italy: "In Italy at the time of unification in 1860, it was estimated that not more than 2.4 percent of the people actually used the Italian language for the ordinary purposes of life; the rest spoke in idioms so different that the schoolmasters sent by the Italian state into Sicily in the 1860s were mistaken for Englishmen" (138).

22. Goldin, "America's Graduation from High School," 350; for general agreement on the nature of the high school curriculum, Reese, *America's Public Schools*, 189. Reed Ueda effectively shows this change in one community in Massachusetts, in *Avenues to Adulthood: The Origins of the High School and Social Mobility in an American Suburb*, Interdisciplinary Perspectives on Modern History (Cambridge, UK: Cambridge University Press, 1987).

23. Charles R. Foster, *Extra-Curricular Activities in the High School* (Richmond, VA: Johnson Publishing, 1925), 5. For the importance of extracurricular activities for immigrants especially, see, Paula S. Fass, *Outside In: Minorities and the Transformation of American Education* (New York: Oxford University Press, 1989), 73–111.

24. An excellent discussion of the problems of youth as they lost their ability to work in the late nineteenth century can be found in James D. Schmidt, "'Rendered More Useful': Child Labor and Age Consciousness in the Long Nineteenth Century," in *Age in America: The Colonial Era to the Present*, ed. Corinne T. Field and Nicholas L. Syrett (New York: New York University Press, 2015), 148–165.

25. Jon Savage, *Teenage: The Prehistory of Youth Culture, 1875–1945* (New York: Penguin, 2007).

26. Kurt Vonnegut, quoted in Reese, *America's Public Schools*, 286.

27. Kate Simon, *Bronx Primitive: Portraits in a Childhood* (New York: Viking, 1982); Simon, *Wider World*.

28. Simon, *Wider World*, 6; Covello, *Heart Is the Teacher*, acknowledgements.

29. Simon, *Wider World*, 10.

30. Louis Wirth, "Culture Conflict in the Immigrant Family" (master's thesis, University of Chicago, June 1925), 11.

31. For a general discussion of the experience of immigrant children and how this process affected them and their families, see Melissa R. Klapper, *Small Strangers: The Experiences of Immigrant Children in America, 1880–1925* (Chicago: Ivan R. Dee, 2007).

32. W. Lloyd Warner and Leo Srole, *The Social Systems of American Ethnic Groups* (New Haven: Yale University Press, 1945), 127–128.

33. Sigmund Freud, *The Interpretation of Dreams*, trans. James Strachey (New York: Basic Books, 1956), 257.

34. For this process, see especially Stephen Lassonde, *Learning to Forget: Schooling and Family Life in New Haven's Working Class, 1870–1940* (New Haven: Yale University Press, 2005).

35. Covello, *Heart Is the Teacher*, 6; Wirth, "Culture Conflict in the Immigrant Family," 46.

36. Wirth, "Culture Conflict in the Immigrant Family," 67 (quote).

37. Simon, *Bronx Primitive*, 51; Robert Merrill, with Sandford Doty, *Once More with Feeling* (New York: Macmillan, 1965), 28.

38. This is nicely captured in Anzia Yezierska's immigrant novel, *The Bread Givers* (1925; repr., New York: Doubleday, 1952).

39. Covello, *Heart Is the Teacher*, 49, 50.

40. Simon, *Bronx Primitive*, 167–168. For the changing mores of American youth, see Paula S. Fass, *The Damned and the Beautiful: American Youth in the 1920s* (New York: Oxford University Press, 1977); Kathy Peiss, *Cheap Amusements: Working Women and Leisure in Turn-of-the-Century New York* (Philadelphia: Temple University Press, 1986).

41. Mary Odem, *Delinquent Daughters: Protecting and Policing Adolescent Female Sexuality in the United States* (Chapel Hill: University of North Carolina Press, 1995).

42. *A Bintel Brief: Sixty Years of Letters from the Lower East Side to the Jewish Daily Forward*, ed. Isaac Metzker (New York: Schocken Books, 1990); William I. Thomas, *The Unadjusted Girl: With Cases and Standpoint for Behavior Analysis* (Boston: Little,

Brown, 1924), 109. For the special animus directed at girl delinquents (mostly immigrant) during the Progressive era, see Steven Schlossman and Stephanie Wallach, "The Crime of Precocious Sexuality: Female Juvenile Delinquency in the Progressive Era," *Harvard Educational Review* 48:1 (February 1978), 65–94.

43. Irving Louis Horowitz, *Daydreams and Nightmares* (New Brunswick, NJ: Transaction, 2012), 102.

44. Warner and Srole, *Social Systems of American Ethnic Groups*, 151–152.

45. Leonard Covello, *The Social Background of the Italo-American School Child* (Leiden: E. J. Brill, 1967), 358–359.

46. See Fass, *Outside In*, chap. 3, for Bay Ridge High School.

47. Covello, *Heart Is the Teacher*, 6. Fass, *Outside In*, especially chap. 3. Lassonde, *Learning to Forget*, 134.

48. Covello, *Heart Is the Teacher*, 71.

49. Gary Orfield, Mark D. Bachmeier, David R. James, and Tamela Eide, "Deepening Segregation in American Public Schools: A Special Report from the Harvard Project on School Desegregation," in *Interdisciplinary Perspectives on the New Immigration*, vol. 5, *The New Immigrant and American Schools*, ed. Marcelo M. Suárez-Orozco, Carola Suárez-Orozco, and Desiree Qin-Hilliard (New York: Routledge, 2001), 121–140.

50. Merrill, *Once More with Feeling*, 46. According to Covello, in many elementary schools in New York City, Italians made up over 90% of the children. He called this "a normal occurrence." *Social Background of the Italo-American School Child*, 344.

51. Horowitz, *Daydreams and Nightmares*, 89.

52. Covello, *Social Background of the Italo-American School Child*, 341.

53. Covello, *Heart Is the Teacher*, 70. Italian Catholics became the objects of intense Protestant missionizing work in the early twentieth century. A good example of how important schooling was for those engaged in this process can be found in Antonio Mangano, *Sons of Italy* (New York: Missionary Education Movement of the United States and Canada, 1917). The volume was edited and supervised by the Missionary Education Movement and was intended to show exactly how Italian youth could be best approached and understood.

54. For another early version of this sensitivity at the same period of time, see Diana Selig, *Americans All: The Cultural Gifts Movement* (Cambridge, MA: Harvard University Press, 2008).

55. Covello, *Social Background of the Italo-American School Child*, 343.

56. Allison Davis, "Socialization and Adolescent Personality," in National Society for the Study of Education, *Forty-Third Yearbook, Part I: Adolescence* (Chicago: Department of Education of the University of Chicago, 1944), 201–202.

57. See Fass, *Outside In*, chap. 3; Fass, *Children of a New World*, chap. 3.

58. Lindenmeyer, *Greatest Generation Grows Up*, 50–77; Fass, *Outside In*, chap. 4.

59. From James Conant, *My Several Lives*, reprinted in *Childhood Revisited*, ed. Milgram and Sciarra, 83.

60. Ferber, *Peculiar Treasures*, 93.

61. Anne Moody, *Coming of Age in Mississippi* (New York: Delta, 2004), 135, 128: Merrill, *Once More with Feeling*, 47.

62. See Mary P. Ryan, *Cradle of the Middle Class: The Family in Oneida County, New York, 1780–1865* (Cambridge, UK: Cambridge University Press, 1981); Joseph F. Kett, *Rites of Passage: Adolescence in America, 1790 to the Present* (New York: Basic Books, 1977).

63. See Dorothy Ross, *G. Stanley Hall: The Psychologist as Prophet* (Chicago: University of Chicago Press, 1972).

64. Louis Starr, *The Adolescent Period: Its Features and Management* (Philadelphia: P. Blakiston's Sons, 1915).

65. Margaret Mead, *Coming of Age in Samoa: A Psychological Study of Primitive Youth for Western Civilization* (New York: W. Morrow, 1928).

66. There is a large literature on the subject and on how it has been studied by American scholars. Good introductions to this literature are Harold Finestone, *Victims of Change: Juvenile Delinquents in American Society* (Westport, CT: Greenwood Press, 1976); and Jon Dundee Snodgrass, "The American Criminological Tradition: Portraits of the Men and Ideology of a Discipline" (PhD diss., University of Pennsylvania, 1972).

67. See Lindenmeyer, *Greatest Generation Grows Up*, especially 46–109; Glenn H. Elder, Jr., *Children of the Great Depression: Social Change in Life Experience* (Chicago: Unversity of Chicago Press, 1974).

68. National Society for the Study of Education, *Adolescence*, v.

69. Howard Chudacoff, *How Old Are You? Age Consciousness in American Culture* (Princeton, NJ: Princeton University Press, 1989).

70. David Riesman, with Nathan Glazer and Reuel Denney, *The Lonely Crowd: A Study of the Changing American Character* (New Haven: Yale University Press, 1950).

71. Quoted in Wirth, "Culture Conflict in the Immigrant Family," 67.

72. Robert S. Lynd and Helen Merrell Lynd, *Middletown: A Study in Modern American Culture* (New York: Harcourt, Brace & World, 1929), 134–135, for school activities in Middletown, 211–222.

73. For progressive toys, see Gary Cross, *Kids' Stuff: Toys and the Changing World of American Childhood* (Cambridge, MA: Harvard University Press, 1997), chap. 5.

74. For progressive parenting and its relationship to schooling and politics, see Julia Mickenberg, "The Pedagogy of the Popular Front: 'Progressive Parent' for a New Generation, 1918–1945," in *The American Child: A Cultural Studies Reader*, ed. Caroline F. Lavander and Carol J. Singley (New Brunswick, NJ: Rutgers University Press, 2003), 226–243. For the use of "progressive" toys during this time, see Cross, *Kids' Stuff*, chap. 5.

75. Amy F. Ogata, *Designing the Creative Child: Playthings and Places in Midcentury America* (Minneapolis: University of Minnesota Press, 2013).

76. Simon, *A Wider World*, 44.

77. See, e.g., the quiz "How Good a Father Are You?" which furnished the "right" answer at the end, in *Parents' Magazine* 10:6 (June 1933), 36, 77, 78. 79, 85.

78. For the loss of a place for fathers in the new homes of the early twentieth century, see Caroline Hinckle McCamant, "Creating 'Dad': Finding a Place for Father in the Middle-Class American Home, 1900–1929" (PhD diss., University of California at Berkeley, 2011).

79. LeRoy E. Bowman, "Making a Parent of Father," *Parents' Magazine* 10 (November 1935), 13. A recent article studies this advice but is more interested in the trends over time than in what it might actually reflect about behavior; see Melissa A. Milkie and Kathleen E. Denny, "Changes in the Cultural Model of Father Involvement: Descriptions of Benefits to Fathers, Children, and Mothers in *Parents' Magazine*, 1926–2006," *Journal of Family Issues* 35:2 (January 2014), 223–253.

80. Bowman, "Making a Parent of Father," 13; Frederic F. Van De Water, "A Father Falters," *Parents' Magazine* 10:12 (December 1935), 48.

81. Lynd and Lynd, *Middletown*, 143.

82. "Mistakes I've Made with My Boy," by A Father (Who Prefers to Remain Anonymous), *Parents' Magazine* 11 (July 1936), 20, 50.

83. Quoted in White House Conference, *Adolescent in the Family*, 258.

84. Quoted in White House Conference, *Adolescent in the Family*, 268; White House Conference, *Adolescent in the Family*, 269.

85. John Muir, *The Story of My Boyhood and Youth* (1912; repr., Madison: University of Wisconsin Press, 1965), 179.

86. Muir, *Story of My Boyhood and Youth*, 161, 162.

87. Muir, *Story of My Boyhood and Youth*, 5, 27, 41, 209.

88. On the national institutionalization of this perspective, see Lindenmeyer, *Greatest Generation Grows Up*. For the experience of high school students in Berkeley, California, during the war, see Natsuki Aruga, "Continuity during Change in World War II Berkeley, California, as Seen through the Eyes of Children" (PhD diss., Stanford University, 1996).

89. Horowitz, *Daydreams and Nightmares*, 63, 56; Simon, *Bronx Primitive*, 49.

90. Ernest Groves was especially active in encouraging parent education in both colleges and high schools, and he frequently summarized progress in this area in the *American Journal of Sociology*. See, e.g., "The Family (Changes in 1928)," 34 (1929), 1099–1107. For an overview of the movement, see Laura Winslow Drummond, *Youth and Instruction in Marriage and Family Living* (New York, 1942); Jessie H. Newton, "The Role of the Public School in Parent Education," in *Papers on Parent Education Presented at the Biennial Conference of the National Council of Parent Education*, November 1930 (New York, 1931), 79–92.

CHAPTER 5

1. For a discussion of innovative designs for children that aimed at encouraging their creativity, see Amy F. Ogata, *Designing the Creative Child: Playthings and Places in Midcentury America* (Minneapolis: University of Minnesota Press, 2013).

2. Tony Judt, *Postwar: A History of Europe since 1945* (New York: Penguin, 2005), discusses Europe after World War II.

3. Dorothy Height, *Open Wide Freedom Gates: A Memoir* (New York: Public Affairs, 2003), 1–23, 3 (quote).

4. Lewis M. Killian, *Black and White: Reflections of a White Southern Sociologist* (Dix Hills, NY: General Hall, 1994), 1–32, 5 (quote). For the experience of race for black and white children, and how it was learned, see Jennifer Ritterhouse, *Growing Up Jim Crow: How Black and White Southern Children Learned Race* (Chapel Hill: University of North Carolina Press, 2006).

5. Height, *Open Wide Freedom Gates*, 12.

6. For the experience of children in the Jim Crow South, see Killian, *Black and White*; and Ritterhouse, *Growing Up Jim Crow*. Recent resegregation has made some wonder about the long-term effects of the ruling. See the report by Gary Orfield, Mark D. Bachmeier, David R. James, and Tamela Eide, "Deepening Segregation in American Public Schools: A Special Report from the Harvard Project on School Desegregation," in *Interdisciplinary Perspectives on the New Immigration: The New Immigrant and American Schools*, ed. Marcelo Suárez-Orozco, Carola Suárez-Orozco, and Desirée Qin-Hilliard (New York: Routledge, 2001).

7. This story is told compactly in Richard M. Abrams, *America Transformed: Sixty Years of Revolutionary Change, 1941–2001* (New York: Cambridge University Press, 2006), 122–125.

8. For a discussion of this matter, see Paula S. Fass, *Outside In: Minorities and the Transformation of American Education* (New York: Oxford University Press, 1989), 139–155; also Ulysses Lee, *The Employment of Negro Troops: Special Studies of the United States Army in World War II* (Washington, DC: Office of the Chief of Military History, United States Army, 1966). For African American schools in the South, see James B. Anderson, *The Education of Blacks in the South: 1860–1935* (Chapel Hill: University of North Carolina Press, 1988).

9. Killian, *Black and White*, 37.

10. Killian, *Black and White*, 9.

11. Killian, *Black and White*, 81.

12. Height, *Open Wide Freedom Gates*, 136.

13. Edwin King, "Growing Up in Mississippi in a Time of Change," in *Mississippi Writers: Reflections of Childhood and Youth*, vol. 2, *Nonfiction*, ed. Dorothy Abbott (Jackson: University Press of Mississippi, 1986), 374, 375 (my emphasis).

14. Annie Dillard, *An American Childhood* (New York: Harper & Row, 1987), 59, 29–30, 81, 82.

15. John Dittmer, *Local People: The Struggle for Civil Rights in Mississippi* (Urbana: University of Illinois Press, 1994); Harvard Sitkoff, *The Struggle for Black Equality, 1954–1992* (New York: Hill & Wang, 1993).

16. Rebecca de Schweinitz, *If We Could Change the World: Young People and America's Long Struggle for Racial Equality* (Chapel Hill: University of North Carolina Press), 224.

17. Robert Coles, *Children of Crisis: A Study of Courage and Fear* (New York: Dell, 1964), 65.

18. Ellen Herman, *The Romance of American Psychology: Political Culture in the Age of Experts* (Berkeley: University of California Press, 1995).

19. Herman, *Romance of American Psychology*, chap. 7. For how the war affected American children, see William M. Tuttle, Jr., *"Daddy's Gone to War": The Second World War in the Lives of America's Children* (New York: Oxford University Press, 1993).

20. Robert Castel, Francoise Castel, and Anna Lowell, *The Psychiatric Society* (New York, Columbia University Press, 1982), 60.

21. Coles, "John Washington," in *Children of Crisis*, 97–122, 102 (quotes).

22. Coles, "John Washington," 107.

23. Coles, "John Washington," 109 (emphasis in original).

24. Coles, "John Washington," 109, 119–120.

25. Anne Hulbert, *Raising America: Experts, Parents and a Century of Advice about Children* (New York: Alfred A. Knopf, 2003), 230–231, 241 (quotes).

26. Elaine Tyler May argues that this Cold War environment seriously influenced the emphasis on and nature of family life; see *Homeward Bound: American Families in the Cold War Era* (New York: Basic Books, 1988).

27. "Paranoid" was a common description of many of the fears and right-wing movements of the time, adopted by sociologists as well as historians. See, especially, the essays in Daniel Bell, ed., *The Radical Right: The New American Right* (New York: Anchor, 1964); also Richard Hofstadter, *The Paranoid Style in American Politics* (New York: Alfred A. Knopf, 1965).

28. For general developments during this period, see Lizabeth Cohen, *A Consumer's Republic: The Politics of Consumption in Postwar America* (New York: Alfred A. Knopf, 2003); Kenneth Jackson, *Crabgrass Frontier: The Suburbanization of the United States* (New York: Oxford University Press, 1988); Landon Y. Jones, *Great Expectation: America and the Baby Boom Generation* (New York: Coward, McCann & Geoghegan, 1980); William L. O'Neill, *American High: The Years of Confidence, 1945–1960* (New York: Basic Books, 1989).

29. On adoption, see Barbara Melosh, *Strangers and Kin: The American Way of Adoption* (Cambridge: MA: Harvard University Press, 2002); Ellen Herman, *Kinship by Design: A History of Adoption in the Modern United States* (Chicago: University of Chicago Press, 2008): and E. Wayne Carp, *Family Matters: Secrecy and Disclosure in the History of Adoption* (Cambridge, MA: Harvard University Press, 1998), which shows how secrecy about a child's origins was essential to the ideal that adoptive families were like everyone else.

30. See Ogata, *Designing the Creative Child*, which makes clear how much the intellectual life of the time emphasized creative individuality.

31. For the general problem of bad mothering, see Molly Ladd-Taylor and Lauri Umansky, eds., *"Bad" Mothers: The Politics of Blame in Twentieth-Century America* (New York: New York University Press, 1998); for child abuse and neglect, Linda Gordon,

Heroes of Their Own Lives: The Politics and History of Family Violence (New York: Penguin, 1988).

32. "Too Much Mother," Medicine, *Time* 39 (February 2, 1942), 47.

33. William Stekel, *Frigidity in Woman: In Relation to Her Love Life*, 2 vols. (New York: Liveright, 1926); Philip Wylie, *Generation of Vipers* (New York: Rinehart, 1946).

34. Edward A. Strecker, *Their Mothers' Sons: The Psychiatrist Examines an American Problem* (Philadelphia: J. B. Lippincott, 1946), 30, 31, 36 (mom-to-mother continuum), 54.

35. See Hulbert, *Raising America*, 229–236.

36. Yale continued to be a major center for psychoanalytic theory and child observation and treatment. For the period of the 1950s, see Linda C. Mayes and Stephen Lassonde, eds., *A Girl's Childhood: Psychological Development, Social Change, and the Yale Child Study Center* (New Haven: Yale University Press, 2014).

37. Peter N. Stearns, *Anxious Parents: A History of Modern Childrearing in America* (New York: New York University Press, 2003), especially 125–162. For the changes in views about childhood in the late nineteenth century, see Viviana A. Zelizer, *Pricing the Priceless Child: The Changing Social Value of Children* (New York: Basic Books, 1985).

38. Richard Ford, "My Mother, In Memory," *Harper's* 275 (August 1, 1987), 49–50.

39. For changes in children's play, see Howard Chudacoff, *Children at Play: An American History* (New York: New York University Press, 2007); Robert D. Putnam, *Our Kids: The American Dream in Crisis* (New York: Simon & Schuster, 2015), 3.

40. On the new middle-class standards, see Cohen, *Consumers' Republic*.

41. Ogata, *Designing the Creative Child*.

42. Erik H. Erikson, *Young Man Luther: A Study in Psychoanalysis and History* (London: Faber, 1959); *Gandhi's Truth: On the Origins of Militant Nonviolence* (New York: W. W. Norton, 1970).

43. Erik H. Erikson, *Childhood and Society* (New York: W. W. Norton, 1950), chap. 7.

44. Erikson, *Childhood and Society*, 254.

45. Erikson, *Childhood and Society*, 261.

46. For the statistics, National Center for Education Statistics, *140 Years of American Education: A Statistical Portrait*, ed. Thomas D. Snyder (Washington, DC: US Dept. of Education, Office of Educational Research, 1993), http://nces.ed.gov/pubs-93/93442.pdf (accessed December 5, 2014). For the comparison with farmers, see Todd Gitlin, *The Sixties: Years of Hope, Days of Rage*, rev. ed. (New York: Bantam, 1993), 21.

47. Gitlin, *The Sixties*, 92.

48. "The Port Huron Statement: August 1962," reprinted in *The Movements of the New Left, 1950–1975: A Brief History with Documents*, ed. Van Gosse (Boston: Bedford/St. Martin's, 2005), 65.

49. On the subject of women at college in this period, see Fass, *Outside In*, chap. 5.

50. Gitlin, *The Sixties*, 98–99.

51. See Beth Bailey, *Sex in the Heartland* (Cambridge, MA: Harvard University Press, 1999), for the period just prior to the activist politics of the late 1960s. For nineteenth-century students, see Richard Hofstadter, *Academic Freedom in the Age of the College* (New York: Columbia University Press, 1961); for the 1920s (during the first serious expansion of higher education in the United States), Paula S. Fass, *The Damned and the Beautiful: American Youth in the 1920s* (New York: Oxford University Press, 1977).

52. For the different kinds of music styles that defined (and also separated) youth in high school culture, William Graebner, *Coming of Age in Buffalo: Youth and Authority in the Postwar Era* (Philadelphia: Temple University Press, 1989).

53. Glenn C. Altschuler, *All Shook Up: How Rock 'n' Roll Changed America* (New York: Oxford University Press, 2003); Paula S. Fass, "The Child-Centered Family: New Rules in Postwar America," in *Reinventing Childhood after World War II*, ed. Paula S. Fass and Michael Grossberg (Philadelphia: University of Pennsylvania Press, 2012), 1–18.

54. Julian Bond is quoted in de Schweinitz, *If We Could Change the World*, 206.

55. Gitlin, *The Sixties*, 83 (emphasis in original).

56. The severity of the break between generations led seasoned social observer Margaret Mead (among many others) to give a lecture series in 1969 and subsequently publish a book on different kinds of generational relations; *Culture and Commitment: A Study of the Generation Gap* (New York: Doubleday, 1970).

57. Terry H. Anderson, *The Sixties* (New York: Pearson/Longman, 2007), provides a good sense of the sequence of events as does Gitlin, *The Sixties*.

58. For high school students, see Gael Graham, *Young Activists: American High School Students in the Age of Protest* (DeKalb: University of Illinois Press, 2006).

59. Eli Ginsberg, introduction to *The Nation's Children (Three Volumes in One)*, ed. Eli Ginsberg (New Brunswick, NJ: Transaction Press, 1987), xiii, xxvi.

60. Henry David, "Work, Women, and Children," in Ginsberg, ed. *Nation's Children*, 3:180, 181, 181–182.

61. In this regard, see James E. Block, *The Crucible of Consent: American Child Rearing and the Forging of Liberal Society* (Cambridge, MA: Harvard University Press, 2012).

62. For these changing definitions and their consequences, see Stephen Lassonde, "Ten Is the New Fourteen: Age Compression and 'Real' Childhood," in Fass and Grossberg, eds., *Reinventing Childhood after World War II*, 51–67.

63. Michael Grossberg, "Liberation and Caretaking: Fighting over Children's Rights in Postwar America," in Fass and Grossberg, eds., *Reinventing Childhood after World War II*, 19–37.

64. On some of the directions that the questioning of parental authority took, see Martin Guggenheim, *What's Wrong with Children's Rights?* (Cambridge, MA: Harvard University Press, 2005); for the United Nations Convention on the Rights of the Child, see Felton Earls, ed., "The Child as Citizen," *Annals of the American Academy of Political and Social Science* 633 (January 2011).

65. Ruth Rosen, *The World Split Open: How the Modern Women's Movement Changed America* (New York: Viking, 2000).

66. For women's work, Alice Kessler-Harris, *Out-to-Work: A History of Wage-Earning Women in the United States* (New York: Oxford University Press, 1982): William Chafe, *American Woman: Her Changing Social, Economic, and Political Roles, 1920–1970* (New York: Oxford University Press, 1972).

67. David, "Work, Women, and Children," 182–183, 185, 187 (my emphasis).

68. David, "Work, Women, and Children," 195–196.

69. See Fass, "Child-Centered Family" 1–18.

70. http://www.infoplease.com/ipa/A0005067.html (accessed June 17, 2014).

71. For live births per year, http://www.childstats.gov/americaschildren/tables /pop1.asp (accessed June 17, 2014); for the US population by year, http://www.multpl .com/united-states-population/table (accessed June 17, 2014).

72. For "Live Births and Birthrate," http://www.infoplease.com/ipa/A0005067 .html (accessed June 19, 2014).

73. http://www.census.gov/hhes/socdemo/marriage/data/acs/ElliottetalPAA 2012figs.pdf (accessed June 17, 2014).

74. Nanette Asimov, "Child-Free Forever," *San Francisco Chronicle*, June 7, 1988, B3.

75. http://www.huffingtonpost.com/robert-hughes/what-is-the-real -divorce-_b_785045.html. The most recent studies indicate that the American divorce rate began to decline in the 1990s, at least in part because fewer people were marrying, but also because older marriages seemed to be formed on more secure grounds and were more durable. Thus, the divorce rate may have been a temporary indicator of the transition in marriage. Claire Cain Miller, "The Divorce Surge Is Over, But the Myth Lives On," *New York Times*, December 2, 2014, A3.

76. "Children Born Out of Wedlock," http://www.cdc.gov/nchs/data/nvsr/nvsr62 /nvsr62_01.pdf (accessed May 12, 2014).

77. Report to Congress on Out-of-Wedlock Births, Department of Health and Human Services, September 1985, p. vi, http://www.cdc.gov/nchs/data/misc/wedlock .pdf (accessed May 12, 2014).

78. Bill Clinton, "How We Ended Welfare, Together," *New York Times*, August 22, 2007, http://www.nytimes.com/2006/08/22/opinion/22clinton.html?_r=0 (accessed May 12, 2014).

79. United States Department of Labor, Women with Children in the Workforce," http://www.dol.gov/wb/stats/recentfacts.htm#mothers (accessed May 12, 2014).

80. Bailey, *Sex in the Heartland*, 13–74.

81. Reed Ueda, *American Immigration: A Social History* (Boston: Bedford/St. Martin's, 1994), 42–116.

82. Elizabeth Loza Newby, *A Migrant with Hope* (Nashville, TN: Broadman Press, 1977), Preface, n.p., 19, 25, 32 (quote), 34.

83. Newby, *Migrant with Hope*, 35, 38.

84. Newby, *Migrant with Hope*, 20–21.

CHAPTER 6

1. *Male and Female: A Study of the Sexes in a Changing World* (New York: William Morrow, 1949), 255–257.

2. Peter Likins, *A New American Family: A Love Story* (Tucson: University of Arizona Press, 2011).

3. Judith Warner, *Perfect Madness: Motherhood in the Age of Anxiety* (New York: Penguin, 2005), 4.

4. Margaret K. Nelson, *Parenting Out of Control: Anxious Parents in Uncertain Times* (New York: New York University Press, 2010); Peter N. Stearns, *Anxious Parents: A History of Modern Childrearing in America* (New York: New York University Press, 2003); Jennifer Senior, *All Joy and No Fun: The Paradox of Modern Parenthood* (New York: HarperCollins, 2014); Warner, *Perfect Madness*; Marianne Cooper, *Cut Adrift: Families in Insecure Times* (Berkeley: University of California Press, 2014).

5. Ann Hulbert, who has written sensitively about childrearing advice, posted a perceptive online review of Warner's book that captures some of the extremely class-blinkered qualities of this literature: "The Real Myth of Motherhood: Reconsidering the Maternal Memoir-cum-Manifesto," *Slate*, March 8, 2005, http://slate.msn.com/id/2114498/ (accessed March 9, 2005).

6. Senior, *All Joy and No Fun.*

7. Mary Ann Mason has been studying the effect of having children on the career trajectories of professional women. For academics, see Mason, Nicholas H. Wolfinger, and Marc Goulden, *Do Babies Matter? Gender and Family in the Ivory Tower* (New Brunswick, N.J.: Rutgers University Press, 2013); for interviews with women from various professions, see Mary Ann Mason and Eve Ekman, *Mothers on the Fast Track: How a New Generation Can Balance Families and Careers* (New York: Oxford University Press, 2007). For the large investment in their children by middle-class parents today, considerably larger than in the past, see Robert Putnam, *Our Kids: The American Dream in Crisis* (New York: Simon & Schuster, 2015), 125–132.

8. For how women can escape from their frustrations at home through workplace life, see Arlie Hochschild, *The Time Bind: When Work Becomes Home and Home Becomes Work* (New York: Metropolitan Books, 1997).

9. For the changes, see Viviana A. Zelizer, *Pricing the Priceless Child: The Changing Social Value of Children* (New York: Basic Books, 1985). Senior is aware of Zelizer's work but somehow misplaces Zelizer's sense of the timing of the change.

10. Katie Zesima, "More Women than Ever Are Childless, Census Finds," *New York Times*, Aug. 18, 2008.

11. For the changes in the postwar period, see the essays in Paula S. Fass and Michael Grossberg, eds., *Reinventing Childhood after World War II* (Philadelphia: University of Pennsylvania Press, 2013).

12. Data on women with children in the workforce in the 1920s scarcely exists, but the data on married women indicates that overall only 9% worked after mar-

riage at all. By 1950, 11.9% of mothers were in the workforce, a figure that rose over the course of the decade to 18.6% by 1960. The comparable figure in 2000 was 65.3%. http://www.freeby50.com/2010/10/historical-look-at-womens-participation.html (accessed September 4, 2014).

13. Warner comments on this matter in *Perfect Madness*, 139–158ff.

14. For the larger cultural phenomenon of which the concerns with unsatisfied desires regarding children are part, see Peter N. Stearns, *Satisfaction Not Guaranteed: Dilemmas of Progress in Modern Society* (New York: New York University Press, 2012).

15. Isabel V. Sawhill, "Beyond Marriage," *New York Times Sunday Review*, September 14, 2014, 1 (quote), 9. For how families of different economic classes manage insecurity, see Cooper, *Cut Adrift*.

16. Linda J. Waite and Maggie Gallagher, *The Case for Marriage: Why Married People Are Happier, Healthier, and Better Off Financially* (New York: Doubleday, 2000); James O. Wilson, *The Marriage Problem: How Our Culture Has Weakened Families* (New York: HarperCollins, 2002). For a liberal historian's appraisal, see Kriste Lindenmeyer, "Children, the State, and the American Dream," in Fass and Grossberg, eds., *Reinventing Childhood after World War II*.

17. This kind of insecurity is discussed in Cooper, *Cut Adrift*.

18. Andrew Solomon, *Far from the Tree: Parents, Children and the Search for Identity* (New York: Scribner's, 2012), 199. For the uneven distribution of contraception and abortion options and especially how protections regarding fetal rights affect working women, see Sara Dubow, *Ourselves Unborn: A History of the Fetus in Modern America* (New York: Oxford University Press, 2011), especially chap. 4.

19. Solomon, *Far from the Tree*, 236.

20. Solomon, *Far from the Tree*, 202.

21. Solomon, *Far from the Tree*, 242–245, 244 (quote).

22. Rebecca Jo Plant, "Debunking Mother Love: American Mothers and the Momism Critique in the Mid-Twentieth Century," in *Raising Citizens in the Century of the Child: The United States and German Central Europe in Comparative Perspective*, ed. Dirk Schumann (New York: Berghahn Books, 2010), 122–140.

23. Dennis Hall, "Moms.com," in *Mommy Angst: Motherhood in Popular Culture*, ed. Ann C. Hall and Mardia J. Bishop (Santa Barbara, CA: ABC/CLIO–Praeger, 2009), 179–195.

24. Alanna Levine, *Raising a Self-Reliant Child: A Back-to-Basics Parenting Plan from Birth to Age 6* (Berkeley, CA: Ten Speed Press, 2013), 3.

25. Warner, *Perfect Madness*, 7.

26. Amy Chua, *Battle Hymn of the Tiger Mother* (New York: Penguin, 2011).

27. For the fears about hurting one child's feelings, see Stearns, *Anxious Parents*.

28. Dorothy Corkille Briggs, *Your Child's Self-Esteem* (New York: Doubleday, 1970), 131, 128. It is worth noting that by 2001, David Elkind was already questioning self-esteem as the right guideline for childrearing. See "Childrearing and Education in a Changing World," in *Changing Childhood in the World and Turkey*, ed. Bekir

Onur, vol. 3 of *Ulusal Cocuk Kulturu Kongresi* (Ankara, Turkey: Ankara University, 2001), 235–236.

29. Jane L. Rankin, *Parenting Experts: Their Advice, the Research, and Getting It Right* (Westport, CT: Praeger, 2005), 64–69.

30. Marilyn Heims, "Tiger Moms vs. Wimp Moms," http://parentkidsright .com/ (accessed August 6, 2014).

31. Rankin, *Parenting Experts*, 33.

32. For some of these changes in a comparative perspective, see Fass and Gross-berg, eds., *Reinventing Childhood after World War II*.

33. In an insightful article, David Brooks has caught the tenor of this tradition without fully understanding its historical roots; see "Love and Merit," *New York Times*, April 24, 2015, A25.

34. Ross Douthat, "The Parent Trap," *New York Times Sunday Review*, July 20, 2014, 12.

35. These quotes are taken from Arthur W. Calhoun, *A Social History of the American Family: From Colonial Times to the Present*, 3 vols. (New York: Barnes & Noble, 1945), 2:53.

36. Warner, *Perfect Madness*, 14; quoted in Calhoun, *Social History of the American Family*, 2:151.

37. Pamela Druckerman, *Bringing Up Bébé: One American Mother Discovers the Wisdom of French Parenting* (New York: Penguin, 2012).

38. *Parenting Beliefs, Behaviors, and Parent-Child Relations*, ed. Kenneth H. Rubin and Ock Boon Chung (New York: Psychology Press/Taylor & Francis Group, 2006).

39. Arthur W. Calhoun, *A Social History of the American Family: From Colonial Times to the Present*, vol. 3, *Since the Civil War* (New York: Barnes & Noble, 1945), 132–135. For an intriguing examination of the ways Americans have often admired this kind of characteristic in children, see Gary Cross, *The Cute and the Cool: Wondrous Innocence and Modern American Children's Culture* (New York: Oxford University Press, 2004).

40. Margaret Mead, *Male and Female* (New York: William Morrow, 1949), 245–246.

41. Quoted in Calhoun, *Social History of the American Family*, 3:144.

42. Jane Hunter, *How Young Ladies Became Girls: The Victorian Origins of American Girlhood* (New Haven: Yale University Press, 2002).

43. Sara Harkness and Charles M. Super, "Themes and Variations: Parental Ethnotheories in Western Cultures," in Rubin and Chung, eds., *Parenting Beliefs, Behaviors, and Parent-Child Relations*, 61–80.

44. In 1936, an article on childrearing in the "Medicine" section of *Time* magazine (February 17, 1936, 55) noted the rapid changes taking place in the area of toilet training as parents were advised to wait until their children were eight months old for bowel control and fifteen to seventeen months for bladder training. Those ages would seem very young to many middle-class parents today. For the great variation

in parents' behavior, see Robert R. Sears, Eleanor E. Maccoby, and Harry Levin, *Patterns of Child Rearing* (Evanston, IL: Row, Peterson, 1957), for a mid-twentieth-century perspective. The situation has become even more complicated more than a half-century later.

45. Rankin, *Parenting Experts*, examines the five most widely read experts. For the multiple styles of parenting in early America, see Philip J. Greven, Jr., *The Protestant Temperament: Patterns of Child-Rearing, Religious Experience, and the Self in Early America* (New York: Random House, 1978); see also Greven's *Spare the Child: Religious Roots of Punishment and the Psychological Impact of Physical Abuse* (New York: Knopf, 1991) for the continuing tradition of severe discipline. For popular fads over time, see Ann Hulbert, *Raising America: Experts, Parents and a Century of Advice About Children* (New York: Knopf, 2003); for how mothers respond to expert advice, see Julia Grant, *Raising Baby by the Book: The Education of American Mothers* (New Haven: Yale University Press, 1998).

46. Lenore Skenazy, "Here's How," *New York Times Book Review*, June 15, 2014, 21.

47. See, e.g., Levine, *Raising a Self-Reliant Child*.

48. Cooper, *Cut Adrift*, 116.

49. David Leonhardt, "The Distinct Geography of Female Employment," *New York Times*, January 6, 2015, A3.

50. Warner, *Perfect Madness*, 6.

51. Annette Lareau, *Unequal Childhoods: Class, Race, and Family Life* (Berkeley: University of California Press, 2003). For class comparisons in parenting, see also Margaret Nelson's excellent *Parenting Out of Control*.

52. Putnam, *Our Kids*, chap. 3.

53. Nicholas Kristoff, "Is a Hard Life Inherited?" *New York Times Sunday Review*, August 10, 2014, 1, 11.

54. For the experiences of American young people in the twentieth century, see John Modell, *Into One's Own: From Youth to Adulthood in the United States, 1920–1975* (Berkeley: University of California Press, 1989).

55. See Modell, *Into One's Own*; also Corinne T. Field and Nicholas Syrett, ed., *Age in America: The Colonial Era to the Present* (New York: New York University Press, 2015).

56. http://www.infoplease.com/ipa/A0005061.html (accessed June 30, 2015).

57. Stephen P. Hinshaw and Richard M. Scheffler, *The ADHD Explosion: Myths, Medications, Money, and Today's Push for Performance* (New York: Oxford University Press, 2014).

58. William Deresiewicz, *Excellent Sheep: The Miseducation of the American Elite, and the Way to a Meaningful Life* (New York: Free Press, 2014).

59. Nelson, *Parenting Out of Control*, 163, 2.

60. One expression of this can be found in polls that are taken to gauge the optimism of parents in the future. See, e.g., Frank Bruni, "Lost in America," *New York Times*, August 26, 2014, A23, which cites the latest *Wall Street Journal*/ABC poll.

61. Paul E. Johnson, *A Shopkeeper's Millennium: Society and Revivals in Rochester, New York, 1815–1837*, American Century Series (New York: Hill & Wang, 1983).

62. For a discussion of the frantic efforts from pre–nursery school through college, see Kay S. Hymowitz, *Liberation's Children: Parents and Kids in a Postmodern Era* (Chicago: Ivan R. Dee, 2003).

63. For the specific calculation among Italian immigrants, see Stephen Lassonde, *Learning to Forget: Schooling and Social Life in New Haven's Working Class, 1870–1940* (New Haven: Yale University Press, 2005); for Polish families, see John Bodnar, "Schooling and the Slavic-American Family, 1900–1940," in *American Education and the European Immigrant*, ed. Bernard J. Weiss (Urbana: University of Illinois Press, 1982).

64. Sidney Hook, *Out of Step: An Unquiet Life in the 20th Century* (New York: Harper & Row, 1987), 11. The literature on the schooling of European immigrant children early in the twentieth century and how this related to their social mobility is substantial. A good place to begin is Michael R. Olneck, "Americanization and the Education of Immigrants, 1900–1925: An Analysis of Symbolic Action," *American Journal of Education* 97 (1989), 398–423; and Michael Olneck and Michael Lazerson, "The School Achievement of Immigrant Children, 1890–1930," *History of Education Quarterly* 18 (Fall 1978), 227–270.

For additional comparison, see Thomas Kessner, *The Golden Door: Italian and Jewish Immigrant Mobility in New York City, 1880–1915* (New York: Oxford University Press, 1977). For a comparison of the aspirations of various groups at school, see Paula S. Fass, *Outside In: Minorities and the Transformation of American Education* (New York: Oxford University Press, 1989), especially chap. 3; Joel Perlman, *Ethnic Differences: Schooling and Social Structure among the Irish, Italians, Jews, and Blacks in an American City, 1880–1935* (Cambridge: Cambridge University Press, 1988).

65. Samuel G. Freedman, "Latino Parents Decry Bilingual Programs," *New York Times*, July 14, 2004, A8.

66. The source for these statistics is the Department of Homeland Security's *Yearbook of Immigration Statistics*, http://www.dhs.gov/yearbook-immigration-statistics-2013-lawful-permanent-residents (accessed August 14, 2014).

67. For a concise overview of changes in American immigration, see Guillermina Jasso and Mark M. Rosenzweig, "Characteristics of Immigrants to the United States: 1820–2003," in *A Companion to American Immigration*, ed. Reed Ueda (Malden, MA: Blackwell, 2003). For the new international quality of some of these immigrants, see David Gerber, "Internationalization and Transnationalization," in the same volume, 225–254.

68. Vikki S. Katz, *Kids in the Middle: How Children of Immigrants Negotiate Community Interactions for Their Families* (New Brunswick, NJ: Rutgers University Press, 2014).

69. The requirement that children of undocumented immigrants attend school goes back to the Supreme Court ruling in *Phyler v. Doe*, 457 US 202 (1982). The right

of all children to education is also part of the United Nations Convention on the Rights of the Child (1989). For this, see Jacqueline Bhabha, *Child Migration and Human Rights in a Global Age* (Princeton, NJ: Princeton University Press, 2014), 271–275.

70. Min Zhou, "Conflict, Coping, and Reconciliation: Intergenerational Relations in Chinese Immigrant Families," in Nancy Foner, ed., *Across Generations: Immigrant Families in America* (New York: New York University Press, 2009), 27; Angie Chung, "From Caregivers to Caretakers: The Impact of Family Roles on Ethnicity among Children of Korean and Chinese Immigrant Families," *Qualitative Sociology* 36 (2013), 279–302.

71. Mary C. Waters and Jennifer E. Sykes, "Spare the Rod, Ruin the Child? First and Second Generation West Indian Child-Rearing Practices," in Foner, ed., *Across Generations*, 80.

72. David A. Baptiste, "Family Therapy with East Indian Immigrant Parents Rearing Children in the United States: Parental Concerns, Therapeutic Issues, and Recommendations," *Contemporary Family Therapy* 27 (2005), 345–366; Jyotsna M. Kalavar and John Van Willigen, "Older Asian Indians Resettled in America: Narratives about Households, Culture and Generation," *Journal of Cross-Cultural Gerontology* 20 (2005), 213–230; Azis Talbani and Parveen Hasanali, "Adolescent Females between Tradition and Modernity: Gender Role Socialization in South Asian Immigrant Families," *Journal of Adolescence* 23 (2000), 615.

73. Victoria Wen-Chee Chen, "Communication and Conflict between American-Born Chinese and Their Immigrant Parents" (PhD diss., University of Massachusetts, 1988), 87, 119.

74. Mohammed Fariudl Alam, "Bracing for and Embracing Difference in America's Majority Minority Metropolis: Bangladeshi Immigrant Children Coming of Age in New York City," *British Journal of Social Work* 43 (2013), 631–650.

75. Karen Pyke, "The Normal American Family as an Interpretive Structure of Family Life among Grown Children of Korean and Vietnamese Immigrants," *Journal of Marriage and Family* 62 (2000), 240; Karuna Sharma and Candace L. Kemp, " 'One Should Follow the Wind': Individualized Filial Piety and Support Exchanges in Indian Immigrant Families in the United States," *Journal of Aging Studies* 26 (2012), 129–139.

76. Cecilia Menjivar and Leisy Abrego, "Parents and Children across Borders: Legal Instability and Intergeneration Relations in Guatemalan and Salvadoran Families," in Foner, ed., *Across Generations*, 160–189.

77. Karen Pyke and Tran Dang, " 'FOB' and 'Whitewashed': Identity and Internalized Racism among Second Generation Asian Americans," *Qualitative Sociology* 26 (2003), 147–172; Sunaina Marr Maira, *Desis in the House: Indian American Youth Culture in New York City* (Philadelphia: Temple University Press, 2002).

78. Some of this complexity is clear in Carola Suárez-Orozco, Marcelo M. Suárez-Orozco, and Irina Todorova, *Learning a New Land: Immigrant Students in American Society* (Cambridge, MA: Harvard University Press, 2008); and Antonia

Darder and Rodolfo D. Torres, eds., *Latinos and Education: A Critical Reader*, 2nd ed. (New York: Routledge, 2014).

79. Ruth K. Chao, "Chinese and European American Mothers' Beliefs about the Role of Parenting in Children's School Success," *Journal of Cross-Cultural Psychology* 27 (1996), 403–423; Guofang Li, "What Do Parents Think? Middle-Class Immigrant Parents' Perspectives on Literacy Learning, Homework, and School-Home Communication," *School Community Journal* 16 (2006), 27–46; Cheng Shuang Ji and Sally A. Koblinsky, "Parent Involvement in Children's Education: An Exploratory Study of Urban, Chinese Immigrant Families," *Urban Education*, 44 (2009), 687–709; Chen, *Communication and Conflict*, 119.

80. http://theivycoach.com/2014-ivy-league-admissions-statistics/ (accessed September 10, 2014); http://opa.berkeley.edu/uc-berkeley-fall-enrollment-data (accessed September 3, 2014); http://studentlife.umich.edu/files/research/demographics2012 .pdf (accessed September 10, 2014).

81. The graduation rate of Mexican American students was 61% in 2006; but in 2009 male completion rates rose to 74.9%, and female were 78.8% compared with overall rates of 88.3 and 91.5. http://nces.ed.gov/pubsearch/pubsinfo.asp?pubid =2012006, specifically http://nces.ed.gov/pubs2012/2012006.pdf, figure 5, see also the decline in dropout rates from 1972 to 2009 in tables 3 and 8 and completion rates in table 11 (accessed September 3, 2014).

82. http://www.pewhispanic.org/2013/05/09/hispanic-high-school-graduates -pass-whites-in-rate-of-college-enrollment/ (accessed August 29, 2014).

83. http://theivycoach.com/2014-ivy-league-admissions-statistics/ (accessed September 10, 2014); http://opa.berkeley.edu/uc-berkeley-fall-enrollment-data (accessed September 3, 2014); http://studentlife.umich.edu/files/research/demographics2012 .pdf (accessed September 10, 2014).

84. Alejandro Portes, "Children of Immigrants: Segmented Assimilation and Its Determinants," in *The Economic Sociology of Immigration*, ed. Alejandro Portes (New York: Russell Sage Foundation, 1995), 248–279.

85. For this pattern, see Margaret A. Gibson, "Complicating the Immigrant/ Involuntary Minority Typology," in *Interdisciplinary Perspectives on the New Immigration*, vol. 5 of *The New Immigrant and American Schools*, ed. Marcelo M. Suárez-Orozco, Carola Suárez-Orozco, and Desiree Qin-Hilliard (New York, Routledge, 2001), 35–58; and Alejandro Portes and Dag MacLeod, "Educational Progress of Children of Immigrants: The Roles of Class, Ethnicity, and School Context," in the same volume, 59–75.

86. Suárez-Orozco, Suárez-Orozco, and Todorova, *Learning a New Land*, 31; John U. Ogbu and Herbert D. Simons, "Voluntary and Involuntary Minorities: A Cultural-Ecological Theory of School Performance with Some Implications for Education," in Suárez-Orozco, Suárez-Orozco, and Qin-Hilliard, eds., *Interdisciplinary Perspectives on the New Immigration*, 1–29.

87. Angela Valenzuela, *Subtractive Schooling: U.S.–Mexican Youth and the Politics of Change* (Albany: State University of New York Press, 1999), 135.

88. See the biography by Dorothy Ross, *G. Stanley Hall: The Psychiatrist as Prophet* (Chicago: University of Chicago Press, 1972). For the prehistory, see John Demos and Virginia Demos, "Adolescence in Historical Perspective," *Journal of Marriage and the Family* 31 (1969), 632–638. For girls, see Crista DeLuzio, *Female Adolescence in American Scientific Thought, 1830–1930* (Baltimore: Johns Hopkins University Press, 2007).

89. Margaret Mead, *Coming of Age in Samoa: A Psychological Study of Primitive Youth for Western Civilization* (New York: William Morrow, 1928).

90. The literature here is vast; a good place to begin is Mary Odem, *Delinquent Daughter: Protecting and Policing Adolescent Female Sexuality in the United States* (Chapel Hill: University of North Carolina Press, 1995), for the historical background; and Franklin E. Zimring, *American Juvenile Justice* (New York: Oxford University Press, 2005), for the legal framework.

91. Rickie Solinger, *Wake Up Little Susie: Single Pregnancy and Race before Roe v. Wade* (New York: Routledge, 1992). Juvenile delinquency was especially prominent as part of the public consciousness in the 1950s when it became the subject of Congressional investigations in Washington, DC. See James Gilbert, *A Cycle of Outrage: America's Reaction to the Juvenile Delinquent in the 1950s* (New York: Oxford University Press, 1986). In the 1960s, attention to youth was refocused on college campuses.

92. For the contemporary attention to cognitive functions, see Barbara Strauch, *The Primal Teen: What the New Discoveries about the Teenage Brain Tell Us about Our Kids* (New York: Doubleday, 2003).

93. *Roper v. Simmons* (2005) ruled against the death penalty for those convicted of commiting crimes before they were eighteen years of age.

94. For sex education in schools, see Jeffrey P. Moran, *Teaching Sex: The Shaping of Adolescence in the Twentieth Century* (Cambridge, MA: Harvard University Press, 2000). For an early textbook on family education, see Ernest R. Groves, *The American Family* (Chicago: J. B. Lippincott, 1934).

95. For the rapid diversification of the high school curriculum as the high school became democratized, see Fass, *Outside In.*

96. Gary Orfield, Mark D. Bachmeier, David R. James, and Tamela Eide, "Deepening Segregation in American Public Schools: A Special Report from the Harvard Project on School Desegregation," in Suárez-Orozco, Suárez-Orozco, and Qin-Hilliard, eds., *Interdisciplinary Perspectives on the New Immigration*, 121–140.

97. Pyke and Dang, "'FOB' and 'Whitewashed'"; Desiree Baolian Qin, "Being 'Good' or Being 'Popular': Gender and Ethnic Identity Negotiation of Chinese Immigrant Adolescents," *Journal of Adolescent Research* 24 (2009), 37–66. See also the discussion of third-generation Asian Americans in Pyke, "Normal American Family."

98. Julie Stein, "Youthful Transgressions: Teenagers, Sexuality, and the Contested Path to Adulthood in Postwar America" (PhD diss., University of California at Berkeley, 2014).

99. For the radical changes in sexual mores at colleges and universities, see Beth Bailey, *Sex in the Heartland* (Cambridge, MA: Harvard University Press, 1999).

100. Jason deParle and Sabrina Tavernise, "For Women under Thirty Most Births Occur Outside of Marriage," *New York Times*, February 18, 2012, http://www.ny times.com/2012/02/18/us/for-women-under-30-most-births-occur-outside-marriage .html?pagewanted=all&_r=0 (accessed September 11, 2014).

101. For the deep influence of the choice of schools, see Putnam, *Our Kids*, chap. 4.

102. Cooper, *Cut Adrift*, 7–8.

103. Karen Sternheimer, *Kids These Days: Facts and Fiction about Today's Youth* (Lanham, MD: Rowman & Littlefield, 2006).

104. Among various books that have tried to assess the effect of the economic recession on family life and to trace the current anxiety to it, see especially Cooper, *Cut Adrift*.

105. On the importance of going off to college as an initial transition into adulthood, see Francesco Duina, *Life Transitions in America* (Cambridge, UK: Polity Press, 2014), 23–40.

106. Jeffrey Jensen Arnett and Elizabeth Fishel, *When Will My Child Grow Up?* (New York: Workman Publishing, 2013); Jeffrey Jensen Arnett, *Emerging Adulthood: The Winding Road from the Late Teens through the Twenties* (New York: Oxford University Press, 2004).

107. For the major changes in sexual behaviors prior to marriage, see Martin King Whyte, *Dating, Mating, and Marriage* (New York: Aldine de Gruyter, 1990), 26.

108. How the new media world has affected perceptions about children and how ideals of childhood have changed in the context of the media are discussed in David Buckingham, *After the Death of Childhood: Growing Up in the Age of Electronic Media* (Cambridge, UK: Polity Press, 2000). Although Buckingham is dealing specifically with Great Britain, his insights into how parents have come to fear the changes introduced by new media and how experts have often used these toward arguments about the meaning and limits of childhood are broadly applicable to the West and certainly to the United States.

EPILOGUE

1. Robert Putnam has most recently addressed just this matter in *Our Kids: The American Dream in Crisis* (New York: Simon & Schuster, 2015).

2. Hendrik Hartog, *Someday All This Will Be Yours: A History of Inheritance and Old Age* (Cambridge, MA: Harvard University Press, 2012).

In writing this book, I have used many kinds of sources: memoirs and autobiographies, tracts and pamphlets on childrearing and education, the records of government panels on children and youth, the writings of social scientists of many kinds, contemporary explorations on the subject of parenting, and magazines and newspapers. For readers eager to learn more from these sources, please refer to the endnotes to each chapter.

Below, interested readers will find a brief guide to the historical literature on the several subjects that comprise this book.

CHAPTER 1

The American Revolution, its origins and its consequences have been addressed repeatedly and and the bibliography is huge. Bernard Bailyn is among its foremost interpreters. The most relevant of his work for understanding how America's environment influenced parents and children is *Education in the Forming of American Society: Needs and Opportunities for Study* (Chapel Hill: University of North Carolina Press, 1960). The literature on the revolution as it affected family issues is more compact. Especially important are Philip Greven, *The Protestant Temperament: Patterns of Child-Rearing, Religious Experience, and the Self in Early America* (New York: Alfred A. Knopf, 1977); Jay Fliegelman, *Prodigals and Pilgrims: The American Revolution against Patriarchal Authority, 1750–1800* (Cambridge, UK: Cambridge University Press, 1982); James J. Block, *The Crucible of American Consent: American Child Rearing and the Forging of Liberal Society* (Cambridge, MA: Harvard University Press, 2012). The best introduction to how the revolution affected all aspects of society is Gordon S. Wood, *The*

Radicalism of the American Revolution (New York: Alfred A. Knopf, 1991). See also the interesting essays on children's experiences during the early republic in James Marten, ed., *Children and Youth in a New Nation* (New York: New York University Press, 2009).

For children's play in the early nineteenth century, Howard Chudacoff, *Children at Play: An American History* (New York: New York University Press, 2007), provides an excellent introduction. For women's changing role in the new republican order and in childrearing, several now classic studies are still relevant and important reading: Ann L. Kuhn, *The Mother's Role in Childhood Education: New England Concepts, 1830–1860* (New Haven: Yale University Press, 1947); Linda Kerber, *Women of the Republic: Intellect and Ideology in Revolutionary America* (Chapel Hill: University of North Carolina Press, 1980); Nancy Cott, *The Bonds of Womanhood: Woman's Sphere in New England, 1780–1835* (New Haven: Yale University Press, 1977); Mary P. Ryan, *Cradle of the Middle Class: The Family in Oneida County, New York, 1780–1865* (Cambridge, UK: Cambridge University Press, 1981). The classic essay on women's special qualities is Barbara Welter, "The Cult of True Womanhood: 1820–1860," *American Quarterly* 18, no. 2 (Summer 1966), 151–174. For the consequences of the revolution on fertility, see Susan E. Klepp, "Revolutionary Bodies: Women and the Fertility Transition in the Mid-Atlantic Region, 1760–1820," *Journal of American History* 85 (December 1998), 910–945. For the revolution and family law, see Michael Grossberg, *Governing the Hearth: Law and the Family in Nineteenth Century America* (Chapel Hill: University of North Carolina Press, 1985); Hendrik Hartog, *Man and Wife in America: A History* (Cambridge, MA: Harvard University Press, 2000). Pavla Miller, *The Transformation of Patriarchy in the West, 1500–1900* (Bloomington: University of Indiana Press, 1998), sets the problem of patriarchy in a larger Western context.

CHAPTER 2

As a fundamental aspect of early American history, slavery has a considerable literature. Ira Berlin, *Many Thousands Gone: The First Two Centuries of Slavery in North America* (Cambridge, MA: Harvard University Press, 1998), tells the essential story. For children and slave family relationships a good place to start is Marie Jenkins Schwartz, *Born in Bondage: Growing Up Enslaved in the Antebellum South* (Cambridge, MA: Harvard University Press, 2000); also Wilma King, *Stolen Childhood: Slave Youth in Nineteenth-Century America* (Bloomington: Indiana University Press, 1995); Brenda E. Stevenson, *Life in Black and White: Life and Community in the Slave South* (New York: Oxford University Press, 1996). The story of Mary Walker and her children is told by Sydney Nations in *To Free a Family: The Journey of Mary Walker* (Cambridge, MA: Harvard University Press, 2012). Still relevant is Herbert Gutman, *The Black Family in Slavery and Freedom: 1750–1925* (New York: Pantheon Books, 1976).

Foundlings and the institutional response are ably examined by Julie Miller, *Abandoned: Foundlings in Nineteenth-Century New York City* (New York: New York University Press, 2008). An excellent introduction to street children in the nineteenth-century city is Timothy Gilfoyle, "Children as Vagrants, Vagabonds and Thieves in Nineteenth Century America," in *The Routledge History of Childhood in the Western World*, Paula S. Fass, ed. (London: Routledge, 2013), 400–418. The same volume also contains a good discussion of the question of social welfare in the Western world at this time: Ivan Jablonka, "Social Welfare in the Western World and the Rights of Children," 380–399. For Charles Loring Brace and the Children's Aid Society, see Stephen O'Connor, *Orphan Trains: The Story of Charles Loring Brace* (Chicago: University of Chicago Press, 2004); and Bruce Bellingham, "Waifs and Strays: Child Abandonment, Foster Care, and Families in Mid-Nineteenth Century New York," in Peter Mandler, ed., *The Uses of Charity: The Poor on Relief in the Nineteenth Century Metropolis* (Philadelphia: University of Pennsylvania Press, 1990). Poverty and the growth of institutional responses are discussed in Eric C. Schneider, *In the Web of Class: Delinquents and Reformers in Boston, 1810s–1930s* (New York: New York University Press, 1991). For how families viewed and interacted with the Societies for the Prevention of Cruelty to Children, see Linda Gordon, *Heroes of Their Own Lives: The Politics and History of Family Violence, Boston 1880–1960* (New York: Penguin Books, 1988).

The new industrial order and its consequences for children are discussed in Priscilla Ferguson Clement, *Growing Pains: Children in the*

Industrial Age, 1860–1890 (New York: Trayne, 1997). For the incorporation of young women into the early factory system, see Thomas Dublin, *Women at Work: The Transformation of Work and Community in Lowell, Massachusetts* (New York: Columbia University Press, 1981). Views on child labor as a problem and the campaign against it are the subjects of Walter L. Trattner's *Crusade for the Children: A History of the National Child Labor Committee and Child Labor Reform in America* (New York: Quandrangle Books, 1970). Hugh Cunningham, *Children and Childhood in the Western World since 1500*, 2nd ed. (Harlow, England: Pearson, Longman, 2005), chap. 6, examines the international response to child labor. For the attempts to save girls from sexual abuse by raising the age of consent, see Mary E. Odem, *Delinquent Daughters: Protecting and Policing Adolescent Female Sexuality in the United States, 1885–1920* (Chapel Hill: University of North Carolina Press, 1995), chap. 1. Brian Gatton and Jon Moen, "Immigration, Culture, and Child Labor in the United States, 1880–1920," *Journal of Interdisciplinary History* 34 (Winter 2004), 355–391, provides a good summary of the different perspectives on child labor.

The classic study of how childhood was reimagined in the nineteenth century is Viviana Zelizer, *Pricing the Priceless Child: The Changing Social Value of Children* (New York: Basic Books, 1985). Anne Higonnet, *Pictures of Innocence: The History and Crisis of Ideal Childhood* (London: Thames and Hudson Ltd, 1998) provides a compelling picture of how children were represented by Victorian illustrators. For changes in family life in the nineteenth century and the new family rituals, see John R. Gillis, *A World of Their Own Making: Myth, Ritual, and the Quest for Family Values* (New York: Basic Books, 1996). Changing attitudes toward mixed-race children are examined in Anne F. Hyde, *Empires, Nations, and Families: A New History of the North American West, 1800–1860* (Lincoln: University of Nebraska Press, 2011). The story of Charley Ross is told in Paula S. Fass, *Kidnapped: Child Abduction in America* (New York: Oxford University Press, 1997), chap. 1.

CHAPTER 3

For the campaigns against dirt, Suellen Hoy, *Chasing Dirt: The American Pursuit of Cleanliness* (New York: Oxford University Press, 1995), is a good beginning. Nancy Tomes, *The Gospel of Germs: Men, Women, and the Microbe in American Life* (Cambridge, MA: Harvard University Press, 1998), shows how science began to inform views about dirt and disease, and how rigorously these were pursued. The story of efforts to control infant mortality is well told in Richard Meckel's *Save the Babies: American Public Health Reform and the Prevention of Infant Mortality, 1850–1929* (Baltimore: Johns Hopkins University Press, 1990).

To understand the world of women reformers, see Robyn Muncy, *Creating a Female Dominion of Reform, 1890–1935* (New York: Oxford University Press, 1991); Ellen Fitzpatrick, *Endless Crusade: Women Social Scientists and Progressive Reform* (New York: Oxford University Press, 1990). The history of the children's bureau is ably recounted in Kriste Lindenmeyer's *"A Right to Childhood": The U.S. Children's Bureau and Child Welfare, 1912–46* (Urbana: University of Illinois Press, 1997). For the settlement house movement, Allen Davis, *Spearheads for Reform: The Social Settlements and the Progressive Movement, 1890–1914* (New York: Oxford University Press, 1967), is an old, but still very readable account.

The best introductions to childrearing advice literature are Anne Hulbert, *Raising America: Experts, Parents, and a Century of Advice about Children* (New York: Alfred A. Knopf, 2003); Peter N. Stearns, *Anxious Parents: A History of Modern Childrearing in America* (New York: New York University Press, 2003) (especially good on the central importance of the new parenting of the 1920s); and Julia Grant, *Raising Baby by the Book: The Education of American Mothers* (New Haven: Yale University Press, 1998) (on how women responded to the advice they were offered). For the scientific study of children and the support of foundations toward this end, see Alice Smuts, *Science in the Service of Children: 1893–1935* (New Haven: Yale University Press, 2006); and Dennis Raymond Bryson, *Socializing the Young, The Role of Foundations, 1923–1941* (Westport, CT: Bergin & Garvey, 2002). Also relevant is Rima D. Apple, *Perfect Motherhood: Science and Childrearing in America* (New Brunswick, NJ: Rutgers University Press, 2006).

A good beginning for understanding juvenile delinquency as an important focus of study in the United States is provided by Harold Finestone, *Victims of Change: Juvenile Delinquents in American Society*,

Contributions to Sociology 20 (Westport, CT: Greenwood Press, 1976). For female juvenile delinquents and their management, Mary E. Odem, *Delinquent Daughters: Protecting and Policing Adolescent Female Sexuality in the United States, 1885–1920* (Chapel Hill: University of North Carolina Press, 1995). Steven L. Schlossman, *Love and the American Delinquent: The Theory and Practice of Progressive Juvenile Justice, 1825–1920* (Chicago: University of Chicago Press, 1977), provides a longer-term prospective. Chicago as a boisterous enterprising city is discussed in William Cronin, *Nature's Metropolis: Chicago and the Great West* (New York: Norton, 1991); for the university in the city, see Steven J. Diner, *A City and Its Universities: Public Policy in Chicago, 1892–1919* (Chapel Hill: University of North Carolina Press, 1980). Jay Martin's *Education of John Dewey: A Biography* (New York: Columbia University Press, 2003) provides a comprehensive introduction to the philosopher and educator committed to the democratic way of life.

CHAPTER 4

William J. Reese, *America's Public Schools: From the Common School to "No Child Left Behind"* (Baltimore: Johns Hopkins University Press, 2005), is a good introduction to the history of public schooling. For the common school and education in the nineteenth century, see Carl F. Kaestle, *Pillars of the Republic: Common Schools and American Society, 1780–1860* (New York: Hill & Wang, 1983); for changes in urban education, Reed Ueda, *Avenues to Adulthood: The Origins of the High School and Social Mobility in an American Suburb*, Interdisciplinary Perspectives on Modern History (Cambridge, UK: Cambridge University Press, 1987); David B. Tyack, *The One Best System: A History of American Urban Education* (Cambridge, MA: Harvard University Press, 1974). The little red schoolhouse is discussed in Jonathan Zimmerman, *Small Wonder: The Little Red Schoolhouse in History and Memory* (New Haven: Yale University Press, 2009).

For immigrant children, see Melissa R. Klapper, *Small Strangers: The Experiences of Immigrant Children in America, 1880–1925* (Chicago: Ivan R. Dee, 2007); for ethnic relations among high school students, Paula S. Fass, *Outside In: Education and the Transformation of American Education* (New York: Oxford University Press, 1989), chaps. 3 and 6.

One of the best discussions of the conflict between schools and immigrant families is Stephen Lassonde, *Learning to Forget: Schooling and Family Life in New Haven's Working Class, 1870–1940* (New Haven: Yale University Press, 2005). The story of how immigrant children combined work and school, and how they resisted the reformers' efforts to stop them from working, is told in David Nasaw, *Children of the City: At Work and at Play* (New York: Doubleday, 1985). In *The Greatest Generation Grows Up: American Childhood in the 1930s* (Chicago: Ivan Dee, 2005), Kriste Lindenmeyer shows how high school education was established as the norm in the midst of the Great Depression. For New Deal programs that helped young people continue in school, see Fass, *Outside In*, chap. 3.

Joseph P. Kett, *Rites of Passage: Adolescence in America, 1790 to the Present* (New York: Basic Books, 1977), is especially good on the history of adolescence in the nineteenth century. For teenagers, Thomas Hine, *The Rise and Fall of the American Teenager: A New History of the American Adolescent Experience* (New York: Avon Books, 1999), is a readable introduction. For a revealing examination of how American teenage culture influenced youth elsewhere in the Western world, see Jon Savage, *Teenage: The Prehistory of Youth Culture, 1875–1945* (New York: Vintage Penguin, 2007). The new consumer desires of immigrant daughters are discussed in Kathy Peiss, *Cheap Amusements: Working Women and Leisure in Turn-of-the-Century New York* (Philadelphia: Temple University Press, 1986), and the problem of female delinquency in Mary Odem, *Delinquent Daughters: Protecting and Policing Adolescent Female Sexuality in the United States* (Chapel Hill: University of North Carolina Press, 1995).

CHAPTER 5

American culture after World War II is explored in a number of books that deal with issues relating to children. See especially Amy Ogata, *Designing the Creative Child: Playthings and Places in Midcentury America* (Minneapolis: University of Minnesota Press, 2013); and Paula S. Fass and Michael Grossberg, eds., *Reinventing Childhood after World War II* (Philadelphia: University of Pennsylvania Press, 2013). The impact of the Cold War is discussed in Elaine Tyler May, *Homeward*

Bound: American Families in the Cold War Era (New York: Basic Books, 1988). For American children during World War II, see William M. Tuttle, Jr., *"Daddy's Gone to War": The Second World War in the Lives of America's Children* (New York: Oxford University Press, 1993); and Lisa L. Ossian, *The Forgotten Generation: American Children and World War II* (Columbia: University of Missouri Press, 2011). Anne Hulbert, *Raising America: Experts, Parents, and a Century of Advice about Children* (New York: Alfred A. Knopf, 2003), provides a shrewd introduction to Dr. Benjamin Spock. For how psychological understandings emerged from World War II experience, see Ellen Herman, *The Romance of American Psychology: Political Culture in the Age of Experts* (Berkeley: University of California Press, 1995).

There is an extensive literature on the civil rights era. A good overview is Harvard Sitkoff, *The Struggle for Black Equality, 1954–1992* (New York: Hill & Wang, 1993). The role of African American children and youth is examined in Rebecca de Schweinitz, *If We Could Change the World: Young People and America's Long Struggle for Racial Equality* (Chapel Hill: University of North Carolina Press, 2009). The experience of race for Southern children is explored by Jennifer Ritterhouse, *Growing Up Jim Crow: How Black and White Southern Children Learned Race* (Chapel Hill: University of North Carolina Press, 2006).

For the Vietnam War and student reaction, see David Farber, *The Age of Great Dreams: America in the 1960s* (New York: Hill & Wang, 1994), chaps. 6–8; high school student activism and protests are discussed in Gael Graham, *Young Activists: American High School Students in the Age of Protest* (DeKalb: University of Illinois Press, 2006). Changes in student culture, especially as regards sexual behavior, are discussed in Beth Bailey, *Sex in the Heartland* (Cambridge, MA: Harvard University Press, 1999). For music, see Glenn C. Altshuler, *All Shook Up: How Rock 'n' Roll Changed America* (New York: Oxford University Press, 2003).

The effect of the 1960s on views of the family is described in Natasha Zaretsky, *No Direction Home: The American Family and the Fear of National Decline* (Chapel Hill: University of North Carolina Press, 2007). Changes in perspectives on children's rights are discussed in Michael Grossberg, "Liberation and Caretaking: Fighting over Children's

Rights in Postwar America," in *Reinventing Childhood after World War II*, Fass and Grossberg, eds. For changes in immigration after 1968, see Reed Ueda, *American Immigration: A Social History* (Boston: Bedford/St. Martin's, 1994). Some of the consequences for schooling are explored in *The New Immigrant and American Schools*, Interdisciplinary Perspectives on the New Immigration, vol. 5, ed. Marcelo M. Suárez-Orozco, Carola Suárez-Orozco, and Desirée Qin-Hilliard (New York: Routledge, 2001).

CHAPTER 6

There are many excellent studies on specific aspects and time periods in the history of family and childhood, but more broadly framed histories of these subjects are less common. The first serious history of the American family was Arthur W. Calhoun's *A Social History of the American Family: From Colonial Times to the Present*, 3 volumes (New York: Barnes & Noble, 1945). More recent studies include Steven Mintz and Susan Kellogg, *Domestic Revolutions: A Social History of American Family Life* (New York: Free Press, 1988); and Stephanie Coontz, *The Way We Never Were: American Families and the Nostalgia Trap* (New York: Basic Books, 1992). John R. Gillis, *A World of Their Own Making: Myth, Ritual, and the Quest for Family Values* (New York: Basic Books, 1996), examines how family life in the United States and in Europe over the past two centuries has become more alike.

For histories of childhood, Steven Mintz, *Huck's Raft: A History of American Childhood* (Cambridge, MA: Harvard University Press, 2004), is very useful. Sheila Cole's picture history book of American children, *To Be Young in America: Growing Up with the Country, 1776–1940* (New York: Little, Brown, 2005), ranges broadly and includes capsule stories of individual children's lives. Peter N. Stearns, *American Cool: Constructing a Twentieth-Century Emotional Style* (New York: New York University Press, 1994), is more limited in scope but offers a refreshing and stimulating way to understand twentieth-century parenting and childhood. Stearns has also put the American experience in a global perspective in *Childhood in World History* (New York: Routledge, 2006); for the Western perspective and how it has evolved over time, see Colin Heywood, *A History of Childhood: Children and*

Childhood in the West from Medieval to Modern Times (Cambridge, UK: Polity Press, 2001); Hugh Cunningham, *Children and Childhood in Western Society since 1500*, 2nd ed. (Harlow, UK: Pearson, 2005). Also useful for understanding American experience in a wider and even longer context is Paula S. Fass, ed., *The Routledge History of Childhood in the Western World* (London: Routledge, 2014).

What makes for success in school has a growing literature. Paul Tough, *How Children Succeed: Grit, Curiosity, and the Hidden Power of Character* (Boston: Houghton Mifflin Harcourt, 2012), looks at inner-city kids; William Deresiewicz, *Excellent Sheep: The Miseducation of the American Elite, and the Way to a Meaningful Life* (New York: Free Press, 2014), looks at the other half of the social spectrum. See also Rhona Weinstein, *Reaching Higher: The Power of Expectations in Schooling* (Cambridge, MA: Harvard University Press, 2002).

The education of immigrant children and their comparative successes in the past and the present has a large literature. A good place to begin for earlier immigrations is Michael Olneck and Michael Lazerson, "The School Achievement of Immigrant Children, 1890–1930," *History of Education Quarterly*, 18 (Fall 1978), 227–270; and Joel Perlman, *Ethnic Differences: Schooling and Social Structure among the Irish, Italians, Jews, and Blacks in an American City, 1880–1935* (Cambridge, UK: Cambridge University Press, 1988). For contemporary immigrant groups, see Alejandro Portes and Ruben Rumbaut, *Legacies: The Story of the Immigrant Second Generation* (Berkeley: University of California Press, 2001); Carola Suárez-Orozco, Marcelo M. Suárez-Orozco, and Irina Todorova, *Learning a New Land: Immigrant Students in American Society* (Cambridge, MA: Harvard University Press, 2008). For a lyrical exploration of the continuing successes of public schooling, see Michael Rose, *Possible Lives: The Promise of Public Education in America* (New York: Penguin Books, 1995).

Note: Page numbers followed by *f* indicate a figure.